THE
KILLING
STREETS

Also by Tanya Bretherton

The Suitcase Baby
The Suicide Bride

THE KILLING STREETS

TANYA BRETHERTON

hachette
AUSTRALIA

Published in Australia and New Zealand in 2020
by Hachette Australia
(an imprint of Hachette Australia Pty Limited)
Level 17, 207 Kent Street, Sydney NSW 2000
www.hachette.com.au

10 9 8 7 6 5 4 3 2 1

A catalogue record for this
book is available from the
National Library of Australia

ISBN: 978 0 7336 4238 8

Cover design by Christabella Designs
Cover photographs courtesy of NSW State Archives (photo of Eric Craig, Waverley streetscape); City of
Sydney Archives (George Street footpath, 032541)
Typeset in 12/18.6 pt Sabon LT Pro by Bookhouse, Sydney
Printed and bound in Great Britain by Clays Ltd, Elcograf S.p.A.

MIX
Paper from
responsible sources
FSC® C001695

The paper this book is printed on is certified against the
Forest Stewardship Council® Standards. McPherson's Printing
Group holds FSC® chain of custody certification SA-COC-005379.
FSC® promotes environmentally responsible, socially beneficial
and economically viable management of the world's forests.

CONTENTS

PROLOGUE

IN LATE 1932, IN THE KITCHENETTE OF A SMALL RUNDOWN FLAT in Sydney's east, a woman prepares dinner. With a large knife she slices into a raw lamb shank, then chops vegetables. She scoops lard from the dripping jar, smears it on the meat, then drops it roughly onto a cooking tray with a metallic thud. The joint of lamb rolls facedown, and the bone protrudes awkwardly from one end. The woman flicks the gas tap, strikes a match and ignites the burners. Small blue flames glow within the warming oven, and she slides the tray inside.

Twilight is approaching but hasn't yet begun to drain the heat from the day. It's stuffy and cramped in this flat, and there's barely room for a kitchen table, a sideboard, a free-standing stove, and two people. A man, much younger than the woman, sits at the table drawing heavily on a cigarette while he looks at a newspaper spread out before him. The ash slips from the end of his smoke, a light-grey snow falling across the column of job ads. The date on the corner of the broadsheet is Friday, 9 December. A bill addressed to Mr and Mrs Edwards lies unopened next to him.

The man sips a beer. The woman sits down at the table and begins applying porcelain-white make-up to her face with firm taps of a powder puff. The man drains his glass and fills it again. The woman holds up a cracked hand mirror and pencils in her eyebrows with severe, sharply curved black lines. Patting her cheeks with crimson rouge, she inspects her handiwork more closely, turning her head left to right.

The woman drops the powder puff, rushes to the oven and tugs open the door. A rush of hot air hits her freshly powdered face, although the room is already so warm she barely notices it. She sweeps the chopped potatoes and tomatoes from the countertop into her bare hands, and they clatter like rain on a tin roof as she drops them into the hot fat surrounding the meat in the cooking pan.

The woman returns to her make-up. The man sips a third beer.

At about 7 p.m. the couple share the meal. Within the hour, the woman has cleared and washed the plates, scrubbed the tray and put all the dishes away. She walks into the adjoining room and selects a forest-green dress from a small rack of coats and frocks. Around nine o'clock she slides into the dress, buttons it all the way up the front, slips into her two-tone black-and-white heels, and brushes and pins her hair neatly into curled rolls on either side of her head. Though it remains warm and humid outside, she pulls on an overcoat. After slamming the heavy wooden door of the terrace on Renny Street, Paddington, she walks the short distance up to Oxford Street, then heads down it for a kilometre or so to enter Greens Road.

The man goes to bed shortly after her departure. He doesn't leave a light on for her.

1

WHITE IRIS

IT WAS EARLY MORNING ON SATURDAY, 10 DECEMBER 1932 WHEN a forest-green dress was spotted, hooked in a spiky thicket of lantana in Queens Park. Nearby was a naked woman lying facedown on a bed of overgrown brambles and weeds, beneath a coral tree.

When local teenager Bernard Green saw the body, he did not, at first, believe his eyes. The air was still cool, and an unseasonal dreamlike mist hung in the valleys of the residential suburb of Waverley as he walked south, away from Bondi and towards Randwick. He'd taken this journey countless times before, and he was very familiar with the short cuts through back lanes, vacant lots and public parks. Coming down a steep hill towards Randwick, he always cut through the grove of coral trees in Queens Park because it was a little quicker and usually a little more pleasant than walking along the road.

The teenager didn't see the body up close, and from a distance the skin seemed to glow eerily in the early morning light. When he realised with horror what he was looking at, he stopped dead in his tracks. He ran from the scene, heading towards the nearest household he knew had a telephone.

David Frame, the foreman of Centennial Park, was the next person to see the dead woman. He too had spied the body from some distance away, and as he approached he had time to consider the woman's exposed back. Her petite frame and the stark white tone of her skin made her seem fragile, like bone china.

As he approached, he noticed details. Perhaps this was because he viewed the scene with a horticulturalist's gaze, but how she was arranged within the scene seemed significant. Her hair looked like twisted willow as it emerged from the bed of bramble on which she rested. He pondered the strange positioning of the woman's legs too. He narrowed his eyes in an attempt to see more clearly from such a long distance away. Her body seemed to be perfect and whole, but strangely plant-like. The woman's knees were bent sharply, and her feet seemed to curl – the way petals might in protection of the reproductive organs of a blossoming flower. Frame could not tell if it was a trick of the early morning light, or due to the unusual pallor of the woman's skin, but she looked like a flower. Her skin seemed to glow – radiating a white light – like an exotic bloom unfolding its beauty to receive the first rays of sunshine.

Frame didn't panic as quickly as the teenager had. As he drew closer, he still wasn't entirely convinced there was a problem. He often arrived at the park in the very early morning, and it wasn't unusual to see curious things – especially at dawn on Saturday. Workers who'd partied on Friday night were known to stumble into Centennial Park or Queens or any of the green spaces throughout the eastern suburbs. They often woke late the next morning and stumbled home – still hangover-groggy, but now with heavy coats damp from a night of dewfall. Prostitutes were known to take clients to the park. Vagrants, too, used the park as a place to camp, at least until police moved them along. Park employees had become accustomed to seeing a side of the city that not many others saw.

The woman's body was in an overgrown part of the park, and Frame had monitored the growth of coral trees in this area for years. Flourishing in the Sydney climate, the subtropical species had multiplied quickly and grown wild. The trees were broad and expansive, and they'd produced impressive canopies of claw-shaped, blood-red flowers. As Frame drew closer, the largest of the coral trees in this grove seemed to provide an eerily perfect backdrop for the scene. He was now so close to the body he could more properly comprehend the true horror of what was spread before him. This woman was not drunk, nor asleep, nor passed out. She had been rained on overnight, and this had not been enough to rouse her, and Frame could now see why.

Raindrops had not been able to wash away the large pools of blood dotted across the ground, and the clusters of red flowers in the branches overhead matched the blood puddled around the woman's body.

Frame finally snapped into action. He ran to fetch the police.

•

The sun rose, bringing the temperature with it. By midmorning the suburb was stirring, its families ready to enjoy the summer weather.

At around 10.20 a.m. Detective Patrick Power of the Waverley police arrived with his kitbag, a constable in tow. Power was cautious as he walked towards the dead woman. By 1932 police were broadly aware of the need to collect and preserve evidence, and protocols were slowly emerging. Power knew not to touch the body, because wherever possible the medical examiner preferred to visit crime scenes and see the dead, and their position, first-hand.

The detective bent over the woman's body and stared closely, his hands firmly clasped behind his back. He was soon left in no doubt about what had occurred. The attack had been brutal and close. It appeared she had been hit from behind and there were several angry triangular-shaped cuts in her head. Her skull was a mess of raw meat and exposed bone. There were pieces of what appeared to be blood and brain matter spattered around. The detective considered the position of the body. Two conclusions were easily drawn. She was lying on her face, so for the moment her identity would remain a mystery. And whatever had come for her, she hadn't seen it coming – someone had struck her squarely from behind.

Power noticed pieces of evidence that would need to be gathered. A deep-green dress hung awkwardly in a lantana bush. A beret was on the ground. While these physical remnants were important, so too was the cartography of the crime. He stepped back to take in the whole scene. To his left was a high cliff with a grand view of the suburb; to his right, a half circle of coral trees in a sunken, scrubby grove. Thorny castor oil bushes and spiky lantana dotted the landscape. Alongside them, angry splotches of the victim's blood were visible.

From his bag the detective removed a large bound diary and flipped it over notebook-style. He began to record his observations and speculations. By night, the darkness cast by the trees would have afforded protection to the killer, shielding their activities from the moonlight above and streetlight to the side. In broad daylight the space felt very open, with bright summer sunshine baking down on the body. Neat houses with trimmed hedges and lovingly tended flower beds were less than fifty metres from a brutally murdered woman. Children were tumbling out of their homes with footballs and cricket bats, billycarts and skipping-ropes. As the senior officer present, Power had to do something, and quickly. He directed the constable to clear the area around Victoria Street and to doorknock in the immediate vicinity of the crime scene – people needed to know that their dead-end street had quite literally lived up to its name, in the most macabre way possible. The body of the woman who had met her end here lay within clear line of sight of the row of white picket fences.

In 1932, the NSW police force believed it had put the best possible structure in place to support the study of complex crime. A Criminal Investigation Branch (CIB) of specialist detectives had been established to guide the examination of homicides in the state, and to develop and refine suspect interrogation and evidence analysis techniques. Some consider this the dawn of modern policing because the structures established in the late 1920s still exist today in the form of State Crime Command. The formation of the unit had emerged in response to a perceived rise in criminal activity in the 1920s which clustered in the inner east. More coordinated criminal threats – highly organised brothels, razor violence between rival gangs, and cocaine distribution – required a commensurate level of coordination by police in response. The state had committed time and money to training NSW detectives in what was believed to be best practice investigative techniques led by Scotland Yard mentors. Detectives had begun to embrace a more diverse range of methodological tools: fingerprinting, sketching, and plaster modelling were all slowly becoming embedded in police practice. By 1932 the CIB in Sydney had amassed such a vast database of fingerprints that high-level policy makers considered expanding it into a Commonwealth or federal bureau of fingerprinting.

As Power carefully examined the dead woman beneath the coral tree, police process was at the front of his mind. He made a note to take fingerprints. If the woman had spent any time in police custody, even if she'd never been formally convicted, it was likely that an inky map of her fingertips was stored in the database.

Power removed a compass from his kitbag. He flipped it open with a flick of his wrist and placed it in the centre of his flattened palm. The woman's face was pointed due west; significant or not, Power noted this too. He then paced out some rough distances, using his stride alone – from the tree, to the street, to the body. He sketched the scene, but he was no artist so it was rudimentary. He removed some small wooden stakes from his bag, each topped with a white flag, and pushed them firmly into the earth wherever he noticed a pool of blood. When he ran out of markers, he used paper from his notebook. He felt grateful for the stillness of the day – each piece fluttered down with the motion of a magic carpet, then stayed precisely where he'd intended.

He narrowed his focus, recording his observations with more detail now. After uncurling a measuring tape from his pocket, he noted the diameters of the blood pools. In the slightly prickly foliage of the nearby lantana, he measured the distance from the body to a singlet, the beret and a garter, and he noticed stockings that he'd overlooked on first surveying the scene. The deep-green dress was threadbare. He listed these details but left most items undisturbed. He did, however, scrape a number of blood-soaked leaves from the ground and pile them up nearby.

Behind him, from the direction of the street, he heard a car door slam, then two more. Detective Inspector William Pryor, head of the Criminal Investigation Branch, and Detective Inspector Jacob Henry Miller arrived, together with more constables. Shortly after, Detectives Campbell and Paton joined them. By eleven o'clock, five detectives had assembled in the grove of blood-red coral trees. The men bore an uncanny resemblance to each other: middle-aged, they wore heavy woollen dress suits complete with buttoned waistcoats and fedoras. They stood in a horseshoe shape, all eyes levelled at the dead woman splayed before them.

CIB Chief Pryor began directing questions at Power. 'Do we know who she is?'

'It's possible she's a vagrant,' the detective answered. 'The state of her clothes is poorly. She may be one of the Greens Road girls who works the strip near the barracks.'

Power didn't need to say anything further on that point: the strip was notorious in the inner city. Only a short drive away, behind the military barracks, it was a popular pick-up point for prostitutes. After peeling off Moore Park Road, a car could slow to a crawl as it moved along the strip. A young woman need only lean into an open window briefly, then jump in just before the driver sped away. Greens Road was the sex industry's equivalent of a fast food drive-through: transactions were quick and cheap, product was taken away to be consumed elsewhere, and extras could be added to upsell an order and meet a customer's unique tastes. Put coarsely, it was not fast food but fast fucks for sale. These business deals could be completed in back seats, but more commonly occurred in public parks.

As Power updated the other detectives, he pointed between the crime scene and his notebook. 'I took possession of the clothing and some leaves that had blown on them. They were in a pool of blood near the coral tree. It is a big tree so it covers a wide area . . . I did not find any bloomers.'

The detectives collectively took a breath and considered the possibilities. Was it significant to the investigation that the woman's underwear was missing? Had this woman come to the park barely clothed? Had she dressed deliberately without underwear, to make sexual services easier to perform? Or had the killer taken the undergarments?

'This looks very much like the other one,' Power said, careful with his words. 'It's much like that White girl.'

Pryor folded his arms, his suit crumpling slightly. He looked at Power expectantly, waiting for more information. But none came.

'We are still gathering evidence, sir, but there are some big similarities.' Power glanced down at his sketch when he said this, realising in that moment how woefully inadequate his drawing must seem. 'I think we need Jardine, sir,' he said.

Pryor nodded. 'Get him down here, would you?' He tucked his meaty hands under his elbows, crossing his arms even more tightly over his chest. When his forehead wrinkled in thought, it seemed a perfect match for the wrinkles across his suit.

William Pryor was a caboose of a man, solid and wide and reliable, with a shag pile of black hair and a thick boomerang moustache balanced atop his rather large mouth. He had two nicknames in the force. Some called him William the Silent for his enduringly quiet but intensely strong presence. Others called him Father, because he had something of a reputation for paternal kindness and was known for giving officers a somewhat free hand in their investigations.

Pryor circumnavigated the woman's body as he stared down at it, close enough that he seemed to be tracing her outline with his feet. He kept his arms folded in firmly against his body as he paced out the crime scene. He thought about the pathways from the road to the park, beyond to the high cliff wall and to the steep set of stairs leading up there. This was a relatively big crime scene, a vast space for the investigation to cover. It was very different from investigating a murder in the confines of a house.

'Have we found anything in the form of a weapon?' Pryor asked Power.

'I've had constables fan out over the park, scanning the ground. The bramble is pretty thick. I've had the boys doorknocking locally as well. It might have been thrown over a fence.'

Pryor nodded, smoothing his moustache with his thumb and forefinger as he thought.

At 11.20 a.m. Dr Arthur Palmer arrived at the crime scene. As a medical practitioner and government officer, Palmer had the responsibility of performing the autopsy in order to formally determine cause of death. Before the removal of the body to the morgue, he'd come to analyse the scene. How was the body found, and where? How was it positioned? He wanted to answer these questions for himself and use that information to build an understanding of the cause and manner of death.

More detectives arrived, their cars packed with equipment. The visibility of this place was increasing, and word of the crime had now spread throughout the suburb. Constables had stopped people from gathering near the body. They'd been unable to prevent spectators from watching if they assembled much further away. A long line of gawkers now stood single file atop the high sandstone wall because of the remarkable vantage point it offered of the entire scene. A mother stood with her hip on an angle, bearing the weight of a child on one arm, while with her other arm she shielded her eyes from the glare of the sun. A line of women stood beside her, the chintz and chequered prints on their dresses bold against the backdrop of the solid blue sky. Men had gathered too; they were dressed casually, many without hats or coats. One man seemed particularly forward – he'd walked halfway down the hill and was leaning over a white handrail to take in a close view of the action. He had a toddler with him, and the little boy swung on the handrail playfully, using it as a monkey bar. His father was seemingly oblivious to the horror of what his son was being exposed to. The dead woman's legs were spread, vulgarly displayed. The crowd simply stared with fascination into the valley of coral trees, no longer a grove but an open grave.

Power gazed up at the crowd, frustrated, then stomped off to a police car parked nearby. He returned carrying a white tarp, like a sail, which he unfolded and began pegging over the lantana to obscure visibility of the scene, at least a little. It isn't clear whether he took this step to preserve some professional discretion and privacy for the medical examiner, who was setting up to begin his examination, or as a meagre gesture of respect for the dead woman.

At first Palmer didn't touch the body – this stage was about observation of the corpse in context. Like other witnesses that morning, Palmer noticed the stunning whiteness of the flesh. He wasn't transfixed by its strangeness. He immediately recognised it as pallor mortis: the first stage of death, when white skin turns unusually pale.

As he worked he spoke to Power, who added medical details to the observations he'd recorded in his notebook.

Palmer leant in close to the body. 'There are scratches on the neck, blows to the head.' He moved locks of hair here and there in the manner of a fastidious hairdresser, careful not to shift the body in any significant way.

Power scrawled a crude outline of the dead woman and made notes very inexpertly, with arrows pointing to different parts of the body.

The medical examiner said, 'The wounds and their place-ment suggest she was bludgeoned from behind. The depressed fractures have a strange shape. Perhaps a tyre lever has caused the injuries. That isn't clear, though.' He removed measuring tape from his bag and dropped one end on the ground near the woman's feet. 'She is only a little over five foot tall.' Palmer had managed to calculate this even though her legs were bent. 'I have no way of weighing her here, but I estimate she is around seven stone.'

The men nodded, both coming to the same conclusion: the woman was so tiny that almost any man could have overpowered her fairly easily.

Two constables entered the scene, one of whom was Cecil Stanley Jardine. Under one arm he carried the past of policing, and under the other he carried its future: respect-ively, a large flat clipboard, an artist's folder and field box, and a camera, a case and a small folding-seat. The other constable was carrying a ladder and a camera tripod. The men unloaded the equipment onto the ground, not far from the dead woman's feet.

Palmer nodded stiffly and formally to the constables, but said nothing to them.

'Palmer won't be long,' said Power to Jardine.

The medical examiner continued. 'Head wounds are trian-gular.' He paused, staring deeply into the incisions. They were jagged and oddly shaped. Whatever the woman had been struck with had etched rune-like markings onto her head. He looked carefully, trying to divine their meaning.

Jardine walked silently, conscious of not distracting Palmer. He mentally tallied how many photos would need to be taken.

'There is brain there.' Palmer continued to call out observations while jotting things down in his own notebook. It wasn't dandruff that flaked through her dark hair but powdery shards of skull. 'It's protruding through the hair,' he added. 'Look for something hard, sharp edges. A stone, perhaps, as a weapon? She has been struck with some force,' he said with a tone of finality. He stepped back from the body, walked around it, leant right down to ground level and stared, almost as if he were trying to look the woman in the eye. 'I will know more when I have a closer examination, but I can tell you for certain – there was intercourse.' He stepped back again and wiped sweat from his forehead with the back of his hand. 'Okay, if you take the photo, I can get started with moving her.'

Pryor, who'd been watching the scene silently, nodded for Jardine to proceed. He stepped in and, with the help of the other constable, unfolded a long ladder. He took several photographs: the crowd, the detectives assembled beneath the tree, a line of palm trees in a street, and the grove of coral trees.

With a colleague steadying the ladder for him, Jardine climbed to the very top rung to get one shot of the body; he then climbed way down, lying flat on the bramble at ground level to get the other. Both images glimmer with the otherworldly silver quality distinctive to early twentieth century photography. One shot is particularly confronting.

The woman's feet are in the foreground and her head is in the background. With her legs awkwardly bent at the knees and her feet turned and then twisted ever so gently outwards like petals, she does indeed look like a strange flower. The woman's genitals, like the swollen pistil of a flower, are the dead centre of the image. The woman's own hand, coated in filth, lies trapped beneath her body. Her hand emerges, as if from the ground, clawing towards her own vulva. It is as if the dead woman herself is trying to leave some clue to the reason for her death. The crime was about sex.

It is unlikely the police photographer would have recognised the artistic mimicry he was engaged in when he took the photo on that day. A few years before, the American artist Georgia O'Keeffe had shocked the world with her modernist studies of flowers. In 1926 she'd released what would become one of her most famous oil paintings: *Black Iris*. An intense study of an iris, it is painted predominantly in black, grey and white, with faint touches of pink and deep purple. White folds at the top merge with the darkened folds of petals in the lower portion. The painting is almost universally regarded by art critics to be a vulva, barely disguised as a flower. Though O'Keeffe's work was not exhibited in Australia, commentaries on her work and the study of geometry, symmetry and sexuality it embodied were given extensive coverage in the press at the time. In a strange way, the constable had created his own, perhaps more clinical, representation and homage to a defining artwork of the generation. It might be said that both are artefacts of the early twentieth century: a time when the female body emerged as a subject of intimate study both artistic and forensic.

Once Jardine's work was done, it was time to take finger-prints. Two junior officers struggled to free the arm trapped beneath the torso. Her limbs were stiffened with rigor mortis, and the rotation of her hands also proved a two-man job. Digit by digit, they rolled her fingertips across an inky piece of tin. The prints were rushed to the CIB for analysis. Its extensive database was stored on index cards in filing cabinets, and arches, loops and whorls were used as shorthand to accelerate the searching process. Police had been remarkably quick at coding and mapping the peaks and valleys of the human finger. They were also continually refining the methods used to take fingerprints.

The woman in the park had been able to keep her fingers; other recent victims had not. In the past when bodies had been found exposed in the outdoors, Sydney police had been required to innovate when taking prints. The geographic location of Sydney as a harbour city could even be said to have led to the innovation, as bodies were so often found in water. Soaked corpses complicated forensics, particularly fingerprinting. In one case, the fingers had been snipped from the hand at the crime scene, so they might be studied more closely in a lab. In another case, investigators had managed to strip the print from a finger as if unsheathing a latex glove from a hand.

At CIB headquarters on that day in December, it didn't take long to match the fingerprints with the name May Miller.

Police weren't surprised by this: May was a common trading name for prostitutes who conducted business in the inner city and the east.

Back at the crime scene, Constable Jardine began sketching. He removed a tin of art pens, of varying widths and tips, a tin of colouring pencils, and a small screw-top jar of water with a tiny pot of watercolour paint. He pulled out a piece of thickly woven art paper, around the size of an A4 sheet, and slid it into a clipboard.

That year he'd supported police briefs of evidence across many important cases around the state. He'd been dispatched to draft landscape maps in Bathurst to support a murder investigation. He'd also been one of the technical experts behind the production of a radical new approach to the prevention of fencing stolen goods across the city. High-end jewellery had traditionally been documented by text alone; Jardine had meticulously sketched every piece from all the finest jewellers in the city, and police now carried a small booklet of these items as a field guide for easy identification. It was tiny, just eight inches by four, contained a thousand illustrations, and was cleverly designed to fit neatly within an officer's vest pocket. Jardine was now well known to be a 'clever pen and ink illustrator'.

No doubt less vibrant than they were eighty years ago, the hand-drawn sketches of the crime scene remain exquisite. Tiny crosshatch marks are used to show texture and shadow. Hedges are delicate curls. Little street lamps glow yellow, streaked with lines to signify illumination. A water wash in pale green signifies grassed areas, a coral-peach has been used for the cottages, a slate grey shows the depth of the drop from the cliff, and a lighter pastel blue-grey represents the streets. If you could view these drawings absent from the violent and debased events that spawned them, they would seem quaint and childlike.

•

By the time officers were packing up and getting ready to leave the crime scene, more information had come to hand about the victim. Criminal records had flowed from the name May Miller. Though she was in her early thirties, her first conviction had occurred only a few years before in 1929. This was an unusual criminal resumé for a prostitute in the 1920s and 30s, as many started in this profession at a horrifyingly early time in life. It seemed that May had been a late bloomer.

The charges against May show a distinct pattern. In the five years she worked the inner city, thirteen convictions were recorded against her. Eight were for the cryptic charge of 'offensive behaviour'. This doesn't give much insight into May as a person, because offensive behaviour charges were laid against people for everything from blowing a trumpet on a public street to wolf-whistling at girls. They were often laid against women for swearing, and this was most likely the case with May. Two offences were for soliciting, and one was broadly described as 'riotous behaviour' (though the details of the criminal act were not recorded). The most serious charge, first brought against her in 1929, was for grievous bodily harm. She was convicted and served twelve months. Very soon after her release she was sent down again for the same charge.

The criminal records tell only part of her story – police interviews with locals, which commenced the day after her death, reveal a lot more. It seems there was no shortage of people willing to share gossip about her. In one version of a story, she'd tried to bite off a man's ear; in another version, she had succeeded. The man was a taxi driver, and apparently his lobe had been taken clear off.

May Miller's records contain one last, but very important, detail – her real name. Given how she was found, and the intimacy of the images taken of her de-flowered corpse, her first name seems not only poignant but fitting.

Her name wasn't May, but Iris.

Iris Marriott.

2

WHITE, HILDA

IRIS WASN'T THE FIRST WOMAN TO BE STRIPPED AND BRUTALISED in a public park in Sydney's east. She wasn't even the first woman to die in this way that year.

In December 1932, in black cursive script, 'Marriott, Iris' was neatly handwritten as a new entry in the official Register of Coroner's Inquests. In the same column, and only a few lines up the page, coronial staff had entered 'White, Hilda'.

At about 7 a.m. on Wednesday, 27 July 1932, a Centennial Park worker walking behind the kiosk and past the stables found Hilda's naked body. She was face up between a park bench and the base of a Moreton Bay fig. With the exception of a few torn shreds of clothing, she was naked except for her beads and shoes.

In the days following the discovery of Iris Marriott, local police reflected on the many similarities between her case and that of Hilda White. But although the detectives must have discussed and compared the cases, no minutes were kept of these meetings.

Hilda had been thirty-three years old, and although Iris's age was more difficult to determine, she was also believed to be thirty-three. Both women had been murdered at night. Their bodies had been discovered in the early hours of the morning on opposite corners of a green space in the eastern suburbs: Hilda in Centennial Park, and Iris in adjoining Queens Park. At the time, Centennial was a large-scale public reserve of over 350 hectares, designed to provide visitors with the opportunity to relax away from the stresses of city life while strolling beside ornamental gardens and fountains, or wandering through forests of exotic trees.

In life, the women appeared to have had a lot in common. Both had struggled to find work and make ends meet. Iris, in particular, had experienced hardship. She'd used the name May Miller for professional convenience and to separate her working life from her private one. To make the tale more convincing and reduce the risk of discovery, she'd even created a backstory for May: May Miller had migrated from Ireland; May Miller had no living family. The truth was quite different. Iris Marriott had come to Sydney from Fremantle in Western Australia. Iris Marriott had living relatives – in fact, she'd left Western Australia in the company of family. And when she'd arrived in Sydney in 1922, she wasn't alone: she was carrying a child.

Iris had two sisters still living in Western Australia, and they'd been willing to confirm some facts to the police. An illegitimate child had been born at some point in 1922. Details about the baby were difficult to confirm, as the birth and the years following were shrouded in secrecy. Iris had relinquished the child – a girl – and she'd been raised with the belief she was an orphan. And, in a sense, she had lost her parents: her father wasn't in the picture, and Iris Marriott had become May Miller. It was May who had worked hard for a decade to bring in extra money. It was May who had dutifully paid for the upkeep of the child. It was May who had died with the stigma of being a prostitute, and with no real recognition that she'd been nobly trying to make provision for her child in the only way she knew how.

Hilda White had also faced significant challenges. Described as 'feeble' and 'weak-minded', she'd likely had an intellectual disability. She'd found it difficult to find steady work. Hilda had been living at home with her widowed mother and her siblings, two sisters and a brother. When she was murdered, the family had already faced a major tragedy that year – her sister had recently died of tuberculosis.

Very early on in the investigations, those closest to each of the women were interviewed then dismissed as possible suspects. Hilda's family members weren't under suspicion, and she was characterised as being a fairly solitary, lonely character who didn't have a boyfriend. Iris lived with her lover, a 23-year-old man called Stanley McGroder. The depressed economy had made unlikely bedfellows of the pair. McGroder was a labourer, and at the time of Iris's death he hadn't worked in two years. Construction was one of the industries heavily affected by the slowed economy, while Iris's line of work had proven to be a little more recession proof. The couple had moved into the cramped front-room flat of 53 Renny Street, Paddington, about eighteen months earlier, and had been calling themselves Mr and Mrs Edwards. Iris had financially supported McGroder throughout much of that time. He was an alcoholic, and police saw him as hopeless. He wasn't ever considered seriously as a suspect. He told police, 'She stayed in the house until about 8 p.m. . . . then got dressed and went out. I did not know where she was going at the time. The next time that I saw her was at the City Morgue.'

Both Hilda and Iris had been prostitutes. While Hilda had never faced a soliciting charge, Iris had faced several. Interviews with locals suggested that Hilda had been seen with men in areas known for soliciting. A newspaper article printed at the time of her death alluded to this: 'Hilda White had many men friends of whom her mother and sisters and brother were unaware. She was a great favourite with some of the members of the Permanent Military Forces . . . She was often seen in the company of soldiers.' Another newspaper printed indiscreet details about Hilda's nocturnal activities in the eastern suburbs: 'The woman had known many men, and it is thought that she was probably lured to the park for some reason, and killed after being there a short time.' Shortly after Iris's death, an article made comparisons between both the women and the crimes: 'The crime bears a curious resemblance to the killing of Hilda White, a girl of somewhat similar habits and age . . . And the men of the CIB are asking themselves whether there is a murderous maniac.'

Both women were found naked. Hilda's underwear was jammed under her chin; Iris's was missing. Both had endured horrible brutality in their last moments. The medical examiner Dr Palmer recorded in his formal notes that Iris had been hit so violently, he'd simply lifted fragments of bone from the brain with his fingers. In some places, the only thing keeping the skull in place was the blood-matted hair. Palmer stated that it wasn't possible to determine which had been the fatal blow, nor precisely how the murderer and victim were positioned at the time of the attack. 'Any one of the wounds could have been caused while she was standing on her feet. I should say that most of them were caused while she was lying on her face,' he noted. There were no strikes to the forehead, and there were scratches and abrasions over the lower part of the back. He determined that someone had killed Iris with 'a piece of wood'.

Photos of Hilda taken soon before her death show a woman with a smooth, broad face, perfectly curved lips around a wide smile, and almond-shaped eyes. She had a beauty mark just off centre above her lip and, with a cloche cap pulled down around her ears to frame her face, she resembled a silent movie star, not dissimilar to Marlene Dietrich.

Hilda didn't look like this when she was found. Based on her injuries, police conjectured that the attacker had 'punched [her] insensible' with a closed fist. Her jaw was busted up, and her lips were cut. However, police believed she'd been awake when the attacker strangled her, choking her with her underwear hard enough to crush her throat. In her desperate struggle to free herself, she'd chomped her jaws violently, biting her tongue repeatedly. The inside of her mouth resembled mince. A bone in her throat had been fractured. Hilda had fought very hard to live.

Hilda's hands and nails were coated in thick dark muck. Her body was black and bloody, and in places police had to scrape back the film of scum to see if the discolouration was superficial or due to bruising. Groundskeepers provided important context by explaining key details about the park. Hilda had died in an area where garden beds had only recently been dressed with topsoil, and almost all of the discolouration on her body could be explained by this. She had writhed and struggled and clawed wildly in the fresh, soft soil as she battled for her life.

Her empty handbag was found tossed not far from her body. Police looked for signs of robbery and ultimately deemed the evidence to be inconclusive. They believed Hilda could have been carrying an empty bag, as she had little money of her own. Police also couldn't explain how her clothes had been torn from her body. It was winter, and she'd left home wearing a lot of clothing, including an overcoat. Was it possible she had removed it herself? If the killer had ripped it off, where had it gone?

Initially, at least, police were unwilling to call Hilda's death a murder, despite the condition of the corpse. Police speculated that cars had been used to drive the women to the sites where they were ultimately murdered. In Hilda's case police believed they'd found evidence of a struggle closer to the roadway, based on foot impressions in the soil. From there it appeared she'd been carried, at least part of the way, and the struggle seemed to have continued at the place where she ultimately died. In an interview with *The Sun* in the month following Hilda's death, police revealed they were exploring the possibility that her strangling had been accidental. According to this theory, Hilda had experienced a violent seizure, and whoever had accompanied her that evening had sought to restrain her. Police conjectured that the tragedy may have occurred because the good Samaritan had exercised 'more pressure than he intended'. Police speculated about how this had led to the abandonment of the body: 'with no intention of killing her, he had fled terrified'.

Hilda's investigation was fragmented, partly due to over-delegation. Many officers within the CIB had handled many different parts of the investigation, and this had spawned many theories. Detective Sergeants Keogh and Barratt had been frontrunners in managing the crime scene, while Detective Sergeants Power, James and Shields processed paperwork, posting rewards and analysing information. Detective Sergeants Matthews and Burns began house-to-house doorknocking, drumming up witnesses who might have seen Hilda with a man on the night of her murder. Detective

Power and Detective Inspector Pryor were the only officers in common to both investigations.

In Centennial Park, Detective Barratt looked at shoe impressions left in the dark earth just near Hilda's body. He noted: 'poor man's shoe'. Because of the size and the flat, wide impression of the heel, officers assumed the shoes belonged to a man. They also surmised that he must be poor: the imprint of the soles offered little in the way of a pattern because they were worn down.

While canvassing for witnesses, James and Shields were stopped by someone in East Darlinghurst who said that yes, they'd seen Hilda out in the company of a man, just near the park, at about eight on the night of the murder. The detectives were hopeful until the witness said it had been so dark, they couldn't provide much of a description. The witness had noticed one detail: Hilda's companion had worn a yellow overcoat. Police then went to the apartment block where Hilda lived with her family, on Liverpool Street in Darlinghurst.

It's difficult to follow the deductive steps that led to the identification of a suspect, as no records are available to provide insight. What's known is that officers arrested a man living in the same apartment block as the White family. His name was Victor Francis Lamerto, but he also may have gone by the names Januschansky or Jamuschersky. He was Russian and had very little English literacy, so he struggled to understand what was happening to him. It was rumoured that he worked as a driver for a local eastern suburbs family, though this was difficult for police to confirm. It had taken about ten days for officers to locate and corner a suspect in a yellow overcoat. Although his arrest had been swift, there was no physical evidence linking him to the crime scene and no witness statement identifying him as the man seen with Hilda. Neighbours in the apartment block said that Lamerto and Hilda hadn't known each other. The arrest was made based on only one piece of evidence: the man owned a yellow overcoat.

Police interrogated Lamerto, who denied his involvement in the crime. They then put forward their evidence brief to the City Coroner, Mr E May. It's hard not to view the decision to arrest Lamerto with immense cynicism. While there was a significant Russian community in Sydney at the time, the Anglo majority tended to view Continental European immigrants poorly and with deep suspicion as 'foreigners'. The coroner responded in a way police hadn't expected: he was furious. He rejected any suggestion that Lamerto had any involvement whatsoever. He ordered the man be discharged due to lack of evidence and publicly shamed the police for the poor brief provided for his consideration. He returned an open verdict.

•

To fully understand why so much fragmentation surrounded Hilda's investigation, it's important to acknowledge some of the challenges faced by police at the time. The department had a backlog of homicides. It had been a busy year for the NSW CIB, and April had been particularly so. One newspaper had mockingly declared April to be the month of murder. Described as 'mysterious murders', Iris's and Hilda's deaths were considered particularly tricky because motive was difficult to determine in each case. They weren't domestic homicides linked to family disputes, but appeared to have been committed by strangers.

William Pryor had been appointed CIB chief on 30 March. 'Big jobs for new chief,' reported one newspaper. By the end of April, another newspaper stated that there was no doubt Pryor had 'his hands full'.

On 17 March, Katherine Sims was stabbed and slashed in a home invasion in Erskineville. Gendered assumptions significantly impeded the investigation. The attack on Katherine had been violent and had occurred in her own house, and there were no witnesses. In less than a week, police had concluded that the type of personal violence showed that Katherine must have been the victim of what they called 'a love tragedy'. Police supposed her lover had killed her, and with nothing to live for had gone off somewhere to kill himself. Because of this assumption, resources were pulled off the case a week after the murder occurred. It was considered a poor use of time and energy to search for a man who was most likely dead. According to the *Labor Daily* newspaper:

> There is none of the feverish excitement and tenseness of the man hunt associated with murders in this case. The men who were assigned to the case are now engaged in other duties. But in case the murderer of Mrs Sims still lives and is in hiding the following description is supplied

by the CIB: 48 years of age, 5ft 6in, medium to stout build, round shouldered, very dark complexion, dark bristly hair turning grey, small dark eyes with a cast in the left one which shows the white, medium to full face, thin lips, good set of natural teeth, though well spaced and discoloured, being black near the gums, clean shaven, has a fresh cut on one thumb. Dressed in blue over-check pattern worsted coat and trousers, greyish coloured felt hat, black boots, no vest and coat is torn up the back.

On 11 April, Dorothy Denzel and Frank Wilkinson, a young couple, were discovered in Holsworthy, a wild and bushy south-western suburb. They'd been buried in separate graves, about three quarters of a mile apart, in dense scrub near a timber-getter's camp. Dorothy had been stripped naked, and her face was so battered that she was almost unrecognisable. Portions of her skull were found twenty feet from the grave. At the local army remount depot, where horses were bred and trained, a worker found the upper plate of her false teeth. Both Dorothy and Frank had been killed at close range with a shotgun.

Next came the murder of Victor Saywell, who was attacked in bed in his Bellevue Hill home and died a few days later on 25 April. Although there were no leads, police could not let the case slide. Saywell was a prominent solicitor and a man of influence in the city. Coronial proceedings were even delayed to give police more time to identify a suspect. Despite their efforts, the police failed to formulate a robust narrative about what had occurred. By the time the inquest was held five months later (an uncharacteristically long period between murder and inquest in 1932) – the police still hadn't formulated any concrete theories. As it had during the investigation into Hilda White's death, xenophobia played a role in police reflections on the case. A report in the *Telegraph* summed up these theories well: 'Foreigner may have murdered Victor Saywell'.

In Glen Innes, almost six hundred kilometres north of Sydney, a fifth mysterious homicide occurred that required the specialist skills of the CIB. On 26 April, dairy farmer Albert Victor Chaffey was found dead with a bullet hole in the back of his neck. The leather pouch in which he carried his change was missing, so robbery appeared to be the motive. His murder was a brutal and shocking event, not only to locals, but to the state executive. Though Chaffey had been a struggling farmer when he was killed, he also happened to be a cousin of the Chief Secretary of New South Wales. Police felt intense pressure to resolve the case. For the CIB detectives who had to commute great distances in order to progress the investigation, the case was an immense challenge. After weeks and weeks of frustrating travel back and forth from Sydney to Glen Innes, a suspect was found – an ex-employee who was familiar with Chaffey's milk run and knew when the man was likely to be alone.

The apparent murder of homeless man Michael Desmond occurred on the night of 26 April, before Pryor had even completed his first month on the job. Aged approximately fifty, Desmond had been killed with an axe in a woodland glade on the outskirts of the national park near Sutherland. The area had become a shantytown for the city's unemployed. Desmond's body was found at the entrance of a canvas humpy. A sleeping woman was spooning the corpse, seemingly unaware that he had passed on.

There is no doubt that the workload of all of these simultaneous cases overwhelmed the CIB. The investigation into Desmond's death can only be described as chaotic. When his body was discovered, there were eight men and two women identified as living at the camp. Police scavenged the site for items that might support a murder charge. A woman's handbag and hat were taken, so too were three bottles of wine and a jar of methylated spirits. A copy of the 1929 short-story collection *Circumstantial Evidence* by Edgar Wallace, which was being read by one of the other homeless men, was also held by police.

The detectives in charge quickly developed a theory: Desmond had been killed during a drunken orgy, therefore every person present was a suspect. The camp's residents – all of whom appeared to be alcoholics – were rounded up and taken into custody. Tempers flared when officers made these arrests, and the situation worsened while the suspects were sobering up in custody. Their cells resounded with abuse and threats – and that was just an officer telling the prisoners to shut up. When individuals were pressed for information, the situation escalated even further. While being interrogated, one man managed to reef a typewriter right off the interview table. It was an impressive effort, given that the style of typing machines at the time could crush a human foot. Police were livid: the machine was broken, its metal keys snapped and bent. A short time later, enraged at the accusations being levelled at him, another interviewee grabbed an inkwell and bowled it overarm and with great precision at a constable's head.

The CIB was stretched to its limits. While constables were dispatched to doorknock at multiple locations across the south of the city canvassing for witnesses, police were also trying to deepen the science of their work as best they could. In the case of Chaffey's murder, the medical examiner extracted the bullet from the back of the victim's head. Police couldn't forensically match a bullet casing to a specific weapon, though they could match it to the style of weapon used. They posted officers along the rivers and roads leading into and out of Glen Innes, and they demand-searched individuals and vehicles looking for the type of rifle used to kill Chaffey. It was a labour-intensive way to investigate and meant the investment of hundreds of man hours.

Constable Cecil Jardine mapped out the crime scenes in a formal and technical way. For the Saywell murder, he also brought his scientific and artistic skills to bear in drawings of the interior fixtures of the home along with a detailed floor plan.

There's no doubt Sydney police had a heavy caseload in 1932, and their exhaustion might help to explain why they failed to solve Hilda White's murder or link it to Iris Marriott's. But it appears that at least one other factor was involved: the investigations weren't just steered by the nature of the crimes, but also by the nature of the victims and the circumstances of their deaths. The authorities viewed Hilda and Iris as immoral. The women had been plying their trade on the nights they were killed, said police. For this reason, their deaths were acknowledged to be difficult to solve and represented a lower order of priority for CIB detectives.

This may explain why several preceding murders in and around Sydney also remained unsolved by police. These crimes bore many similarities to the murders of Hilda and Iris. A pattern of what at the time were known as 'lust killings', albeit a sporadic one, had been established long before 1932.

3

DAISY CHAIN

IN THE DECADE BEFORE 1932, THREE WOMEN WERE BRUTALLY
murdered in eastern Sydney. Each was sexually assaulted
in a public place, then left for dead in an inner-city park.
The murders were spaced apart by a few years; however, the
number of similarities between them is remarkable. There
are the hallmarks of a pattern – what we might today term
serial killing – though no tangible connection between the
crimes was ever made by police.

The first in the sequence was in May 1921, though the
horrible discovery would not be made for over a year. It was
the middle of October 1922 when Waverley police received
a telephone call. The caller, who insisted on remaining
anonymous, left a message with the switchboard. It wasn't a
murder they were reporting, but something far more mundane.

Police didn't have much to go on. Someone had been seen 'loitering suspiciously' in an area of Moore Park known locally as the sandhills. A member of the public had been concerned enough to report it. In the 1920s, the term Moore Park was used to refer to the dense residential zones south of Kings Cross, the showgrounds in the east, and also the terraces and industrial pockets of Redfern. At the time, this parkland included vast green space, bushland for walking, and recreational areas for sport, including golf, cricket and football. Of all the public parks in Sydney, Moore was one of the most popular. But not all of its visitors came in search of the wholesome fun of footy.

Police assumed the loiterer was most likely a flasher in an overcoat, or a pickpocket. Petty thieves were also common in parks. Given the lack of information provided by the caller, and the high frequency of 'pervert in the park' reports, no one identified the call-out to be a high priority. While indecent exposure and stealing were both indictable offences, those committing them weren't generally perceived by police to be dangerous criminals. Charges were processed quickly, and convictions attracted a fine of a few pounds – or a week or month in prison for those who couldn't pay.

A range of local slang terms had emerged to describe indecent exposure in Australia by this time. Men caught flashing their genitals or masturbating publicly by dropping pants or popping a penis through a buttoned fly were said to be playing the 'willy willy wagtail game'. A 'dirty old man doing a dirty trick' or a fella pulling a 'wicked willy' were also terms used informally by police and by the general public. This gives some indication of how society viewed these behaviours at the time. They were certainly considered deviant and weren't condoned, but the humorous tone dilutes the sense of societal condemnation that could follow from such an act. Court records from this period indicate that sex-related offences were fairly common. All of these offences fell under the informal label of 'peeping Tom' charges, but the configuration always seemed to be the same: male perpetrators preying on female victims who were often unaware they were being used as an object of sexual interest. The impact of these behaviours on the victims wasn't given much consideration, and the acts were dismissed as 'practically harmless libidinous gambol', so long as the indecent exposure remained 'contained' and didn't progress to physical contact, such as 'interfering with young girls'.

By the mid-1920s, 'peeping Tom' had become such a common part of the vernacular that newspapers felt it was in the public interest to publish the history behind the idiom. In 1926 the papers highlighted that peeping Toms weren't necessarily dirty men in parks. In the original peeping Tom story, Lady Godiva rode naked through the streets of Coventry to protest her husband's unfair treatment of the local tenants. A public proclamation instructed townspeople to stay indoors and shut their blinds so no one could see aristocracy in the nuddy. A local man defied the order and bored a hole in his window shutter. Legend has it that he was struck blind, but this didn't deter 1920s society from championing his story.

In 1927, an illustrated version of Lady Godiva's ride was promoted in Sydney: 'Peeping Tom, famous in history, was the only person who saw Lady Godiva ride naked through the streets of Coventry . . . be a stickybeak and see what Peeping Tom did through the keyhole'. A copy of this book could be bought from Mortons on Valentine Street in the city, a purveyor of skin mags where a customer could also admire 'beauty books of actresses'. If the customer should prefer a little more discretion, Mortons even offered to send the Lady Godiva book by mail order 'posted in a plain wrapper'.

All of this gives some insight into the ways in which so-called 'lust crimes' were seen at the time: conducted by men and boys against women and girls, they were a nuisance but not dangerous.

When police arrived at Moore Park on that evening in October 1922, they may have been expecting to find a loitering peeping Tom. They certainly weren't expecting any danger. They also weren't expecting to discover a body partially buried in the sandhills.

Geographically, Moore Park is located in the part of Sydney known as the Botany Basin. This includes the Botany Sands, a natural land formation comprising earth above and a layer of groundwater just below the surface. The topography of the eastern side of the city is defined by this water table. In the 1920s, undeveloped parts of the landscape still included rolling and gentle slopes, with lots of sandy soil and swampy, marshy peat.

Careful disposal of the body may not have been part of the killer's design for the crime. The body may have been partially buried because it was easy to do so. Now the body was partially rotted. The hair had decomposed much more slowly than the soft tissue, so it was the pretty hairdo atop the skeleton that led police to their first important conclusion: the bent figure was that of a woman. Given the limits of forensic science at the time, it was difficult for officers to determine how long she had been dead. But the medical examiner determined cause of death: someone had delivered savage blows to her head, much like what would be done to Iris and Hilda a decade later. The examiner identified six distinct depressed fractures of the skull – a 'solid instrument' had clearly been used. The largest fracture was over the left temple.

Police measured the body and based on height and bone structure they made an identification: she was an eastern suburbs woman who had been reported missing. The woman was notably tiny. Her little arms were folded delicately down her body like some varieties of flowers close their petals in repose come dusk. She was buried up to her waist in soil. Her top portion protruded from the ground, weakly, akin to a wilted flower in a cultivated bed.

Looking back now, and it seems macabre to say it, but she could not have been more aptly named. Her name was Daisy. Daisy Maude Kearney.

From the outset, police found it difficult to settle on an investigative approach. Daisy's husband, Patrick, was briefly under suspicion. She had fled the marriage because of his violence. He admitted to police that he'd unleashed a torrent of filthy abuse on his wife and had made the tiny woman cower when he belted her. Then he argued that she had driven him to it: she'd been a drinker, and his violence was intended to curb her, not kill her. Besides, he added at his police interview, he had only ever smacked her with an open hand, never a closed fist. The officers believed Patrick, and he wasn't seriously considered to be a suspect.

Police posted a reward calling on witnesses for information. Two local thick-as-thieves men – Jimmy Ellicombe and Teddy Redi (real name Edgar Read) – came forward. They claimed to have been at Moore Park a few months before, and to have seen a man acting strangely over a woman's prostrate body.

Police wondered why the men hadn't come forward sooner. And how had they seen so much on a pitch-black night? The men said they had night-vision glasses that they carried with them to the park in the evening because they were peeping Toms and liked to watch 'naughties'. They also admitted to being pickpockets. While a couple was otherwise engaged, the thieves helped themselves to any wallets and bags cast aside with the underwear on the ground. 'I steal only money and I leave the handbags in the park,' said Ellicombe.

Reading the story today, it is hard to believe the police accepted the credibility of Ellicombe and Read's account. Night-vision goggles were an ingenuity of the Second not the First World War, so the men could not have been using surplus military equipment or war memorabilia from the recently ended war. For reasons unknown, however, police found their story compelling and set about to find evidence which might substantiate their claims. The men said a shovel had been used to conduct the partial burial of Daisy; police found a shovel near the crime scene but couldn't verify if it was the one involved. The pickpocket peeping Toms also claimed to have seen a pair of earrings on the ground; these were never recovered. Every possible lead culminated in a dead end, yielding nothing in terms of hard evidence that might support a police case.

Officer William Thomas O'Brien claimed to have conversed with Daisy about a week prior to her death. Apparently she'd told him she was working 'on a scam on a guy'. Daisy was a prostitute, and rumour had it she'd been flirting with danger by courting a man involved in organised crime. The lead seemed credible but virtually impossible to follow. If anyone knew to whom she'd been referring, they weren't willing to talk to police about it.

Then a local van driver, John Carl Jensen, was identified as a man known to keep company with Daisy. They'd been seen drinking ale together in an east-side oyster saloon. Police concluded that Jensen had perhaps been the last person to see Daisy alive. Multiple witness statements (from eastern suburbs locals and bar owners) were collected, but they conflicted with each other. There was even disagreement between the key witnesses over what they believed they had seen on the night of Daisy's murder. Ellicombe said it was Jensen he had seen in the sandhills with Daisy, while Read said the man resembled Daisy's husband, Patrick.

At the inquest, the legitimacy of witness testimony was called into question. The coroner found the accounts of Ellicombe and Read to be spurious and forced them to admit they were serial offenders who gave eyewitness statements in exchange for money. Both men had received reward money in other cases, in exchange for statements.

John Carl Jensen was put on trial for Daisy's murder, but ultimately found not guilty. To this day, her case remains unsolved.

•

Two years later, in May 1924, another dead woman was found in a public park, this time a little further east in a parcel of native scrub known as Long Bay. Like Iris Marriott would be in 1932, this victim was discovered by a teenager: a young male shop assistant taking a short cut through the bush. The body was found lying facedown in sandy soil, surrounded by banksia scrub.

Police identified the woman as Rebecca May Anderson, her married name, although she had many other aliases. These included May Hardy, Rebecca May Sadler and May Richmond. Rebecca was a prostitute, and like many in her profession she used multiple monikers – having more than one name reduced the likelihood of being convicted multiple times for the same offence. Prostitution charges, particularly several of them, were viewed very dimly by the judiciary, and harsher sentences were given the more convictions one had. Judges believed that increasingly harsher sentences would reduce recidivism. They did not. Many women were soliciting because they had no access to alternative sources of income.

Monikers were also a means of signalling availability, akin to an open-for-business sign. Women who worked the streets were often called Dot, Ivy, Daisy or May (like May Miller). Women also used aliases to protect themselves. An alias preserved their anonymity. They could lead double lives.

When officers rolled Rebecca's body over, they were horrified by what they saw. The lower section of her body had sustained deep cuts and lacerations, her wounds clotted with sand and debris. Her orifices, including her mouth, had been filled with sand. Rebecca had been in her early thirties, and like Daisy she had an exceptionally small frame. Police noted that teeth were missing from her upper jaw, but this was later found to be due to decay.

Her body had been stripped, and there had been no attempt by the murderer to remove, hide or destroy evidence. A blue straw hat with green imitation-silk thread, a fake crocodile skin handbag and black lace-up shoes were scattered around the scene. A sad bunch of artificial flowers and ferns, threaded together with steel wire, was found not far from the body, along with a glass of whisky. A pocketknife had also been discarded. The device normally had a toothpick and a pair of tweezers attached, but police noted that these instruments had been broken off and were missing. A dark-blue jersey silk dress, trimmed with crocheted lace on the neck, sleeves and skirt, had been tossed into the bush. A brown woollen golf coat was found close by as well, along with a camisole. Police concluded that the latter had been removed after the attack had begun, because it was the only item soaked in blood. Most of Rebecca's blood had spilled on the ground.

The police soon had a wealth of information, because rumours about Rebecca were circulating. Word had spread throughout the inner-city street gangs that she'd been seen in the company of a man called Snowy. Though this was a common nickname for a pale-skinned man with exceptionally blond hair, it was also the name of one of the most notorious gangsters in Sydney: Snowy Cutmore. The second rumour was about Rebecca herself. Some said she was a 'dog' – a slang term used to describe someone always sniffing around for information, retrieving it and taking it away. In other words, a police informant. If either one of the rumours was true, it meant that she'd had enemies.

The constable charged with inspecting the crime scene noted the unusually large amounts of blood on the sand and beneath the trees. Rebecca had experienced something unspeakable.

An examination of her body revealed that her murderer had stabbed her with pieces of wood torn from the banksias abundant in that area of the park. The attacker had also wounded her internally, leaving abrasions and tears. Dr Palmer, the medical expert who would later examine Iris's body, said that death had been due to shock and internal haemorrhage caused by the brutal use of an instrument. It confirmed what police suspected. The woman had not died because of a single injury, but due to the cumulative impact of many.

The eastern suburbs scrubland is unique, and beautiful, and somewhat unforgiving. Melaleuca, acacia and grass trees were common throughout the area at the time. Though the area is now heavily developed, where the native scrub still grows it is dense and barbed and low to the ground. The eastern suburbs banksia native to Long Bay and La Perouse has a distinctive foliage and blossom even within the coastal varieties of banksia. Known for its abrasive leaf and woody shrub structure, its wildflowers have a unique structure and texture. The seed-bearing part of the eastern banksia comprising the flower spikes and fruiting cones are, in effect, the plant's sexual organs. Superficially at least the banksia blooms do not look much like a cultivated English flower but might be said to bear closer resemblance to a spiky oversized corncob. To kill Rebecca, different parts of the plant had been creatively refashioned as murder weapons. Much of the stabbing, scratching and thrusting appeared to have occurred after she was dead, although the medical examination couldn't confirm this.

Though it was beyond the scientific testing of the time and Palmer could not categorically prove it, the medical report alluded to what everyone was thinking: the killer had improvised using the local materials available in order to torture Rebecca. The police constable who had found her camisole and the clots of blood also found a cob. Pieces of banksia branches were found within her vagina, and the banksia cob discovered nearby had probably been forced inside her too. In all likelihood, the killer may have raped Rebecca with the cruellest phallus it was possible to lay hand on – a makeshift dildo fashioned from a banskia cob.

Rebecca's death was a crime of 'unprecedented brutality', wrote one newspaper, and 'disgusting', 'insane' and 'bacchanalian', wrote others. Sir John Macpherson, the Professor of Psychiatry at the University of Sydney, created a proto-profile of the killer (the language of profiling didn't exist yet). According to him, her murder involved 'a sub-normal mind and indicated bestiality of the lowest type'.

None of this helped police solve the crime. They hoped that a witness would be the key, but although many people came forward with information, most of it was unhelpful.

Rebecca had been lodging at a flat in Ultimo, but she had only moved there two days before her death. However, she'd been a prostitute in the Ultimo area for some time. 'She was dirty, usually drunk, and in the company of men of all nation-alities,' it was said. In 1920s Australia, non-Anglo migrants experienced extreme marginalisation and exclusion, so this was a harsh condemnation that implied she was so immoral she would have a go with anyone, even those people deemed inferior. She met men in Belmore, Prince Alfred and Hyde parks, and frequented bars all over the inner east. She was an alcoholic. Less than a month before her death, she'd been charged with vagrancy.

Police tried to retrace her steps on the day leading up to her death: Saturday, 10 May 1924. A witness confirmed that she had left her home at about 11 a.m. She'd then been seen in a local wine saloon with a man everyone knew as Bill Edwin. Bill, a regular customer and Rebecca's on-off boyfriend, had been there with her many times, and they'd been seen to brawl in the street together. The saloon's proprietor, Charles Stonehouse, had often seen her get drunk in his establishment, although he wasn't absolutely sure if she'd been there on the day before her death. He recalled that she had, on one occasion, turned up at the saloon with two black eyes.

Mrs Ethel Wagner, a housewife living in Kensington, had seen Rebecca climb into a tram in the company of a man. Ethel remembered because both Rebecca and her companion had been hammered drunk, and the companion was notable because he 'looked like a seafarer'.

A detective named Jake Miller, who eight years later would be involved in the investigation of Iris Marriott's murder, played a role in managing Rebecca's case. Throughout the investigation, police interviewed close to two hundred people. The brief presented to the coroner was woeful, and the police inspector deemed responsible for oversight of the case, a man named Leary, openly admitted that they had no prospect of an immediate arrest and no evidence to support one.

A suspect has never been identified in Rebecca May Anderson's murder.

•

Five years passed. In the early morning of Saturday, 23 March 1929, police found a woman partially naked, dead, and lying on a bed of white calla lilies in Hyde Park. Newspapers were found partly draped across her body. A bottle of methylated spirits and a bottle of whisky lay nearby. Her hands were posed in the shape of a cross, which prompted one journalist to suggest the murder might have had a 'spark of religion' about it.

This time the cause of death was difficult to determine. The killer had tied her wrists with silk stockings, neatly in a bow. The killer had choked her – her face was blue and distorted. The killer had also beaten her, as there were bloody wounds on the back of her head. There was evidence that the killer had smothered her. Cuts across her hands suggested she had struggled with her attacker.

Police identified her as an eastern suburbs local known as Vera. They eventually connected many aliases to her: Vera Stirling, Vera Ryan, Vera Ross, Vera Lorraine and Vera Gray. She had operated as what police called a 'lone worker' because she had no known connection to any local brothel. Vera was not the only woman who worked this way, but her working life seemed particularly tragic.

It seemed that every eastern suburbs local could recall a sad vignette of Vera. It was reported that she struggled with alcoholism. Her frequent attempts at temperance, and then unfortunate relapses, all occurred very publicly. She was rumoured to be a woman of 'good breeding' who'd come from a reputable English family and had been, at one time at least, the wife of a New Zealand sea captain. There had been periods of sobriety for Vera, and hoteliers in Darlinghurst and Woolloomooloo reported having seen a very different side of her at those times. 'She would disappear for about six months at a time. Then she would just turn up one day, walk into the hotel, well dressed. She seemed to have her life together again. It didn't last for long . . .' said one hotelier. In the months preceding her death, she'd been spotted wandering the streets in odd shoes and stockings, or with just one shoe on as she stumbled drunk on methylated spirits. All the while, she was soliciting for clients. While misery and addiction were not uncommon along the strip where she worked – the streets bordering Surry Hills and Hyde Park – Vera's story seemed particularly tragic. Everyone, it seemed, had seen her at one time or another completely obliterated by alcohol. Vera was the prostitute who the other prostitutes, even with their own tales of woe, felt sorry for. 'She had no enemies and there was no reason why anyone would want to harm her,' said one of the women who worked the same beat. Only hours before someone murdered her, Vera had been seen dancing and singing Irish songs near Hyde Park.

The *Sunday Times* – which saw her as a casualty of the illegal sex and illicit drugs industries rife in the eastern suburbs – described her murder in the following way: 'The slain woman was driftwood on the sea of the underworld's misery.' Vera's murder was quickly regarded as a cold case by police, and it remains so to this day.

The murders of Daisy, Rebecca and Vera slipped quickly from the public consciousness and from police consciousness too. In the early twentieth century, the term 'serial killer' did not form part of the criminal lexicon and certainly not in the way the term has entered common usage in the early twenty-first century. From the police standpoint, they were difficult murders to solve. And while police didn't know who was responsible, they believed they knew why the murders had occurred – in their eyes, the victims had been attacked because they were engaged in dangerous and immoral work; their deaths were almost regarded to be a kind of occupational health and safety risk. Sex in exchange for money was hazardous.

Lots of jobs were high risk in the 1920s and 30s, and in Sydney the building of the Sydney Harbour Bridge had made this work very visible. The dogman riding the crane hook as it swung forty storeys over Sydney Harbour, with absolutely no safety line, was admired by the public for the risks he was willing to take to feed his family. The prostitute who risked her life with dangerous and violent clients in order to feed her children was not viewed in quite the same way. Prostitutes were immoral, and this shaped attitudes to their deaths. Their murders were unfortunate; however, the pitiful circumstances of the women's lives, and their own poor choices, had made them easy pickings – or so it was believed at the time. For these reasons, NSW police dismissed the deaths and overlooked them, as other criminal matters consumed their attention.

By early December 1932, five women had been killed in parks and gardens across the city's east over eleven years, two of them within the previous six months. Women were being picked and plucked like flowers, and soon another one was added to the daisy chain.

4

PENNY IN THE SLOT

IT WAS LATE AFTERNOON ON WEDNESDAY, 14 DECEMBER 1932, and Patience O'Connor was waiting for her daughter to come home. Although she was alone, it was anything but peaceful inside the tiny terrace on Holden Street, Redfern.

Patience didn't need to look at the position of the sun or the clock on the wall to guess the time – the rhythm of industry that surrounded her home told her what hour it was. During the working day, the striking and grinding and twisting of metal echoed out of the deep valley of the railway mainten-ance yard nearby. As the day came to an end, the quiet that fell across the rail yard was quickly replaced by the regular rumble of trains carrying commuters home.

Where the O'Connor family lived in Redfern was also the gateway to the less salubrious part of east Sydney. The suburbs of Alexandria, Rosebery, Zetland and Waterloo were all considered to be east of the city. But these areas hadn't been subdivided to accommodate grand gabled homes, like those surrounding Centennial Park, and there were no cultivated parks through which locals might stroll. More refinery than refined, this part of east Sydney was noisy and dirty because blue-collar men from all over the city flocked here to work, and they all migrated through Redfern on their commute. The O'Connor family lived in a rush-hour thoroughfare.

At about six o'clock Patience grabbed a skillet to begin preparing dinner. The percussion of family life inside the home, and the economic drudgery outside of it, could be heard as a discordant clash inside the very kitchen where Patience stood. The tap dripped incessantly into the sink, hot dripping sizzled in the pan, and the tinny whistle of the kettle pierced the air. Without warning, the distinctive powdery tone of a locomotive horn blasted out from the railway tracks. Shortly after, a train squealed with a deafening scream as a driver hit the brakes on station approach. The industrial complex set the tempo for the city, like a metronome for a metropolis, and the family had little choice but to try to keep time.

From the kettle Patience splashed boiling water over the cold, wet leaves already in the pot. While waiting for the tea to draw, she looked around her. Every week she noticed more damage. Cracked walls framed a cracked window, and the fissures in the wall were growing, creeping diagonally upward at an alarming rate. The rickety window wouldn't completely close, and although it offered a view it wasn't much of one – family laundry was strung along a wire running across the yard, beyond which lay a broken fence. When Patience had hung the calico bedsheets out that morning they'd been wet and clean; now, in the late afternoon sun, they were fluttering dry and black. Factory soot had settled across them and the yard and the windowsill as if something dark and ominous had swept through Redfern on an easterly breeze and had now settled on the O'Connor home.

Patience counted out sausage links and portions of potatoes sufficient to feed her family. These days she always rationed carefully. But she hadn't always lived like this. The family had never been wealthy, but Patience had been hit harder than most by the economic depression of 1932. Neighbours had once envied her. Arthur, her husband, had been a successful hairdresser in Waterloo. And while many in the neighbourhood had known him as a charismatic local identity and business owner, even more people knew him as a champion swimmer.

As parents, Arthur and Patience had raised four children. As a trainer, Arthur had raised four accomplished swimmers and divers. Stanley, Albert, Arthur junior and Elizabeth Isabel – known as Bessie – had been encouraged by their father from an early age to be fearless in the water. When interviewed by a newspaper about the sporting prowess in the family, Bessie said she didn't remember a time when she couldn't swim.

Arthur's parenting philosophy was simple: he paid his children to be good. In a bound notebook, kept on a special shelf, he stored a behaviour diary. The book was ruled up just like a ledger – with credits (good deeds) and debits (bad deeds) listed. But it wasn't Arthur senior who wrote in the ledger – he relied on his children to be honest by recording a full account of their good and bad deeds. Arthur wanted them to be humble, and he discouraged them from making overstated claims just to earn money. A good deed could be something as simple as turning up to school a little early; a bad deed might be arriving late for a training session at the beach. With this method, Arthur believed he was teaching his kids an important lesson: the grandeur of an act isn't important but, rather, the level of honesty in your heart. At the end of the week, Arthur paid the surplus of good deeds over bad, at the rate of ten shillings per hundred. He paid the balance directly into the children's bank accounts. It was 'striking proof of the innate goodness of the young O'Connors,' wrote one journalist. The system cost him about seven pounds a year: an absolute fortune to a child in the 1920s.

Arthur's system seemed to work effectively not just as a behaviour management approach, but as a coaching technique as well. His children trained, and trained hard. They were competitive, committed and successful, and they loved and respected the water. The front window of his hairdressing studio didn't contain stylised pictures of models with neatly trimmed hair but was decorated with his children's swimming medals and diving trophies. He said, 'I don't believe in bullying children and beating them . . . Trust a child, put him on his honour and you will never regret it. While at the same time you will be building up his character as you could never hope to do with Solomon's spare the rod ideas.'

The O'Connors achieved a local celebrity. They were very successful athletes, and they were also a stalwart Redfern family. The children were champion divers at Cleveland Street High School. Arthur junior, in particular, was considered a prodigy. His springboard diving was so good he would go on to compete in the prestigious Empiad trials: the British Empire Games, a precursor to the Commonwealth Games. To this day, photographs of his death-defying exploits are stored in the state archives. He participated in one of the most dangerous events there was: high tower diving. The black-and-white prints show a small but strong little boy, in short swimming trunks, beside a terrifyingly tall ladder, many storeys high, leading up to a narrow diving board. It's estimated that high divers can reach speeds of almost a hundred kilometres per hour. In another photo, Arthur junior hurtles towards water resembling a thick sheet of hard and shiny glass.

Arthur junior participated in competitions but he also travelled with carnivals. In the 1920s and 30s, open-air events designed to attract large crowds – like circuses, football games and mass beachside picnics – were popular because the organisers could make a profit while still only charging a penny entry fee. Wonky backdrops, shonky stages and crooked trapezes were swung on, leapt off and somersaulted from by anyone fearless enough to perform the stunts. It was affordable entertainment for cost-conscious families. If a child was the performer, it only intensified the thrill of the event because the public could marvel at a child seemingly so willing to face death. One photo of Arthur in particular captures the very moment that would have had the audience enthralled. Tiny Arthur is a dot in the air, caught in mid-flight – plummeting from the top of the high tower. It is a genuinely dangerous moment that has been captured, yet the skill of the young diver is evident. His arms are curved back elegantly, like the wings of a bird in upstroke. Somehow, the photograph has managed to capture both the strength and control of the leap upwards, and then the deadly gravity of the fall. With diving training, the water would save the boy's life. Without training, the water would have broken his back. A caption at the bottom labels this act of death-defying risk for public entertainment simply 'the wonder boy'.

Swimming and diving had defined the life of the O'Connor family, and in 1932 they faced a very different kind of dive – an economic one. By December of that year, they were in financial freefall.

At some point in the mid to late 1920s, Patience had separated from her husband and moved into the Holden Street terrace. While marital separations were deeply disapproved of in Australian society at the time, Patience did something that was considered even worse than seeking a divorce – when she left, she didn't take the children. In making this choice she breached social norms surrounding women's behaviour: she was both a wife unwilling to fulfil her conjugal responsibilities and a mother who'd abandoned her children.

Very soon after, Arthur senior brought a new spouse into the family home, and father and stepmother assumed responsibility for the care of the children.

Then, in 1930, Arthur senior suddenly died, and the children came to live with their mother. Patience had struggled financially after leaving Arthur, but the situation now got significantly worse because he'd been providing her with a monthly stipend. As most of the children were now old enough to help support themselves, under normal circumstances the family might have made a financial recovery – unfortunately, the NSW economy was in decline. Even Arthur junior, who'd been able to scrape together money in the hardest of times by putting on diving shows at carnivals, found himself out of work without his father to manage his act. Bessie had worked for a while in a local factory, but there were so many unemployed men across the city that employers were quick to fire a sixteen-year-old girl and give the job to a bloke with children to support.

Since the death of her estranged husband, Patience had lived on 'book-up', a credit system run informally by local businesses and provided only to neighbourhood clientele. By December 1932, Patience owed her landlord forty-six pounds in rent – a huge debt for a single mother with access to only rudimentary social welfare support. So she counted every teaspoon of tea, every ounce of oats, every link of sausage, and even every cubic foot of gas down to the very last penny.

On that day, 14 December, Patience had borrowed a shilling from the woman who ran the local corner store. The money was to cover the tram fare and entrance fee for Bessie to swim in the Coogee Baths. The amount wouldn't be enough for her to catch a tram all the way to the beach – she'd have to walk part of the way – but this at least made it possible for her to attend training. The shilling sat on the table next to Patience as she waited for her daughter to arrive home.

Gas heating was a luxury, so Patience covered a dish of sausage and mash with an upturned plate and placed it in the cooling oven. She had only cooked for herself and Bessie; Arthur junior was at swimming training, and Bessie's two other brothers were working long shifts for the local cab company. Sitting there with a pot of warm tea, Patience traced the rough indentations of the letters BOC on the surface of her dining-room table. She vividly recalled how, as a young girl, Bessie had dug her initials into the table top with a kitchen knife. It was the only table Patience owned, and she'd been furious with Bessie at the time. They'd quarrelled terribly over it, along with many other things over the years – including Bessie's friends, her spending and how much she went out. But Patience believed that their relationship was finally improving.

When the phone rang, Patience startled momentarily. The caller was one of Bessie's girlfriends, Daisy Moffatt. When Patience advised the girl that her daughter wasn't home, Daisy didn't leave a message, she just hung up.

At about six-thirty Patience heard the turn of a key in the front door. It wasn't loud, but somehow she always heard it. The door rattled in its frame as Bessie struggled to release the sticky lock. Then a slender young woman ran through the house, her fashionably bobbed wavy hair bouncing as she picked up speed. The large trophies displayed in the hallway rocked back and forth on the sideboard as she tore along the hallway to her room.

Bessie's love of swimming had never abated. She remained a member of the Randwick and Coogee Ladies' Swimming Club, and she attended training without fail every Wednesday and Saturday. On this evening, she quickly grabbed her swimming costume and towel from a hook near the back door. She shoved the items into a bag, swept right past her mother still waiting in the kitchen, and slid the shilling off the table. Before Patience even had time to say hello, Bessie raced out the front door. Patience, ever frugal, transferred the plate of food from the cold oven to the cooler so it at least might keep till later.

It wasn't until 9.30 p.m. that Bessie returned again. Patience was now upstairs in bed, but awake. 'Bessie?' she called out. She heard her daughter run through the house, and then shortly after heard the clack of court shoes in the hall. 'Bessie?' she called again. Silence. Patience jumped out of bed and was on her way downstairs when Bessie answered, 'I'm going out for a little while, Mum. I won't be long.' Based on the speed with which Bessie was moving, Patience assumed that someone was waiting outside for her. Just as Patience reached the bottom of the stairs, Bessie was closing the door. Home less than five minutes, she'd somehow managed to change, apply make-up and fix her jewellery.

60

Later, Patience recalled in vivid detail what Bessie had been wearing that night. The dress was one of her daughter's favourites: a deep vieux-pink party frock with darts at the waist, a squared-off neckline and short, neatly capped sleeves. Bessie had also put on a choker of red and white beads, though Patience couldn't understand how she'd had time to do it because the clasp was tricky to close. Patience even remembered her daughter's shiny black patent-leather court shoes with striking white trimmings – where had Bessie got the money to buy them? The click-clack of those shoes across the floor as Bessie left the house was the last thing Patience would remember clearly about that night.

The door slammed. Patience stayed up for a while, padding around the house in her slippers. Bessie sometimes put on a pretty party dress but was only out for a short time. This wasn't one of those nights. At about 10.45 p.m. Patience went to bed. Quiet had fallen across Redfern, although the odd train rattled through, and Patience eventually dropped off to sleep.

At six-thirty the next morning she woke and went downstairs to brew a pot of tea. To do this, she needed gas for the stove. In poor suburbs like Redfern, where tenants were known for doing a moonlight flit without paying rent or utilities, the gas provider had developed an ingenious way of ensuring their bills were always paid on time. Customers shelled out on the spot for any gas they used – they had to push a penny in a slot machine and spin the lever until the gas was released from the pipes into the household unit. That slot machine was in Bessie's bedroom, so Patience had to tiptoe in each morning.

On the morning of Thursday, 15 December, Patience knocked lightly on Bessie's door. Work at the nearby rail yard was already in full swing, so it was far from quiet inside their little terrace. But inside Bessie's room, it was silent. Patience knocked again. Keen to get on with the morning, and in need of a cup of tea, Patience pushed the door ajar. The bed was empty. Almost immediately Patience realised this wasn't because Bessie had left for the day. The bed hadn't been slept in. Bessie's swimming bag, wet bathers and towel were still in a pile on the bed. In fact, Patience could smell the sour scent of the ocean as soon as she opened the door – she knew the wet bag had been sitting there for the entire humid summer night.

Patience wasn't alarmed, at least not at first. Bessie had probably stayed at Daisy's, as she sometimes did – this was the first conclusion her mother drew. But the more she thought about it, the more uneasy she became. Bessie usually let her know if she was going to be out all night. Patience wanted to call Daisy, but she didn't know the number and wasn't entirely certain of the girl's name. The more she thought about it, the more the idea that Bessie hadn't come home didn't sit well with her. Her fear grew.

Unsure what to do, and with her boys already at training, Patience ran to ask the nearest neighbour for help. She banged as loudly as she could on their front door. It was still only 6.45 a.m. but her panic had grown so much by this point that she didn't care. After only a short explanation, and many attempts by the neighbour to reassure Patience that she was probably overreacting, the kindly neighbour and the nervous mother came up with a plan: the neighbour's teenage son would go to the police. Within a few minutes, the boy was on his bike pedalling hard to the nearest police station, Redfern.

He returned sooner than anyone expected – the police had dismissed his request for help and sent him away. There was no real evidence the girl was missing, officers said. Patience thanked the neighbours for their help, but ignored the advice from the police. She grabbed her handbag, hat and gloves, and marched down to Redfern police station herself. Again, officers rejected her request for help. One was particularly dismissive. 'The girl will turn up all right,' he said, 'just go home.'

But Patience wouldn't leave. It took convincing, and a considerable number of tears, but the police finally agreed to take a formal report on Bessie as a missing person. They didn't believe the girl was genuinely missing – they wanted the agitated mother out of their station. They sent Patience home, this time with the reassurance that if the girl turned up, they would be in contact. They told Patience to wait at home. She did.

•

George McNamara was living rough, like many people in Sydney at the peak of the Depression. He was one of hundreds who had settled in the shantytown in the Sutherland scrub, just off a dirt road called Farnell Avenue. George was living partly on the land but also on what he could scavenge from the suburbs around him. He'd taken up the habit of scrounging in the early morning – specifically on the hunt for cigarettes. He walked up and down the main roads and side tracks, salvaging butts piffed from the windows of passing cars.

In the early morning of 15 December 1932, George found something unexpected. There were no cigarette ends on the road, but a pool of something dark. And it wasn't the only one. He followed a trail of wet stains off Farnell Avenue into the red earth of the national park, where it kept going through the bush. Plants had been pushed over; the woody scrub of grevillea had been broken with some force. There were tyre marks too.

Not far off the road, but not directly visible from it, George stumbled upon the naked body of Bessie O'Connor. 'I wanted a smoke and that is why I was watching the road to see if I could find a cigarette butt or a cigar end. I was broke. When I came to the dark patch on the road I thought it was oil. Then I saw the dark trail into the scrub and I walked a couple of yards into the bush. I almost stepped on her . . . She was pale, like marble . . .'

Around Bessie, birds hopped in short, stubby trees and probed native flowers. A wattlebird, attracted to the sweet nectar, bounced onto a low branch and swung slowly just above her. The bird drank, paused, then scratched a mournful song across the girl. Cicadas hummed a shaman-like chant. The air shimmered, the sunlight bending as waves of heat rose from the red dirt just beyond Bessie and towards the horizon.

The first thing George noted was Bessie's youth. She was naked, her torso clean and smooth and unmarked. Her attacker had dropped her, perhaps unwittingly, atop a large ant nest. Small black specks scurried in long neat lines across the girl's limbs, and with the summer heat the flies were working on the many openings in her face. Her ears and eyes and mouth moved rhythmically with the metallic green-and-blue backs of flies busy with their work. Bessie had only been there a few hours when George found her, but nature had already begun to reclaim her.

The man was transfixed for a moment, stunned by the scene before him. Then he saw, to his utter surprise, the shallow rise and fall of Bessie's chest. As soon as he realised the girl could be saved, George ran as fast as he could back to the main road. He flagged down the first car that passed and told its occupants to fetch help. He waited near the road, the only entry point into the park, to ensure any rescue party could be directed to the location of the girl.

Officers from the local Sutherland unit were the first to respond. An ambulance arrived shortly after, and Bessie was taken swiftly away. The CIB headed towards the scene.

Detective Sergeant Joseph Geldart, a local to Kogarah, arrived before any other officers. With Bessie in the hands of ambulance personnel, he began examining the scene. He took preliminary notes and observations, conscious of disturbing as little as possible, and careful not to leave too many footprints. Of course, there had already been a lot of disturbance during the struggle to carry the young woman safely out of the dense scrub.

Geldart was focused. But in his intensity, he wasn't as mindful of the scrub as he might have been. He also wasn't very quick on his feet. He had served in World War I, and after suffering a septic leg in Malta and being gassed on a field of battle in France, he'd never been quite the same. This was sometimes interpreted as clumsiness. He tripped on branches as he surveyed the scene. He struggled to unhook his jacket from the brittle undergrowth as he sought to work out the entry and exit points of the tyre tracks that led to the place of Bessie's attack. Had she been hit by a car as well? It was difficult to tell. He got down on his haunches and closely studied the patterns in the ground. He wasn't a tracker, but he could tell the investigation would be assisted by one – though the suburbs weren't far away, this bushland was impenetrably dense. He reflected on how utterly terrifying the young woman's journey to this place must have been. At night, away from the streetlights, he speculated that the area would have been very, very dark, even beneath moonlight. She could have screamed; no one would have heard. Running away would have been impossible – on one side was unpassable scrub, and on the other a rough red-dirt road presented an opportunity to be run down by a vehicle. There was no doubt that Bessie had been brutally attacked in a particularly brutal place.

As Geldart was bent over, eyes downward, he didn't hear the soft slither through the foliage just beside him. A flicker of grey–green appeared in the corner of his eye, so quickly he had no time to react. When he realised, it was too late. A large death adder, unused to being disturbed by foot traffic and out enjoying the morning sun, pounced from beneath a grevillea and struck hard. Startled, Geldart fell backwards on the ground and skittered away awkwardly on his hands and feet.

The detective was lucky. The snake had struck just a fraction too low, its fangs bouncing off the hard leather of his boot. If the venom had entered his bloodstream, the bite would almost certainly have been fatal.

Shaken, Geldart dusted himself off, struggled to his feet and sought to restore what was left of his dignity. He then called for more officers to be sent to the scene.

The process of searching and clearing the bush yielded evidence. A small toll-road ticket with a number was on the ground near the body. A beer bottle lay about fifty to sixty yards away; however, there was no way of knowing if it was connected to the crime.

When CIB officers arrived around midmorning, the mood at the crime scene immediately changed. Local officers were in deference to the more experienced senior officers reputed to be the best investigators in the state. It also became very clear very quickly that their presence was about more than just the discovery of Bessie O'Connor. With the murder of Iris Marriott having occurred less than a week before, and the investigation into her death barely underway, everyone at the Sutherland crime scene that morning felt that something bigger was going on here, though no one could say exactly what they were dealing with.

The similarities between Bessie's attack and Iris's, and indeed Hilda's, didn't go unnoticed by the officers present. Iris hadn't lived to reveal the name of her attacker, but perhaps they could get Bessie to talk.

First they had to identify her. This was a slight challenge, as she had no criminal record or prints in the system. Ironically the thing that had caused aggravation and distance between mother and daughter was the very thing that would reunite them: Bessie's compulsive spending. Though her shoes were a relatively affordable and mass-produced item, they were still beyond the budget of a widow mother and a daughter with no income. The prominent maker's stamp on the shoes made them easy for police to trace. The retailer had kept thorough account details of those who were unable to pay upfront – and Bessie was one of them. She'd still been making penny payments on her shiny two-tone pumps.

•

Around 3 p.m., two police officers drove to the terrace on 3 Holden Street. One knocked on the small wooden door of the O'Connor home. The other was holding a string of red and white beads.

Patience opened the door.

'Bessie is alive,' one constable said.

The other added, 'But she is not doing well.'

Bessie had been taken to St George Hospital. Patience rounded up Bessie's brothers and rushed straight there. On her arrival she was given instructions. She counted the room numbers as she walked the hospital corridor. When she reached what she thought was the right place, she felt she must be mistaken. A female patient was lying in the bed, in the room that Patience had been directed to, but she didn't recognise the woman as her daughter. Bessie's face was so badly beaten and the swelling on her head and skull was so pronounced that her features were altered.

Patience sat with her daughter. She held her hand, stroking it gently. It was the only part of the girl's body that wasn't bruised. Hospital staff had little in the way of comfort to offer the distraught mother. They claimed that Bessie had rallied weakly, just after she was brought in, long enough for her to mutter something. By the time Patience arrived, several hours later, the girl had lapsed back into a coma. It was second-hand information and not verifiable, but it appeared the word Bessie uttered was 'Frank'. Patience informed police that her daughter did indeed have a friend with that name: Frank Curtis. The police tracked him down, but on interviewing the teenager, they dismissed him as a possible suspect almost immediately. Frank claimed he hadn't seen Bessie for some time, and that he hadn't known much about her movements on Wednesday or even in the weeks leading up to the tragedy.

At St George Hospital, Patience, her sons and a party of officers waited. The mother prayed that her baby would wake. Police prayed too.

Bessie died at 6.20 the following morning. Though her killer had attacked her on 14 December, the date of her murder was officially recorded as 16 December.

As soon as Bessie died, police moved in to gather as much evidence as they could. Attention turned from the landscape of the crime scene, and towards the site of Bessie's body. The way they managed this process would have implications for the entire investigation.

When Bessie died her body was transferred to the morgue. Police from the CIB called Patience there, but did little to support the woman through the process. While CIB detectives were inside the morgue with her daughter's body, Patience was told to wait outside, alone, on a small stool. The detectives may have been engaged in the act of serious, technical and very necessary police work, but it would still have felt like yet another grave indignity for her daughter to endure.

This was a serious public relations misstep. While Patience sat outside, alone and unsupervised, with only dark imaginings of what had been done to her daughter to occupy her thoughts, the press seized an opportunity. Journalists had assembled at the morgue in great numbers, knowing the body was to be brought in – the widowed and grieving mother alone was an opportunity they couldn't pass up. With no money to pay for her daughter's funeral Patience was particularly vulnerable. The *Truth* newspaper made a deal with her, in exchange for unprecedented access to her story: they would pay for her daughter's funeral in full, but she had to give them an exclusive.

Bessie's story was written with one purpose in mind – to stoke public fear about what appeared to be a growing problem in Sydney: what was then known as the 'sex slaying' of women in public parks. While newspapers had widely reported the deaths of Hilda and Iris, the perception of the women as wicked meant their story was a more difficult sell to a sanctimonious readership. But *Truth* immediately knew how to package Bessie's death, and repackage the other murders that year with it.

Bessie wasn't like the other women, who had lost their lives through a series of immoral choices for which they were partly to blame, wrote *Truth*. Bessie was a good girl – an athlete, a Sydney surf girl from a battling Redfern family. 'Not only would it seem that the monster is a man using modern methods, but he must also be a personable man. It was doubtless easy enough for a fiend to attract the attention of frail women like poor Hilda White and debauched May Miller [Iris Marriott].' Newspapers had to confirm that Bessie was an 'innocent' victim, and to do this they felt it necessary to heavily imply she was chaste: 'A pathologist examination . . . disclosed that Bessie O'Connor was an innocent girl.'

Patience shelled out photo after photo and detail after detail to *Truth*. She was desperate to keep her daughter in the public eye, hoping that anyone who had information would come forward. She provided photos of Bessie as a child, dressed in swimming trunks, standing tall and straight with her arms rigidly at her sides like a cute little soldier. There were photos of swimming trophies. Pictures of an adorable nine-year-old in a bobbed haircut, and a twelve-year-old dressed and ready and hopeful as she headed into adolescence, were all spread across the front page. In the minds of the public this took the tragedy to a much greater depth than stories about prostitutes in the park. Patience's words created fear in the minds of every Sydney mother: 'She fairly danced from the house and I thought that she was probably going out front to have a chat to some of her swimming friends. It appears now that she must have met the maniac in the car as he cruised about looking for a fresh victim.' The words didn't sound like those of a mother, but more like editorial fear-mongering. The words were attributed to Patience just the same. The story embodied the deepest fears held by any mother and served as a cautionary tale for all.

Patience offered her opinions about the police. She had tried but failed, on more than one occasion, to have a missing person's report filed, she said. On the most awful day of her life, when she had received the terrible news that her daughter was in a critical condition, the police had left her to make her own way to the hospital. This was a huge embarrassment for police, given they'd been boasting about the brand-spanking-new van bought less than a year before. It had been bought to replace a broken-down car nicknamed 'the bug' which was said to be held together with string and rope. The public didn't begrudge police their purchase of a powerful Hudson tourer, but they did look rather unkindly at a force seemingly unwilling to use that vehicle to drive a distraught mother to the bedside of her dying daughter. Worse still, the police didn't have just one new vehicle, but had purchased a fleet of motor cars for the exclusive use of the CIB.

For the press, this was an ideal story. While her daughter lay dying in hospital, and time was running out, Patience had borrowed money from the woman at the corner store in order to afford the train fare for her and her sons to make their way to St George. 'She did not have her fare to the hospital and the police with cars rushing backwards and forwards to the hospital did not offer to take her there ... She borrowed the train fare and trudged from the station to the hospital supported by her 18-year-old unemployed son, Arthur O'Connor, who, when a small boy, used to give diving exhibitions from the highest tower at the Domain, thrilling thousands.'

Once *Truth* had an angle, the other papers followed suit. They stoked public fear with reminders that there was at least one maniacal killer on the loose. 'Who lured Bessie O'Connor to her doom?' asked one headline. The *Daily Telegraph* proposed, in an article titled 'Startling Theory in the Park Murder Case: Police May Link Slayer with Three Crimes', that everyone had something to fear as the killer was now not only targeting immoral women. 'Bessie O'Connor was a girl of clean reputation,' the article warned.

'I never had any fear. I was not worried,' said Patience in an interview with a journalist. 'From the time that Bessie was a baby I have told her never to speak to strange men.

I suppose every mother does that.' The paper asked the question that everyone in Sydney was asking: 'Why didn't she heed her mother's ceaseless warning?' And then the paper answered itself: 'Not until the police lay their hands on the maniac will those problems be solved.' The articles published just after Bessie's murder were written explicitly to feed fear and spread terror. The papers provided affordable, low-cost thrills – less than two pennies for the *Daily Telegraph*, and three for *Truth*.

While Patience had negotiated with the media because she needed a solution to a financial problem, this ended up creating further problems for her. In keeping with funeral customs of the time, she wanted Bessie to be brought home. This would allow her to spend time with her daughter's body, for family and friends to have viewings, and for the funeral cortege to respectfully leave from the family home. But the state refused to release the body.

A corpse was now stranded at the morgue, up for grabs, and every undertaker in Sydney knew about it. One approached Patience directly with what looked like official papers. He claimed he had the government contract to authorise the burial of the body; all Patience needed to do was sign the papers, he said. In her weakened state, and not cognisant of what she was signing, she conceded. It turned out he wasn't a government undertaker – Patience O'Connor had signed loan forms that required her to make regular weekly payments on an extravagant funeral for her daughter. The charlatan undertaker had just swindled a grieving mother.

The problems didn't end there. The depressed economy created ruthless competition for business in the funeral trade. Fisticuffs broke out at the morgue between two undertakers, both of whom claimed they had rights to Bessie's body.

When the crooked undertaker turned up at the O'Connor home, Patience refused to pay. Not taking no for an answer, she was spirited away in a car to the undertaker's office where he tried to bully her into payment. When locals heard about what had happened, they contacted *Truth*.

The NSW Ladies' Amateur Swimming Association, in conjunction with *Truth*, paid for the funeral. And the state finally agreed to release the body directly to Patience.

Unlike Iris, Hilda, Rebecca, Vera and Daisy, who had left their homes never to return, Bessie would go home one last time.

•

No one predicted the size of Bessie O'Connor's funeral, and the police had significantly underestimated the need for crowd control. The strong solidarity of the local blue-collar worker community in Redfern added to the numbers, so too did the school community and the widespread press coverage of the event. Everyone seemed to know an O'Connor, or had gone to school with an O'Connor, or knew someone who had.

A funeral procession was arranged. With the involvement of *Truth*, it was carefully orchestrated to generate the most publicity possible. Hundreds of people not only lined the streets but also shuffled through the narrow little terrace to view Bessie's body, which was laid out in the front room. Then the procession left Holden Street and walked the long stretch of Eveleigh. Although the work of the railway yard pressed on, some of its workers stood to attention for a moment or two, and the mechanical din of the suburb slowed and fell ever so briefly silent. Just for an instant, the air of Redfern seemed still and clean and clear.

Bessie's brothers played an important role in the event. Arthur junior, Stanley and Albert O'Connor were all involved in local sporting clubs including football as well as diving and swimming. The guard of honour was composed of the Randwick and Coogee Ladies' Swimming Club, the NSW Ladies' Amateur Swimming Association and the Green Cabs company where the O'Connor boys worked. 'Redfern is not a locality in which the people calmly accept such brutality as was displayed by the devil in human shape,' wrote one journalist.

Bessie O'Connor's public funeral was stage-managed by newspapers in an effort to create maximum impact. Yet the emotion of the event remained all too real, and deeply personal for Bessie's family. Much like the coma that her daughter had experienced, Patience had endured a trauma so great that her body began to shut down in order to protect itself.

In the late afternoon of 14 December, a mother had waited patiently for her daughter to come home. In the late afternoon three days later, that same mother tried to wait patiently beside her daughter's casket at Rookwood Cemetery. As the pallbearers lowered Bessie's body into the ground, the despondent mother stared dumbstruck at the freshly dug darkness of the grave. Her knees gave way to the gravity of her grief. She fell forward, almost straight onto her daughter's casket. Redfern locals rushed to hold her up. Patience screamed. She took a step back from the grave and dropped to her knees as she completely surrendered to her grief. For a moment it seemed she was about to pray. Instead, she simply wept.

5

TRAFFICKING

IT TOOK HOURS FOR CONSTABLES TO CLEAR THE TRAFFIC CONGES-
tion left in the wake of Bessie O'Connor's funeral procession.
As darkness fell, a traffic jam of a very different kind began
to build in eastern Sydney. A cortege of police cars crawled
through the streets, picking up officers along the way. The
cars were all headed in one direction – towards CIB headquarters in the Central Police Station complex. Every available
officer in the inner-city precincts had been told that they may
be required to assist in an investigation.

Police Commissioner Walter Childs wanted answers.
He had summoned the most experienced detectives in the
state, including Detectives McRae, Parmeter and Pattinson;
and Detective Sergeants Miller, Keogh, Power, Barratt, and
Matthews. Detective Swasbrick and Constables Bell and Smith

from Paddington police attended to provide local knowledge about the streets surrounding two of the murder sites, Centennial Park and Queens Park. Detective Constable William Payne and Detective Geldart – the officers who'd spent the most time scouring the scene of the attack on Bessie – were there as well. The meeting was convened by the CIB chief, Pryor.

The senior leadership team had assembled to talk strategy, like generals in a war room. An army of constables had also been marshalled. They all crowded into a meeting room and huddled around a large desk. Detectives were seated, and constables stood at the perimeter listening and making notes in anticipation of what the next steps of the investigation would be. No formal record, or minutes or transcript was retained. From the investigation that ensued, however, we know something of what was discussed that evening.

At first police were tight-lipped and didn't admit to the press that they believed the murders of Iris and Bessie were related. Their responses to media questions were guarded. But journalists observed the movements of key personnel. Based on their attendance at meetings, the press concluded that police knew the murders were linked, even if they publicly refused to admit it when the investigation began. Detective Inspector Jake Miller was a chief within the CIB of what was known as B area, which took in the eastern part of the city. From the very early stages of the investigation into Bessie O'Connor's murder in Sutherland, Miller took the lead, yet this suburb technically fell into the zone catchment for C area, the city's south. As one journalist pointed out at that time, 'His participation . . .

has given rise to the belief that the murder is linked to that of May Miller [Iris Marriott] in Queen's Park last weekend.'

Hilda's investigation had been abandoned months before due to lack of evidence, but now three startlingly similar murders had occurred in a short space of time, within a relatively close geographical area. All three shared two factors: sex and a car. Both factors were linked to the economy of Sydney at the time.

There is no doubt that privately the police believed the three cases were linked in some way, though publicly these admissions rarely came. Police believed private motor vehicles had transported the three women to their respective murder sites. From a police standpoint, however, using this information to progress the investigations would prove challenging. To understand the obstacles facing police, it's important to understand how Sydney was slowly transforming into a motoring metropolis.

•

In the 1920s and 30s, cars were reshaping not only the landscape of Sydney, but also the way residents were engaging with their city and with each other. Though data on vehicle ownership from this period isn't entirely reliable, counts of vehicles give some insight. In 1921, the official statistics on motor vehicle ownership put car registrations at 99 270. Data from 1927 ranks Australia fifth in a world census of vehicle ownership with 365 651 cars and 70 228 motorcycles. By 1939, however, this had grown to 562 271 private cars and 258 025 commercial vehicles. This indicates the remarkable cultural fascination with cars in Australia from the moment they were available for sale. In less than ten years, by 1930, it was roughly estimated that for every eleven people in Sydney there was at least one motor vehicle. This is particularly remarkable given retail prices: motor vehicles were luxury items, and very few people who had regular jobs and regular incomes would ever have been able to afford to own one. Which perhaps explains the other interesting trend data from this period – while few people could afford to own a car, almost everyone had the ability to steal one.

Data is sketchy, but police certainly perceived a rise in car theft in the 1930s. In 1929 they publicly released crime statistics: 2300 cases of grand theft auto had occurred in one year, in the metropolitan area alone. In 1932, owners routinely left their keys with their vehicles; stealing a vehicle only required walking up to it, knowing how to start it, then driving away. Thieves were also hard to catch as number-plates could easily be switched. By the mid-1920s the Motor Traffic and Railways Traffic Department in New South Wales had introduced tighter regulation of numberplates, though it seemed to have little impact.

Sydney began to be reshaped, moulding social, cultural and economic life around the motor vehicle. The 1930s were the dawn of the modern era of road expansion, in which strands of streets became woven together into the web of roadways that define Sydney to this day. It might also be said that 1932 was the year in which the city became truly defined as a motoring metropolis. To link the city centre to its west, a serviceable road was needed for the larger volumes of faster motor vehicle traffic heading along old Parramatta Road. To better connect George Street to the expanding frontier of suburbs to the west, a wide intersection was needed. In the 1930s George Street West became 'the Broadway' and it is still considered Sydney's motor gateway to the Great Western Motorway (Parramatta Road and the M4). In 1928 what had been known as the Great South Road (connecting Sydney to Melbourne) was renamed the Hume Highway and remains so to this day. Significant construction work was done to better connect Newcastle to Sydney by road between 1925 and 1930. The sections of road which hugged the Pacific Ocean and connected towns all the way up the east coast of Australia were also transforming into a high-speed corridor for motorised transport. In 1931 the highway heading north, which to this day constitutes almost 800 kilometres of continuous road, was named the Pacific Highway.

The year of 1932 is also often informally known as the year of the birth of modern Sydney because of the defining moment that occurred: the completion of the Sydney Harbour Bridge. Sydney had historically been cut in two by a body of water, and some believed the opening of the bridge finally made the city whole. It did more than this: all capitals and major regional centres along the east coast were now connected by road.

From the start of the motoring age in Australia, macho culture drove the love of these vehicles and the fascination with horsepower and sleek duco. Every year, men competed to record the shortest travel time down the east coast. In December 1928, two men made the trip from Brisbane GPO to Sydney GPO in the record-breaking time of fifteen hours and eight minutes. Crowds cheered when the duo pulled up right in front of the grand post office building in the centre of town. In that year the winner was an Oldsmobile, but the record had been broken twelve times over sixteen years by several makes and models, including the Essex, the Vauxhall and the Overland. Speed and thrills and pleasure and conquest quickly became synonymous with cars.

If Ford is the father of motoring, Essex might be labelled the mother. Essex made cars accessible to the mass market by providing a closed-top vehicle at an affordable price for families. The major distributor for these cars in New South Wales, Messrs Dalgety and Company, pushed the closed-cabin sedan hard in Sydney in the late 1920s, and sales boomed. Up to 1928 only about 10 per cent of cars purchased had been closed cabin, but the balance tipped towards them from then on.

Private car owners began leasing their vehicles as an altern-ative income stream – and to cover the exorbitant capital cost of the vehicle and its ongoing maintenance. With no formal regulation governing vehicle rentals, the hirer set the terms. Some didn't allow anyone under twenty-one to hire a car. For others, 'no one smelling of drink may secure a vehicle' (noted the copy of one private car rental advertisement). Car owners enjoyed the after-hours income stream that rentals provided. Members of the general public enjoyed the new night-time recreations offered by temporary access to a car. While the Ford still remained popular, the closed-cabin Essex was used for racier undertakings. One editorial claimed that vehicles were hired for 'petting parties' involving 'whispered words of tenderness broken by long silences'.

Cars offered unique opportunities for sex to take place at a time when sexual activity outside of marriage was still taboo. The Essex sedan gained popularity because it offered a more spacious enclosed cab with four doors, privacy, and shelter from the weather. Marketed as a family car because it made long journeys relatively comfortable, the closed cabin also allowed long nights to pass in relative comfort.

Police knew these vehicles were linked to sex, and theft. The slang term 'joyrider' was used to describe car thieves. It was perhaps a particularly appropriate epithet because of the nature of the joy being sought.

Cars not only reshaped urban planning but also the daily commute to work, the nature of leisure, the way that commerce was transacted, and the delivery of goods to and from and within the city itself. They also affected how crime was undertaken. Cars offered speed. Cars offered pleasure. Cars offered new business opportunities for sex. Cars had begun to transform the lives of both the lawful and the lawless in Sydney in ways which would shape the rest of the twentieth century. Traffic was becoming a way of life in Sydney, and so too was trafficking.

•

Back at the Central Police Station complex, police officers considered how to move the investigation of Bessie's murder forward, and this inevitably led to comparisons with the other two recent murders. The vaginas of all three victims had been swabbed, and semen was found in each case. The officers present at the meeting reviewed the known facts. Iris Marriott had supported herself, her partner and her child with earnings from sex work – this had been fairly easy for police to establish, given her criminal record and local reputation. Hilda had been moonlighting as a prostitute, sneaking into an area of the park known to be 'used by couples'. It hadn't taken long for police to obtain information that Bessie had also engaged in escort services. The night of her murder was not the first time that Bessie, along with her friends Daisy Moffatt and Dot O'Dell, had been driven by men to the Sutherland bush.

One detective, it isn't clear who, posited that the killer may have borne a grudge against prostitutes. In 1932, syphilis and gonorrhoea were identified to be significant public health risks, and testing was readily available for both diseases. Police conjectured that perhaps the murderer was infected with an STD, and under the belief he had contracted the disease from a prior sexual encounter with a prostitute. The motive for murder, therefore, might be revenge. This was informally coined 'the grudge theory'. Police believed that grudge attacks were driven by what was speculated to be the 'insensate rage' of a male perpetrator.

•

The fact that police gave the grudge theory serious consideration says much about the attitude of police towards women, but also reveals how public the sex industry had become in Sydney by this time.

Red-light districts had flourished in the east of Sydney, and the streets there were described as having an infestation of 'footpath flossies' and 'street tarts'. By 1932, the police presence in the east had grown stronger in an attempt to stop the sale of sex on the street.

Networks of brothels existed in Surry Hills, Darlinghurst and Paddington. Tilly Devine was known for her premises in Palmer Street, Woolloomooloo, and Kate Leigh operated hers in Devonshire Street and Fitzroy Street, Surry Hills. But brothels still needed to draw men indoors to 'do the business'. A prostitute known as White Lily, for example, had the job of soliciting men on Elizabeth Street, then bringing them back to a row of residentials. 'In the vicinity of the railway can be found more than one hundred girls who occupy their time from dusk till dawn tramping the streets in search of victims . . .' wrote one newspaper. If stopped by officers who asked what she was doing, White Lily could simply point to her wedding ring, a common tactic used to throw police off the trail. The proximity to Central Railway Station was important because both domestic and country rail lines converged there, so men looking for sex in the city only needed to hop off the train then wander the eastern Sydney streets before being approached by a woman.

In Surry Hills and Woolloomooloo, the calls of girls and women posted out on the street – 'Are you lookin' for a girl?' or 'Hello, love' – were coded signals to passing men. In modern economic theory, this pattern of economic activity might be labelled 'clustering': groups of businesses with similar interests and markets gather in a common geographic area because it's mutually advantageous for both buyers and sellers. Surry Hills was a popular retail district in the 1930s for sex, not fashion or coffee as it is today.

As the depression intensified in 1932 working women, in particular, felt the pinch. Many astutely adapted to remain competitive. Prostitutes had to look for new ways to access new markets. They had even begun accepting food coupons from unemployed clients as payment for sexual services rendered. The depression may have changed the pricing structure, but it had been consorting laws that had re-defined the business model. In 1932, the impact of consorting laws was still being felt on those working in brothels. As one paper reported, 'Sydney police with the aid of the consorting act have driven most of the infamous womenkind from the streets ... Rejoicing in the fact that the street girl has been swept from her domain, the public found for a short period that they could enjoy a stroll about the city without being harassed.'

Consorting laws allowed police the opportunity to tackle the problem of soliciting in two ways. First, women could be charged directly for engaging in the selling of sex; second, any women consorting or fraternising with women known to engage in the act of selling of sex could be charged as well.

Though leaders of the underworld Kate Barry (Leigh) and Tilly Devine had the reputation for engaging in a range of criminal activities, it was often consorting laws which offered police the latitude to charge and build a viable case against them.

With consorting laws came new risks for the women involved. Women could be charged for habitually consorting even if they tried to argue they were not soliciting themselves. Inside the criminal enterprise there were risks too, as women found it impossible to leave brothels owned and managed by gangs. Some described it as a form of sexual 'semi slavery'. The conditions were documented to be filthy in some places where sex work was known to take place. One newspaper noted that 'in several of these places the rooms are nothing more than tiny cubicles partitioned off with sheets of asbestos. Gaping holes in the partitioning make privacy an impossibility.'

•

The mean streets of eastern Sydney, for a range of reasons, were developing into places where sex work was becoming more difficult. The car, however, opened up a range of new business opportunities. The retail trends of sex and sedans were becoming increasingly intertwined. Not only did cars offer a site where sex could take place discreetly, but they also gave the driver access to motels, boarding houses and the great outdoors. While city parks had always been used for sex, cars helped facilitate this. Couples were caught by police in cars and in parks, and so too were people engaged in sexual commerce.

The nature of solicitation changed with the arrival of the motor vehicle to the Sydney scene. Negotiation of the sexual act to be performed could occur in the car. The couple could arrive at a destination, perform their business transaction, then be gone before local residents had time to switch on their outdoor lamps to snoop on the unfamiliar vehicle parked near their homes. Cars also made it much more difficult for police to establish if a woman had been soliciting for sex on the street. Coded signals like 'Hello, love' were usually no longer needed; indeed, very little needed to be said – an escort could just hop into a car as it cruised past. And if the prostitute and customer were caught in the act in a park, or in a parked car, they could just claim they were an overly amorous couple. Cars could take the business of sex away from the organised brothels and beyond the reach of the consorting laws and the throbbing and insatiable metropolis, to the quiet and tranquil streets and parks of the suburbs.

On an even darker note, police knew that the greater number of cars in circulation made the collection and transfer of women in international sex-trafficking rings easier as well. Only the previous year, eastern suburbs police had pursued the prosecution of a French couple, posing as husband and wife, who had established a network of men in Sydney to scout for 'talent'. The men were called trappers, and the practice was known as skin buying. The destination for the human captives could be the export market, as far away as Paris, or to elite buyers locally. When police located the traffickers they were found with a half-dressed man and a very young woman in the midst of an advertising shoot to promote the business; provocative photos of the woman had been taken to compile what appeared to be a buyer's catalogue.

There was also active local trading of girls and women. In 1930 police had investigated what they described as a white girl slave trade, 'in which white girls are paraded before the gaze of buyers'. The girls were sold for two pounds each. These human auctions were said to occur in a range of locations across the city, and their underground nature made them difficult for police to track. Again, a network of agents charged a finder's fee to buyers, and motor vehicles enhanced the ability of nego- tiators to manage their criminal activity in secret. 'After the girls pass under the control of their buyers they are spirited away from the city in closed motor cars with curtains drawn.'

•

As prostitutes, Iris Marriott, Hilda White and the very young Bessie O'Connor had their commercial activities greatly facil- itated by the motor vehicle, as all three operated outside the organised brothel system and turned towards what might be called the mobile sex industry. They were freelancers, each driven into sex work out of economic desperation.

Detective Sergeants McRae and Power addressed the officers assembled at HQ, and discussed the many rumours surrounding Iris. One informant told police that her life had been mowed down long before her final drive to Centennial Park: apparently a love affair with a motor-car salesman had sealed her fate. With sales booming, the man had every prospect of a lucrative career, and in the 1920s this usually meant that a wife and family followed. But when Iris got pregnant before they were married, the man put pedal to the metal and fled. It was rumoured that her earnings were secretly sent to an orphanage for the upkeep of the child.

Under the name May Miller, officers confirmed that Iris Marriott had indeed worked the Greens Road strip, popular with soldiers from the nearby military barracks. She often stood right in front of the giant 'McWilliams 99 Port' billboard. It was a sweet fortified wine pitched to be one of the most affordable.

Detective Sergeants Keogh, Barratt, Power, James and Shields all spoke to issues associated with Hilda's murder. Her situation too had been a vulnerable one, but her activities on the night of her death, and in the weeks leading up to it, were more difficult to track than Iris's. The last sighting of Hilda had been with the man in the yellow overcoat, who was said to be a car-sitter for a local wealthy family.

To the officers assembled that night, in the war room at CIB headquarters, Detectives Swasbrick and McRae provided preliminary information about Bessie's case. They knew for certain that she had been driven to the site where her body was found – there was simply no other way to get there. She too had faced economic vulnerabilities.

The area in which Bessie had been found was well known to her and her friends Dot and Daisy. They'd travelled there on what they called 'night-time runs'. Police had managed to corner Daisy on the day of the funeral. The young woman had been careful to characterise the activities as nothing more than social dates or 'harmless fun'. 'We had been told hundreds of times by our mothers never to go out for car rides but we thought it was all right as long as the three of us were always together,' Daisy reputedly stated to one officer. But what their mothers had believed was joyriding was in fact a bespoke escort service run by three teenage girls. They were, in the modern sense of the term, the uber escorts – they had developed a marketing and delivery model that operated outside the established and more institutionalised services. What the police couldn't work out was why, if the girls had a routine to escort together safely, Bessie had broken away and taken a ride alone. Or had she been taken unwillingly?

Daisy shared conflicting stories with police and the media. Untrusting of the authorities, and most likely fearful of getting charged, she wouldn't admit to much. On one occasion she said the girls had accepted rides regularly with men as harmless and wholesome fun. 'We went for short rides with them,' she admitted, adding, 'we never told our mothers because we knew that there would be a rumpus.' On another occasion she claimed that the girls had been 'pirated' – snatched from the street without their consent and 'mashed by men in cars', she reported to one journalist.

As the meeting wore on into the night, police put the investigation into high gear. One factor seemed critical in navigating the road ahead: all three victims had disappeared from the same dimly lit corner of Sydney.

6

THE DARK TRIANGLE

IN THE WEEKS FOLLOWING THE MEETING AT CIB HQ, POLICE were driven by the understanding that the three recent murders were, in all likelihood, connected. The three victims had all experienced a similar kind of brutal and sexual attack. As one newspaper at the time described it, these crimes were the product of timing, approach and the 'Slayer's demeanor'. But it was the factor of place that came to be seen by the police as perhaps the most significant. All three women were from the same part of Sydney, and two had died only streets away from home.

Police narrowed their focus to the deaths of Iris and Bessie. But it's worth noting that one piece of forensic evidence seemed important to all three 1932 murders. When lab testing was completed, the grudge theory was discounted: the vaginal swabs taken from the victims had been tested for common STDs and the results came back negative.

The medical pathologist also made basic, generalised observations about suspected blood samples. Red blotches could be tested and confirmed as human blood, but not much else. Samples of blood could be taken from a suspect, or a victim, to confirm blood type, but not much else. After Hilda's murder, police had gathered a coat discarded nearby. At the scene of Iris's murder, police picked up a beret only a few feet from her body; it had been slashed across the top, and hair and a sticky red substance were sent for testing. Red-stained leaves were gathered up for further analysis as well. These specimens, along with Iris's blood and nail parings, were all sent to the assistant microbiologist at the Department of Public Health, Dr Stanley William Milton King. He was an accomplished pathologist and doctor, a Member of the Royal College of Surgeons in England, and his skills were accredited by a diploma of Licentiate of the Royal College of Physicians London. Red blotches on the beret, leaves and coat 'gave the human reaction' and 'no blood was detected in the nail parings,' wrote King, in his official medical report. It took weeks for police to get even this basic result.

The crime scenes yielded little. A beer bottle was held for a short time until it was determined that the slippery glass neck couldn't catch fingerprints. The bottle was destroyed. For weeks police continued to scour the Sutherland area, searching for a weapon and for clues that might be used to identify and implicate a suspect. It was dense scrub and police believed they might have missed something.

Police had more luck with the cars. Two separate vehicles were linked directly to the murders, one to each crime. Not only did this help detectives to form a picture of what had happened on the nights of the murders, but it also narrowed their investigation to a specific part of town.

•

At about 5.30 p.m. on Friday, 9 December 1932, Edward Gallard parked his royal-blue Essex sedan on Elizabeth Street. With only two weeks to Christmas, it was retail high season and people had flocked to the city. Gallard was there on business, but it was mostly shoppers and tourists who crowded the streets. His car was one of many parked outside Mark Foy's grand flagship Piazza store; its display windows and ornate gold and polished green tiles dominated the triple frontage on Liverpool, Elizabeth and Castlereagh streets. Despite the bleak economic conditions prevailing across the city, people had gathered to window-shop, peering covetously at the Christmas hams and fruitcakes, and the Mark Foy's signature hampers brimming with delights like canned sheep tongues, sweet jellies and bonbons. Lots of other people were jumping into their cars and driving away, their boots loaded with shopping. Iris Marriott's killer couldn't have chosen a better time or place to steal a car.

The theft occurred in broad daylight, and no one even noticed. When Gallard returned to look for his car, sometime after eight that night, it was gone. He reported the theft to the police immediately.

An hour or two later, in the quiet, dead-end street adjacent to the grove of coral trees in Queens Park, a resident noticed a blue Essex sedan parked just near their house. The car was unfamiliar, and the resident noticed it only because it happened to be parked right under a street lamp. The next time the resident happened to look out their front window, about an hour later, the car was gone.

A little later on, sometime around eleven-thirty that same night, local Bronte electrician Leslie Egan was walking along Cuthbert Street in Waverley. It was only a few streets away from Queens Park but not within line of sight of Iris's body. On a small plantation of palms in the middle of a large traffic island, Egan spotted something shiny in the grass. He stopped to look more closely. The object was a fork. And there were other things with it: spectacles, a jam jar, a slide rule, and further away a kitbag with some electric testing equipment. Being an electrician, Egan knew the value of the testing meter and the other equipment, and took special care with them. Opening the bag he found the address and contact details of the owner stamped inside: E Gallard. He gathered up all of the strange little objects and placed them in the bag. On returning home he called Gallard and made arrangements to return the items.

On the same street, during a search a few days later, police found torn pieces of women's clothing and what they assumed were Iris's lost bloomers. This was near to where Gallard's kitbag had been thrown. Police were now certain they had identified the specific stolen car that the killer had used to pick up Iris and drive her to the site where he had murdered her.

A car had also been reported stolen on the evening of Bessie O'Connor's disappearance. Lionel Downey, eastern suburbs businessman and resident of Centennial Park, arrived home at about 6 p.m. on 14 December. He parked his car in the small garage adjacent to his house, not bothering to lock the door. He went inside, changed out of his work clothes, had dinner, and fed the dog. When he went out to walk the dog around eight that night, the garage was empty.

Downey's car was spotted the next morning by a neighbour. The thief had kindly returned the car very close to the location of its theft. It was parked in a narrow lane, running behind a row of private garages that culminated in a dead-end street. Police concluded that this was significant: the car had been dumped there precisely because it was an ideal place for the driver to slink away on foot.

Detective Constable Payne was sent to gather more evidence from Bessie's crime scene, sometime after the site had been closely inspected by senior detectives. He studied about 150 yards of tyre-track marks along Farnell Avenue and into the national park. Downey's car had mismatched tyres that apparently matched up with these tread marks.

More compelling was what Downey claimed to have found when he opened the door of his car on the morning of its discovery. Something unspeakable had occurred within the closed cabin of the automobile. Blood was smeared thickly across the seats, the floor and doors, and across the dashboard panel. Hair was found too. But this was a different time, and the public had little understanding of the notion of forensic evidence. Downey claimed that he'd simply cleaned the car when it was returned to him. When he'd retrieved a small fragment of what appeared to be human bone from the back seat, he had promptly handed it over to Detective Keogh. But all of the other evidence was gone, and so too an opportunity for officers to photograph and therefore verify Downey's claims.

Downey also claimed to have found gravel, sand and small particles of tea-tree – all things present at the crime scene. He said a Texaco oil tin was also sitting on the seat, and claimed it did not belong to him. Police deduced that the killer must have driven from the scene absolutely covered in blood. The use of the vehicle had provided him with the opportunity to inconspicuously glide through the streets with the evidence of slaughter still splashed upon him. *Truth* called it 'the vehicle of death'.

Downey's car was also a royal-blue Essex sedan, but the fact that an identical make and model of vehicle had been used in both murders was perceived by police to be both significant and insignificant at the same time. On one hand, it was a particularly common car; thousands of them cruised the streets of Sydney every day. On the other hand, police now believed that the exact same make and model of car had been used to commit more than one murder.

•

The discovery of the vehicles became central to the investigation. The cars had been stolen then dumped within a
cross-section of streets that included many of the parks in
the east of the city. On the map it looks like an equilat-
eral triangle with its apex at Hyde Park; the base runs from
Redfern across to Centennial Park. In a public statement,
police explained their strategy:

> The secret of the park murders is held, perhaps innocently,
> by some person or persons who formerly lived and may
> still live in the residential area bounded by Lang and Cook
> roads and Mitchell street, Centennial Park . . . The CIB chief
> Inspector Pryor has contended all through that somebody
> in the Centennial Park residential area – not necessarily
> a relative – knows the murderer and perhaps unwittingly
> is withholding information calculated to remove from the
> community a ruthless slayer who may possibly repeat his
> heinous crime.

Police released photographs of streets and even aerial shots
of the geographic area of interest. Hand-drawn maps of the
parks were also released to the press.

Truth employed a clever device in their presentation of the
story. The press had photos of Iris, but they were mugshots.
They also had photos of Hilda, but she was heavily made
up like a starlet. Editors focused their copy entirely on the
story of the innocent Redfern girl, Bessie. To subliminally
reinforce that three women were dead, and that the city was
in the midst of what it called a murder spree, three copies of

Bessie's face were printed side by side across the broadsheet. They were recent photos of a happy girl with a wholesome smile, her hair neatly curled into a glossy fashionable bob. The message was clear: no young woman in the inner city should feel safe.

In reporting on the brutal killings of women, journalists offered up a brutal assessment on the level of police competency in New South Wales. 'Three brutal unsolved murders in 8 months leave a feeling in the mind of the community that the police department is, to say the least of it, slipping,' wrote one newspaper.

But police now knew where to start looking: they would have to shed light on the dark triangle of streets where they believed the fugitive had been lurking. They theorised that he would have moved recently, driven by the desire to get away from what he'd done – and perhaps make it more difficult for police to locate him should anyone suspect him.

In the absence of any other strategy, the CIB knew how to knock on doors. Due to the high-profile nature of the case, the commissioner had provided them with access to a huge amount of manpower. The CIB mobilised additional constables and detectives, and blitzed the inner east. It was the biggest house-to-house ever mounted by the metropolitan police. Their strategy was simple and unsophisticated: bang on doors and keep banging on doors until you get a result

While police concentrated their search for a perpetrator in the dark triangle, they also focused on their search for the weapon used to murder Bessie. Constables were combing the crime scene at Sutherland. After the detective's near-miss with the death adder, police had been proactive in their approach: each day, constables were instructed to thrash through the bush and scare off any venomous snakes before the murder-weapon search continued. Officers marched shoulder to shoulder, in the style of an emu parade, as they beat the scrub to see if they could flush out a predator.

Meanwhile, back in the suburbs, officers would ask two questions when the door to each house was opened: 'What were your movements on the evening of 14 December? Now what were your movements on the night of 9 December?' Police believed they had the answer to locating the suspect or suspects involved, and their claims regarding the effectiveness of the strategy weren't modest. They said they anticipated interviewing 'possibly 1000 men in the course of house to house visits'.

Police had also visited Gallard, the engineer whose stolen car was believed to be involved in the murder of Iris. He was still missing items from his car that hadn't been tossed into the street along with his kitbag. Officers were most interested in the work tools: they were unique – not everyone had electrical-testing equipment. A circular was printed listing some of the items that Gallard had identified as stolen. There were enough copies to saturate the dark triangle. Police prepared many circulars about the case over many weeks. In the era before social media, handbills represented an important way to very directly and instantly reach the public without having to rely on journalists and editors to distribute, and perhaps distort, the message. The strategy reinforced to the public that somewhere in the eastern suburbs someone might be housing a fugitive, though they most likely didn't know it. Locals were warned that police firmly believed the 'sex slayer' lived somewhere in their midst. 'The police believe the car was used to take Iris Marriott to the fatal spot and the tools were taken out of the car and then abandoned. If the tools have been sold, the detectives are hopeful somebody will recognise them. The fact that the second car was stolen is further support for the theory that two, if not all three of the Park murders were the work of one man.'

7

MOVING PICTURES

THE BIGGEST HOUSE-TO-HOUSE EVER MOUNTED BY THE SYDNEY police yielded nothing. But police had a second strategy: use images to garner public interest and solicit information. They needed photos of a royal-blue Essex sedan.

In 1932, crime photography was becoming important to police practice in Sydney. It wasn't just about the scene and the body. A wide range of images were used to illustrate crime and create the telling of vivid narratives in court. Photos formed an important part of the physical evidence collected because they allowed the prosecution to display subjects or objects critical to the investigation, in context.

To aid in their dual investigation, officers drove a royal-blue Essex sedan to significant sites across the city. It was photographed where the cars had been stolen, and also where they'd been dumped.

Other photos feature locations where it was believed the killer had discarded items associated with the crime. One shows a plantation of palms in the centre of a roadway: it is the traffic island where Gallard's kitbag washed up like a message in a bottle. In most cases the images were deliberately taken early in the morning because it was best to snap them when the streets were clear; it produced a better exhibit for evidentiary purposes because the image was generally free of clutter and distractions like pedestrians or traffic.

Although the images were produced to clinically chronicle the crime, almost ninety years later it's hard to view them with an entirely scientific gaze. They convey sadness not science. What we are left with are artefacts of a bleak 1932. A silvery monochromatic emulsion coats the streets in a cool dark charcoal, and the sky has transformed to a flint colour that is so grey it throws purple. Rather than capturing Sydney as it truly was – a busy, vibrant and dangerous metropolis – they convey something else entirely. The photos have captured lonely scenes of still and silent streets devoid of the souls that make the city pulse. Telegraph poles stand Hopperesque above empty homes and empty cars. Large billboards cast shadows menacingly over streetscapes. While death may not be represented in these photos, life is not to be found here either.

Where photographs couldn't provide the level of detail the police needed, they turned to drawings. Hilda's crime scene was never sketched, and the bush setting of Bessie's attack was not captured because it was considered too vast and too dense. The scene of Iris Marriott's murder, however, was exquisitely drawn by Constable Cecil Jardine. These pen-wash sketches were considered pieces of physical evidence that elevated the science and rigour of the investigative process. Again, however, science is not what the pictures convey.

Jardine drew from the perspective of the eye in the sky. A crime scene has been shrunk to a page, at scale, with topographical features carefully noted and measured. A tiny fleur-de-lis and a crucifix-like compass marker have been inked in the corner, to give the viewer their bearings. All the features of a map are present, but they are artful, almost playful scenes. Streets are drawn in neat lines with soft pastel washes of colour. House plots have been shaded and crosshatched. Complex trees have been reduced to evenly curled florets of green. In these images, Sydney of the 1930s seems pocket sized and pretty. At first glance, they resemble childlike re-imaginings of the city – Sydney retold as *Tintin's Adventures in the City of Sin*.

Officers also had images of the victims that would prove vital to the case as well. Crime scene photographs were taken of all six women who formed the daisy chain of victims spanning 1921 to 1932; however, only the photos of Iris have survived to this day. The photos of her are confronting, and not just for the violence of the scene, but because her vulnerability seems brutally captured by the image. The bright white imprint of her body looks like a pressed flower, carefully preserved as it is crushed between the pages of a heavy book. She looks frightfully small and childlike, tangled in a tumble of grey weeds.

•

The police moved forward with Bessie's case but with only a few pieces of evidence. They had a photograph of a royal-blue Essex sedan, and a picture of a smiling teenage girl. They also had a small paper toll-road ticket found near the body.

Investigators knew the road the killer had travelled. This insight wasn't derived from superlative police work, but was determined by the geography of Sydney. In 1932, if heading south from the city there was only one way to get to Sutherland. The killer had travelled along the Princes Highway through the growing suburbs of Rockdale and Kogarah. It was common for travellers to stop at the popular beachside suburbs of Ramsgate and Dolls Point because there were service stations and refreshment rooms along the route.

As Sydney sprawls down the coast away from the metropolitan centre, it's cut in half abruptly by a watercourse at Blakehurst. Spanning a hundred kilometres, the Georges River slices east to west across the city before turning sharply and flowing south. Anyone heading south out of Sydney on the Princes has to cross the Georges.

Up until 1929, the usual way to make the passage across the Georges was by ferry. A vehicular barge capable of taking people, then horses, then buggies, then cars, punted back and forth throughout the day and night. Trains passed over the

Georges at the Como Bridge, but no other form of traffic could use it. The Captain Cook Bridge, a major connector in the twenty-first century, wouldn't be built until the 1960s. In 1929, the Pratt truss toll bridge was built to connect the local fishing spot known as Tom Uglys Point, in the St George area of Blakehurst, to Sutherland across the river. It didn't have the architectural beauty of the Sydney Harbour coathanger: it was utilitarian – flat and functional, iron and steel. Indeed, some said the crossing barely resembled a bridge. At night, road and water seemed to merge into a wall of blackness, and drivers commented it was almost impossible to see the depth of what lay ahead.

In 1932, police knew the killer had crossed this bridge.

Officers visited the toll booth operator who'd been on shift the night of Bessie's attack. Herbert Cook had been rostered on from about quarter to three in the afternoon until about quarter to eleven that night. He recognised the ticket immediately and could even confirm a rough timeline. 'I would have been the one to issue this toll ticket for a vehicle that night. You can tell by the numbering system on the toll ticket roll. It would have been between twenty-five past ten and a quarter to eleven. It was for a car and it was going south towards Sutherland, I can tell you that for sure,' said Cook. This confirmed what police had mapped out: Bessie had been picked up in Redfern, somewhere very near her home, and the killer had driven fairly directly to their destination in the park.

If the estimates were right and Bessie had jumped in the car sometime after nine-thirty, the sun would already have set.

That evening had been gloomy and overcast, and the moon hadn't been full. As the driver turned out of Redfern towards Newtown and then onto the Princes Highway, it would have been completely dark. Trapped in a beast of steel, Bessie was hurtled further and further into that darkness.

At the toll booth, engine idling, the driver leant out the window and handed over the coins. Cook had stared him in the eye, perhaps even brushed his hand.

But Cook couldn't offer police much information about the suspect. 'I do not know the make of the car nor the name of it or what kind of car it was at all. I did not take that much notice . . . If they have the right amount of toll they do not stop at all.' Cook had sold tens of thousands of tickets to drivers as they rolled slowly through the booth; in any one day, as many as four hundred. To Cook, the suspect was nothing more than a blurred face and a shadowy shape, looming from a window only momentarily before he sped away.

One small but important fact fell into place for police: the man who had paid for Bessie's passage away from the city and towards the underworld had been completely unremarkable, because the toll operator remembered nothing unusual about that night. The person the authorities were looking for seemed to be an ordinary man.

•

To find this ordinary man the senior leadership of the police took an extraordinary step: they harnessed the power of mass media in a way that had not occurred before in Australia.

Newspaper articles, letterbox drops and the cinema were all used to share images about the case. The media events were timed to provide the biggest exposure possible to the case.

On Christmas Day 1932, Bessie O'Connor's story was splashed across the front page of the *Truth* and the *Sun*. This was an ideal day to reach the public as people had plenty of time to read the paper. Large photos of Bessie featured: it was the same photo artfully tilted at diagonals, and slightly touched up to accentuate her lips in one, her costume jewellery in another. A photo of the Essex was also included.

On 27 December, the police commissioner called on the public to help. A circular was issued, and local police stations were asked to distribute it widely across the east and to the south. It featured the same photograph that had appeared in all the newspapers. Bessie was young and fresh faced. Her hair was brushed neatly across and fell forward almost sensually on one side. Her neat bob curled beneath her chin and was pinned behind one ear. Around her neck were the red and white Galalith beads that her mother had seen her leave the house with.

Galalith is synthetic; a plastic of casein and formaldehyde. It was popular with girls like Bessie not just because it was affordable but because it was versatile. It could resemble the creamy luxury of ivory, horn or bone but could also be vibrant. It matched the colourful polka-dot and floral party dresses popular at the time. Often bright and cheerful-looking, Galalith was memorable.

Newspaper articles featured details of Iris's murder too, but the stories continued to be devoted largely to Bessie. And on New Year's Day, another holiday when people lazily read the paper over breakfast or while out on a picnic, the police soaked Sydney in images of her murder again.

On the first day of 1933, Sydneysiders were confronted with a detailed account of Bessie O'Connor's horrifying death at the hands of the 'The Sex Slayer' and the 'Park Killer'. Not all papers published on New Year's Day, but those that did (the *Truth* and the *Sun* in particular) devoted multiple articles to the story. Newspaper editors hadn't settled on a single moniker for the murderer. The *Sun* and the *Labor Daily* preferred the 'Slayer', while the *Arrow* went with the imaginative and more folkloric title of 'The Satyr of the Park'. Readers were also reminded that the man was still unidentified, wandering the streets, looking for more victims: 'In less than six months he has taken three lives and he is still at large in Australia's greatest city. Women and girls fear to be abroad at night. They turn livid with fright if a stranger speaks to them. They know that a human gorilla who stalks abroad at night kills without mercy or pity. First he seizes his unfortunate prey, satisfies his evil desires, then destroys them, and casts their bodies aside. Nothing comparable with these crimes has happened in the history of Australia.'

Editors posed a confronting question to the public very directly: 'Who is he? A vital throbbing crime story from real life, strange but true. *Truth*, which hitherto has refrained from publishing the full facts, now reveals everything in the hope that other persons whose timidity has sealed their lips may come forward.'

Police also made use of state-of-the-art communications technology to broadcast their messages. In the 1930s, cinemas weren't just sites for entertainment. Before television, newsreels presented the public with breaking news and major sporting events. Road safety warnings were also considered of significant public interest and the demon on wheels needed a very special kind of road safety alert. In an all-Australian newsreel service called the *Cinesound Review*, Inspector Pryor appealed to the nation throughout the popular holiday season of Christmas and New Year. Rather than only casting a net over the dark triangle in the eastern suburbs, he instead tried to 'cast the net over the Commonwealth'.

Police reinforced the visual campaign with a mass radio broadcast. Only ten years before, radio had been a field dominated by hobbyists. In the early 1920s, broadcasters and listeners experimented with the new communication technology which meant broadcasts lasted only a few hours per week. Participants required licences, and the content was produced by amateurs and shared only by fellow enthusiasts. Within only a decade, national broadcasting had been born. The Australian Broadcasting Commission (ABC) had formally aligned as an entity in July 1932, and it already had a network of stations across six capital cities and several regional sites as well. On the evening of Monday, 2 January 1933, police made a national broadcast calling for information about the park killer and offering a reward. This radical step by police provides insight into the level of importance the case had reached. It was the first ever public call for help on a criminal case broadcast on national radio in Australia.

For Sydney police, the use of media served two important purposes. First, it helped to improve their public image by demonstrating that they were actively working difficult cases that local residents were greatly concerned about. Second, public exposure offered some hope for the police to obtain something they desperately needed in order to push the case forward: more witnesses.

And witnesses came forward. There was just one problem: everyone now miraculously remembered the girl and her plastic pearls with a remarkable degree of detail, but no one seemed to recall much about her male companion. Members of the public contacted police saying they'd seen the Essex with a girl like Bessie in it, and their memories of her seemed to be improving rather than fading as time passed – and as more information was broadcast. Some described the shape of her lips or her hairstyle. Many described the pretty beads around her throat. Witnesses began to report as if they'd known Bessie personally, speaking with confidence about the personality and qualities of the girl whom they'd only observed from a distance. She'd been a happy girl, they said. That wide, smiling face was a sign of a friendliness. She was 'charming', and 'athletic': they were terms used by newspapers to describe her.

Police at first perceived this to be a stroke of luck and didn't foresee any issues with witness contamination. In fact, the media had helped people to remember 'better', or so police believed at the time.

All kinds of descriptions of the man in the Essex were being offered up to the police as well. Some said he was tall, others said short. Some said stout, others thin. Some described an Irish skin tone, another said the man was rather swarthy.

A vast number of officers were working on the case, and CIB detectives were running an investigation at the same time that local police seemed to be running one in parallel. Then one of the worst possible things that could have happened, did.

Detective William Payne circulated one description of the suspect to the general public. Detective Jake Miller circulated another.

•

In the weeks following Bessie's death, the police had received thousands of letters from the public suggesting that they'd seen 'the man' – in their town, in their street, in their neighbourhood. This took up precious police time and resources as most of the leads proved worthless. A vindictive mother-in-law phoned in to report a daughter's husband whom she didn't care for. A landlord dobbed in a tenant as an easy way to assure an eviction. Neighbours turned on neighbours.

One lead, however, piqued the interest of police, largely because more than one person reported seeing the same thing. A blue Essex had been seen parked on the side of the road on the way to Sutherland on the night of Bessie's disappearance. One witness stated that the driver, a man in a suit, had said 'the car is out of fuel'.

Police were also still looking for the items that Gallard claimed had been stolen from his car: some photographs, as well as tools, a pocketbook, and women's clothing. Police checked with pawnshops, as the killer might have tried to fence the items. Although it seems a foolhardy strategy, as so many calls and letters were already being received by police, officers approached the media again. They urged the public to come forward with information about the murders of Iris and Bessie, and to keep an eye out for any commonplace items they might find in their home that seemed out of place (like a woman's cardigan, men's spectacles or an engineer's work tools).

The more news stories that were printed, the more leads rolled in. The wild goose chase continued. A motel keeper in Corrimal, a town just north of Wollongong, had been following the 'sex slayer' stories as though they were serials. When a mysterious man who described himself as a gold buyer blew into the small bayside town only a few days after Bessie's murder, it raised suspicion among some locals. Gold buyers were perceived to be slightly shonky at the time. Gold-buying laws in New South Wales were somewhat more lenient than in other states, particularly Victoria (which required operators to be licensed). As a result, lots of people posed as gold buyers in an attempt to swindle. The man had been travelling up and down the east coast, doorknocking in local towns and offering to pay cash on the spot in exchange for golden rings, bangles, necklaces and watches. The early 1930s was a good time to be in that line of business, as tough economic times meant desperate housewives were often willing to sell their personal items, right on their doorstep, to strangers. The gold buyer struck the local motel keeper as a little shady, and the moment he observed the man driving a royal-blue Essex, he called the police. The gold buyer was interviewed thoroughly by Detective Sergeant Keogh, who had the nickname of 'The Bull' for his tough treatment of suspects. Although heavy pressure was applied to the man in a fierce interrogation, he didn't crack. He was dismissed without charge, his evasiveness chalked up as a personality attribute typical of his somewhat shady occupation.

Witnesses continued to come forward. A set of anecdotes about Bessie's attack began to coalesce into a sensible story. A blue Essex had overheated – there had been a problem with the fanbelt. The car had broken down on the side of the road for a period of time. Downey, the Centennial Park resident whose car had been stolen that night, confirmed that the fanbelt was tricky and the car was prone to overheating.

Gerald Stiff, a labourer, had been out cruising the streets with mates Tom Moatt, Alf Brown, and brothers Jack and Ron Dufficey on the night of Bessie's attack. They'd been for a swim at Brighton-Le-Sands, then they'd parked at a roadhouse stop on the way to Sutherland. A man had come up to them and asked where he might get some petrol. 'I told him the garage was closed, he might have more luck at the restaurant. Then I saw the bus pull up and the bus driver spoke to him,' said Stiff.

A local bus driver, Percy Weekes, confirmed the broad story sketched out by the cruising boys.

Although this helped police put together the sequence of events on the evening of Bessie's attack, they were still no closer to arresting the suspect. Witnesses had met the man, they had even shaken hands with him, but they didn't know his name. And police still needed witnesses who could offer consistent statements. One had seen an Essex that night but remembered it as greenish with a black hood; others recalled blue.

From late December, police had advertised a reward in the NSW Government Gazette – 250 pounds each – for any information which would lead to an arrest in the murder of either Iris Marriott or Bessie O'Connor. As the investigation rolled on through January, the rewards remained posted in public spaces.

And the CIB cinema newsreel continued to roll. It played for weeks, at locations throughout Sydney. Drawn from the only information they had to go on about the suspect, and cobbled together from an array of witness statements, they wanted the public to be left with a visual image of the killer. Detective Inspector Pryor, neatly suited and with hair firmly greased into place, stared intensely into the camera lens as he delivered his instructions. 'He had on the early morning of 15 December 1932, two scratches on his face, believed to be on the left side, extending from the cheekbone down to the mouth. Try to impress the description on your mind. Carry a copy of it where you go – it is your duty.'

'Watch for this man,' the newsreel voice-over implored.

8

THE CONFESSION

POLICE LOCATED THE SUSPECT. THERE IS NO RECORD OF THE precise steps they took to identify the man they believed to be responsible for killing Iris and Bessie. The suspect may have been identified because police received an anonymous tip-off. Officers may have identified a target based on their background checks of criminal records, or perhaps a local eastern suburbs resident provided a compelling report on a suspicious neighbour or relative. When it comes to details of the man's capture, however, much is known.

At about 5 p.m. on Friday, 6 January 1933, Detective Swasbrick, Detective Constable James Wiley, and Constables Bell and Smith waited at 386 Moore Park Road, Paddington. On a stake-out under direct instructions from a superior officer, Detective Sergeant McRae, they were in an unmarked vehicle on the other side of the road and a little further away. The wide, curved street offered clear visibility of the front entrance.

Police had already searched the subdivisions of the area. The terraces on that section of Moore Park Road had front entrances, and the backs of the properties emptied into Leinster Street at the rear. Police had also researched the lease arrangements governing the property; the suspect occupied only the front room of the terrace, and so used only the front exit.

The officers waited patiently for any flicker of life or light from within the property. It was the peak of summer, and the men sweltered in their suits as the afternoon sun beat down on the force's Armstrong Siddeley tourer.

For two hours, no one arrived at or left the property. Around 7 p.m. a man exited. He was dressed in a smart and well-fitted pinstripe navy-blue suit and a neatly knotted midnight-blue tie striped with bold diagonal lines like a candy cane. He walked quickly down Moore Park Road towards Surry Hills.

Police didn't waste any time. The officers separated and split off. The man walked for about ten minutes, unaware that he was followed by police the entire way. They watched closely. Just as the man was about to turn at the next intersection, officers converged. Detective Wiley approached him from behind; Swasbrick surged quickly in front of him. The constables waited, poised and ready to give chase if the man took off.

When it was clear he wasn't a flight risk, the two junior officers – Bell and Smith – doubled back and headed towards the property that the man had just left. One of the constables knocked. A young woman, described as 'child-like' with 'pale milky white skin', answered the door.

While the two constables entered the property on Moore Park Road, the gentleman in the navy-blue suit was led away and taken to the police car, flanked on each side by an officer.

The suspect was driven to Central Police Station and led into the wing designated for the CIB. While Pryor was the public face of the investigation, and the local Detective Wiley had helped bring in the suspect, Detective Jake Miller was the key decision-maker. The suspect was led into the interview room sometime after 8 p.m. It was Miller who locked the door between the CIB offices and the rest of headquarters. The CIB wasn't usually a high-security unit, but rather another department within HQ. On any normal day, officers could simply pass freely through. On this particular night, Miller took the unusual step of instructing all officers to keep the door locked. No one would be allowed to enter the unit without Miller's personal approval.

As Miller and the suspect approached each other in the corridor, they eyed each other closely. It was an encounter between very different men.

The suspect was cool and clean, perhaps twenty-five, with smoky grey eyes, neatly slicked-back hair and a closely shaved face. The distinctive woody scent of cologne hung in the slipstream of the man as he passed through the corridor and into the interview room. His hat was suavely dipped at an angle, in the manner of one taught how to dress well. His suit was expertly fitted, the cuffs resting elegantly so just the glimmer of a cufflink was exposed. The tie had been knotted with impeccable precision and sat with beautiful symmetry on his chest.

In contrast, Detective Inspector Miller was, superficially at least, everything that the suspect was not. Miller had the look of a man whose mind was consumed with concerns far more important than a striking tie, a well-pressed shirt, or a polished shoe. He was an officer known for his silhouette, which wasn't so much portly as disproportionately shaped. With the widest point of his body in the very middle, narrow shoulders that sloped sharply, topped with a long pinhead and tiny feet known for a measured step, Miller's shape was akin to a spinning top. Because the watermark of his belt rode up somewhere around Harry Highpants, the breeze on his ankle would have been significant and ventilating.

When Miller entered the interview room he had no evidence linking the suspect directly to the crime. He had a proto-profile of the suspect so vague and general that thousands of men would have conformed to the composition of characteristics. Yet, when Miller left the room that night, he held a typed confession in his hand. The signature at the bottom of that confession had been written by a man named Eric Roland Craig.

•

Though we can't ever be sure precisely how Craig made it onto the list of suspects, what is known is how he stayed on this list. Craig fitted the 'proximal zone' theory that police had used to shape their investigation. And other facts about his life further solidified him as a person of interest.

The suspect was young and male.

He lived inside the dark triangle of east Sydney, the target zone for the police investigation.

He had also moved house. Craig had moved from 12 Victoria Avenue, Woollahra. However, he had then moved straight back into the same area. Craig had remained within the dark triangle – this didn't fit with the police theory about the killer, but they seemed happy to overlook that fact.

When Miller entered the interview room that evening, he was holding a file. The first sheet within the file-folder was stamped with the letterhead of the Victoria Barracks, Darlinghurst. It was an admission form for Eric Roland Craig. The second sheet was a conviction record: with a prior conviction for car theft. The third sheet was a discharge form from the army, at Victoria Barracks. The reasons for the discharge were thoroughly outlined. On a night in April 1930, Craig had taken an officer's car without permission. Craig was severely reprimanded and warned by the senior ranks of the military to never do it again.

He'd done it again, a year later. Military officials reported him. In April 1931, he was charged with theft and for driving without a licence.

The fourth sheet detailed Craig's conviction. He'd been sentenced to serve one month of hard labour for the theft of the vehicle, or he could elect to pay a fine of ten pounds. For driving without a licence he was sentenced to four days in gaol, or he could pay the state twenty shillings. Craig had paid the fines.

What occurred in the CIB interview room that night remains contested to this day. The two men present left behind very different accounts of what transpired.

'Please state your name and your place of residence,' said Miller.

'My name is Eric Roland Craig. I live at 386 Moore Park Road, Paddington.'

'What portion of 386 do you occupy?'

'I have the front room with my wife and two children.'

'How long have you resided there?'

'A couple of days.'

'Where were your accommodations before that?'

'Twelve Victoria Avenue.'

'Have you any property currently in your accommodation that you cannot account for?'

'No.'

'Do you know of a woman called Iris Marriott?'

'No.'

'Do you know of a woman called May Miller?'

'No, I've never known anyone called by that name.'

Craig's first statement was then made to the police. Miller asked him to give an account of his movements over the week in which both murders occurred, Iris's on 9 December and Bessie's on 14 December. Craig's first statement is as follows.

[On Friday 9 December] I was at home. I laid down in the afternoon. I ate tea at six. I went out at about quarter to seven, in my blue serge suit and black shoes with no hat. I went to the billiards room opposite Lowe's in Pitt street. I never saw anyone I knew. I watched people play billiards, walked up William street to the Cross. I got home about 11pm. My brother in law Bob Campbell was there. He was throwing up in the bathroom. He said 'by Jesus I am crook. I have been on the plonk with Mac'. He dipped his head under the tap and I got him a towel. Bob left to meet his wife who was working at Sargents in Market street. She was due to finish shift at 11.30. After Bob left, my wife and I went to bed.

On Saturday I was at home all morning and played cricket in the afternoon. Then on Sunday I went to Rushcutters Bay about 10.30am, played cricket all day, then came home about 6pm. I never left the house on Monday 12 December. On Tuesday 13 December I polished the floor. I never left the house. On Wednesday 14 December I remained at home all day. At 6pm I went out in my blue serge suit. I said to my wife 'I am going for a walk'. I kissed her goodbye and left. I was wearing black shoes and no hat. I walked along Victoria avenue into Ocean street. I intended going to Woollahra Pictures but I changed my mind and went back home. I arrived about 8.10. My wife was there with her friend Lily. Jack Wonders, my friend, had been there. He had just left so I went looking for him. I knocked on his door at Oxford Street. There was no one home. I got home about 10.15. I did not leave home again. On Thursday 15 December I stayed home all day. I went to bed with my wife about 9pm. I got up on Friday at 7.30am and commenced work at Lowe's at 9am. I worked until 5pm. I did so every day until 23 December.

After Craig had made his statement, police didn't release him. They allowed him to have cigarettes – many cigarettes, in fact. They allowed him to lie down on a bench fixed along the wall. They didn't take him back to a holding cell. The officers seemed to be waiting for something. They left him alone for a short time.

•

Back at Craig's home, a different kind of interrogation was underway.

With the suspect in custody, Detectives Wiley and Swasbrick returned to 386 Moore Park Road. A young woman, waifish, struggled as two children huddled in fear, grabbing at her skirt while a line of strange men marched through the house. Their heavy leather boots scuffed black marks across the floor. The men opened cupboard doors and knocked objects out. They removed drawers from wardrobes and cabinets. They stripped linen from the beds.

Wiley zeroed in on the young woman and began to ask a series of straightforward questions. The woman was silent. It was that quiet fear distinctive of someone so terrified they can barely speak.

'What is your name?' asked Wiley.

'Mary-Caroline Craig,' she answered in a soft tone.

'What is your relationship to Eric Roland Craig?'

'He is my husband.'

Mary-Caroline Craig was asked about her husband's whereabouts, his employment, their relationship and the kind of man he was.

Officers undertaking the search had been put on notice to look for some specific items. Although there were lots of items on the list provided by Gallard, police seemed particularly interested in finding a woman's cardigan, and a torch missing from the engineer's kitbag. To this day, it is not entirely clear why. Police were also searching for anything that might be the murder weapon. Both women had been struck about the head, so they knew the object would be hard and flat. It would show evidence that it had been damaged or bent, given the injuries the women sustained. Officers were also told to look for a bloodstained suit.

Mary-Caroline Craig was asked some questions identical to those posed to her husband: Where did they live? Had they moved recently? What was Eric doing in the week of 9 to 14 December 1932?

Mary-Caroline described a family situation that most likely paralleled those of many men in Sydney that year. Craig was unemployed. His prospects for employment were very dim. He'd been kicked out of the army. He had no trade skills and no real training. In an economic recession, when people had little to no discretionary spending money, Craig was in the worst possible field: retail. He'd gone from department store to department store looking for work. First Lowe's and Murdoch's, then in David Jones' he'd worked in the mercery department, specifically in the tie section. For most of their married life, Craig had been one of thousands of men queuing at the local harbour pier to draw the dole.

Mary-Caroline began to recall the week in question, in large part because they'd moved house in the past month, and so dates and details had mattered to her at the time.

'On 14 December last you were living together in Victoria Avenue, Woollahra? This is a residential place?'

'Yes.'

According to Mary-Caroline, her husband had gone out that night, but only briefly, before returning home. She said this with certainty, because this was how her husband spent most evenings. He polished the floor. He drank tea. She seemed eager to create the impression of a teetotalling husband, who despite his unemployment was not idle.

The detectives then took a more aggressive approach. As Mary-Caroline wrangled a fussy baby in her arms, police peppered her with questions. Husband and wife were asked some of the same questions, but others were posed to Mary-Caroline alone.

In a drawer with Craig's socks and ties, police found a small black notebook. Initially, they thought it was an address book and quickly scanned through it in vain for the names May Miller, Iris Marriott, Bessie O'Connor or Hilda White. The officer was about to set aside the item, dismissing it as a waste of time, when he noticed a pattern. The little black book was filled only with women's names.

'What is this?' Wiley brandished it right in front of Mary-Caroline's face.

Expecting that she would either know nothing about the book or deny its existence, Wiley wasn't hopeful she would offer up much of an answer. What happened next stunned the detective.

Mary-Caroline knew all about her husband's little black book. Police were even more surprised to learn that she wasn't taciturn about it, nor resentful nor threatened. She wasn't ashamed by the little black book. She was matter-of-fact in her response. 'That's my husband's dance book.' The tone of her voice didn't shift, and she didn't sound upset or alarmed.

Wiley looked incredulously at the young woman who didn't seem suspicious of her husband. 'Does he ever take you dancing?' he asked. He raised his eyebrows at her, trying to get a rise out of her.

'No.' Her face was open, plain. She showed no hint of resentment.

The detective looked the young woman up, then down. He looked at the stains on her blouse, and at the misshapen cardigan that folded over the ends of her hands. Wiley couldn't get a read on the girl; she seemed completely without guile. He asked, 'When were you married?'

'Nineteen twenty-nine.'

'And you have two children.'

'Yes, Valma and Robert.'

'And is your husband employed?'

'No.'

'So what does your family live on, what is your income?'

'My husband draws unemployment.'

'That's not very much, is it? How does your husband have the money to go dancing?'

'His mother helps.'

The issue of money was of particular interest to police because the killer had apparently handed over a ten-pound note to a bus driver. It was an extremely generous amount of money for anyone to have in 1932, let alone an unemployed man supporting a family on the dole.

'You say he was out of work. Do you know how much money your husband had?'

'I gave him a shilling,' said Mary-Caroline. Now she was scared – the detective could see it. Though of what, he couldn't precisely tell.

'Do you work? Do you earn money for yourself?'

'No.'

'So, how is your family getting money? Are you getting money from your people?'

'No, the money comes from my husband's people.'

'Where are they?'

'Sydney.'

'How long have you been getting money from your husband's people?'

'His mother gives me money every week. I don't exactly remember when that started.'

'But that is for housekeeping purposes?'

'Yes. And to help pay the rent.'

'So where does the rest of the money come from, Mrs Craig? Surely your mother-in-law doesn't have enough money to be supporting her son's family every week.'

Mary-Caroline simply didn't answer. The woman's hands were small, and she struggled to wrestle with the little child who was now fussing at her feet. The detective didn't press the issue.

'Does your husband drive a car?'

'I have seen him drive a car,' she said.

'Whereabouts?'

'In around Paddington. He drives for a friend of his.'

'Is it a pleasure run?'

'I don't know,' she replied. It was clear that Mary-Caroline didn't know what a pleasure run was, so the inference went over her head.

'Are you ever in the car when he goes on a pleasure run?'

'No.'

Police continued searching, then they left with armfuls of objects. Some items of women's clothing were confiscated, and a few items small enough to fit in the hand. The black book was taken, and a few notebooks. Mary-Caroline didn't know exactly what was taken, and police didn't tell her.

She did see officers looking closely at her husband's suits. Though she probably didn't know it at the time, they were inspecting the fabric for red spots, dirt, holes or tears, or any terracotta-coloured stains – anything that resembled dried blood. As he was leaving, one officer commented to

Mary-Caroline, 'Your husband sure does have a lot of suits.' Detective Wiley commented formally later on, in his notes regarding the case: 'I formed an impression of a man who barely seemed to behave in a way that was married. For a man with very little money, he still seemed to find money to spend on himself. His wife and children seemed to have very little.'

One constable, the name isn't recorded, picked up a sheaf of suits and carried them with great care towards the door. He draped them flat, with one arm supporting the shoulders, the other supporting the legs, in the manner of one carrying the ailing. Just before he exited, he turned to Mary-Caroline, who was standing by the door watching police take her life apart right before her eyes.

'Are these all of your husband's suits?' he asked.

'Yes, they are all my husband's.'

'But is this all of them?'

'No.'

'Then where are the others?'

And the response was difficult for police to interpret. Was she being evasive? Was she naive? The officers couldn't tell.

'You've come too late,' she said. 'My mother-in-law came and took them away for cleaning.'

●

About an hour later, back at the CIB headquarters, the suspect was exhausted. His clothing was crushed, and his body seemed crushed too. He had removed his jacket, and although his shirt was soaked with what appeared to be sweat, he seemed to be shivering. His knees were crunched up on the long wooden bench in the interview room and a heavy grey blanket was bunched beneath his head as a pillow. His once neatly knotted tie was now askew. He stirred as he heard the heavy footfall of men's shoes in the corridor outside.

Miller entered the room. He took tiny, precise steps. Another officer came with him this time. This man had a broad, thick face and a heavy chin, and he swaggered in.

Miller was carrying something. He walked over to the table in the centre of the room and placed a small electric torch and a taupe-coloured cardigan on it.

'Do these two items belong to you?' Miller asked.

Eric Craig now had the blanket around his shoulders. The suave demeanour was gone, and he stooped over as he looked at the items. 'No,' he said.

'Is this your torch?'

'No.'

'But it was found at your house tonight.'

Craig thought for a moment, then said, 'Well I forgot about that one. I found it. I was walking my daughter Val through Centennial Park and I found it near the gates at the entrance.'

The police account of what transpired that night is as follows.

'That particular torch was stolen from an Essex car on Elizabeth Street on 9 December last,' said Miller firmly.

'I know nothing about that,' said Craig.

Miller then did something that Craig didn't expect: he walked out of the room and closed the door. Craig was now left with the man the police themselves nicknamed The Bulldog – Detective Sergeant Thomas Walter McRae.

'I understand that the only time you were away from your home on 9 December was between 9 and 9.45 p.m.?' McRae posed it as a question, though it was really more of a statement.

'Yes,' said Craig.

'What about the other item on the table? This cardigan was found in your apartment tonight.'

'That belongs to my wife,' Craig responded quickly.

'Your wife doesn't know anything about it.' McRae raised his eyebrows, mocking the man.

'Did she tell you that?' Craig replied.

The officer didn't answer.

Police claimed that Mary-Caroline had given a formal statement saying the items were not hers – but this statement can't be found in any of the surviving files associated with the case.

'These were stolen from an Essex car on 9 December. How do you account for your possession of the torch and jumper?'

'Well,' Craig hesitated. Then, 'I did steal a car.'

'What time did you steal it?' asked McRae.

'Can't say the exact time,' responded Craig.

'We have reason to believe that car was used in connection with the murder of Iris Marriott, also known as May Miller.'

Craig didn't answer for a moment, and then, according to the officers present, he said, 'I know what is coming next.'

'What do you mean?'

The police account of what occurred next is very detailed. McRae claims that Craig confessed, that this occurred spontaneously, and nothing had been done to provoke it. There were other junior officers present, assisting with the statement, or so McRae claimed. The officers described Craig's demeanour in detail. He put his head in his hands, in the manner of a man broken. 'I must have been mad. I killed her,' he is reported to have said over and over. Immediately after that, according to police, he offered his confession. 'Craig then agreed to make a voluntary statement, which he then signed,' said McRae. That confession is reproduced below – it was a typed statement.

I am a salesman and I live at 386 Moore Park Road, Paddington. About 7 p.m. on 9 December, I left home. I walked along Queen Street and other streets to Pitt Street where I entered a billiard room. I was in the billiard room about half an hour. I left and walked up Pitt Street to Goulburn Street where I saw an Essex tourer standing between Goulburn and Liverpool streets. I got in the car and drove by way of Oxford Street to Greens Road. May Miller was standing in Greens Road. She whistled at me. When I rolled the car alongside her, she called out, 'Will you drive me home?' I said, 'All right.' I drove to Queens Park. At the corner near the park she said, 'Turn this way.' I turned up to the left along Victoria Road to a dead end. She said, 'I live over there,' and pointed to a house on the opposite side of the street. She said, 'What about coming into the park for a while, love?' I agreed. We got out of the car, which was left on the right-hand side of the road facing the steps. We walked through some long grass under a white railing. She led the way. We went under a coral tree and sat down. We talked for a while and she said, 'What about a naughty? Give us a dollar.' I said, 'I have no money.' She said, 'Come, you have a dollar.' I said, 'I have not any money.' She said, 'Haven't you any money at all? You didn't bring me out here for nothing.' I said, 'I did not bring you. You said you lived here. You asked me to drive you home.' With that she stood up and said, 'You are a bastard of a man bringing a woman all this way. For two bloody pins I will give you a kick in the balls.' I started to laugh and she slung a punch at me. I said, 'You dirty bitch.' I stepped in close to her. She brought up her knee and hit me in the thigh with it. I knocked her down with my fist and I lost my head. I think I must have gone mad. I picked up a piece of wood and hit her. When I saw what I had done I was frightened and tried to hide her in the bush. I took off her clothing as I thought I would not know her. I wrapped the clothes in a piece of newspaper and got into the car and drove away.

The statement contains everything the detectives needed, covering all of the main plot points in the police-conceived narrative of that night. It conveniently provides a motive, it explains why the clothes had been left in the street, and it offers a reason for the car being parked in Fullerton Street.

At some point, though it is not clear when, Inspector Miller entered the room with McRae. Inspector Miller claimed that he issued the requisite warnings to Craig by saying, 'You are not obliged to say anything.' Miller also claimed that in response to this, Craig freely said, 'I will make a full statement.' Miller's account, as might be expected, asserts that police protocol had been conformed to, completely and correctly. He claimed his words to Craig were, 'Are you prepared to make a voluntary statement giving the full details of how the offence was committed?' Miller further claimed that Craig willingly answered, 'Yes.' According to Miller's account, he asked Craig, 'You can either write it yourself or I will type it.' Craig replied, 'You type it and I'll sign it.'

What officers didn't record in their official statements is that Craig was put in the back of a police car and driven to the scene of Iris Marriott's murder as part of the interrogation process. What is unclear is what elements of the confession were extracted before or after visiting the crime scene.

•

In the eyes of the officers assembled in the dawn light, the sight of the man shivering in the back seat, like a child, was all the evidence they needed that he was guilty. According to officers, Craig quaked with shame in the back of the police car.

Craig bent forward, his arms wrapped around his knees in an effort to warm himself. He asked, 'Can I have a coat, please?'

A constable walked around to the back of the car, turned the handle and opened the boot. He took out two blankets, then handed them to Craig through the open window.

It took less than twelve hours for police to obtain a confession in the murder of Iris Marriott. If the confession had been offered in order for Craig to get relief from police pressure, it did not work.

Wiley saw Craig again at about 4.15 a.m., he said, when he returned to the interview room. 'I was the one who led him to the yard where we got into a police car. I sat in the back seat next to him.' Craig sat crowded by officers in the car in the early hours of the morning. If he thought the ordeal was over, he was wrong.

He later claimed that he had chain-smoked in the back of the police car. Police didn't disagree. But he also claimed he'd been so exhausted that the cigarettes fell out of his mouth as he was nodding off. Police said nothing of the kind had occurred.

Police claimed that Craig took them on a tour of the crime scene. 'We sat down here.' He was said to have pointed to a spot a few feet from a tree trunk. 'I happened to be sitting on a log of wood, a piece of three by two, pointed at the end. When she made to kick me I picked up the piece of wood and hit her over the head.'

According to police, Craig claimed to have taken the piece of wood with him when he left the scene. He said, 'I threw it away.' Where and how this occurred was never fully explained, so it couldn't be verified.

In 1933 police didn't record interviews. The two statements – both of which, according to police, represented a verbatim transcript of Craig's words – couldn't have been more different. In one, he was a floor-polishing, wife-doting homebody. In the other, he was cruising for prostitutes and beating them to death.

Inspector Miller claimed that Craig had indicated a preference for the statement to be typed rather than handwritten, and had consented to officers typing while he recited. Handwritten at the bottom are the words: 'I have read over this statement. It is true and correct, being made of my own free will. There has been no promises or threat or inducement made to me by Inspector Miller to make this statement, signed Eric Roland Craig.'

It was in the early hours of the morning when the police car pulled away from Queens Park and headed down the hill towards the major intersection on the border of Centennial Park. Instead of turning right, which would have taken the car towards headquarters, the driver took a left and began heading away from the city.

Craig waited for the policeman behind the wheel to correct himself and realise that he'd taken a wrong turn. It never happened. The driver kept heading south until Craig finally realised that the police had not finished with him at all. If he had not travelled this road before, with Bessie, as police had supposed, he was certainly re-creating her journey now. He was trapped, hurtling further and further south, spinning wheels away from the city lights, and towards the darkness – captive in a beast of steel headlong for destruction. And so too had it been for Bessie.

9

STAIN REMOVAL

THE MEDIA REMAINED FOCUSED ON BESSIE. STORIES ABOUT THE innocent Redfern teenager and the faceless beast that had taken her life stayed in the news for a month.

The media blitz had certainly given the investigation exposure, for good and ill. The scale of the challenge facing police featured often in news reports. 'It is known that the detectives are worried over the crime for clues are so few . . . most of their searches have proved fruitless.' They were under significant pressure to solve the very public murders of Iris and Bessie very quickly.

By the second week of January, the investigation had progressed, but not in the manner in which police would have preferred. They had a signed confession for the murder of Iris Marriott. What they really wanted was a confession for the murder of Bessie O'Connor. But Eric Craig wasn't giving one up.

Inspector Miller changed tack. In the absence of any real evidence to confirm what had occurred on the night of Bessie's attack, he needed witnesses to identify Craig as the man seen on the road to Sutherland.

Miller had tried taking Craig to the place where Bessie's attack had occurred and where bloodstained pools of dirt were still visible. Officers had pressed Craig in that location; they had interrogated him, trying to prompt an answer. He'd given them nothing.

Miller wasted no time – he immediately made arrangements for a line-up to be held back at CIB headquarters, and Craig was ushered into the back of a police car and taken there. Meanwhile, witnesses were rounded up and brought into HQ. Miller, with McRae at his side, issued directions to his bevy of officers about how to line the men up, and how to parade the witnesses through. He waited eagerly for a response. Would any of the witnesses recognise Craig?

None of them did. Much to the chagrin of police, the media reported the failure in detail. It isn't clear who among the officers spoke to journalists.

Detective Inspector Miller and Detective Sergeant McRae bided their time. A parade of potential witnesses now carried with them a mental image of the suspect that police wanted to line up for the murder of Bessie O'Connor. Officers orchestrating the investigation knew this would be important for the case down the road.

Miller changed tack again. He had to. In early 1933, a number of forces were converging to create immense personal and professional pressure for the detective inspector. Firstly, Miller had a new boss – William Pryor had ascended the police ranks quickly and had only just been promoted. Pryor, like any police chief, wanted a strong success rate during his period of incumbency.

Secondly, Miller had a lower success rate than most when it came to closing cases. Though it wasn't public knowledge, he still carried the stain of failure on his reputation within the force. And it was a failure that could only be removed with a successful conviction.

Thirdly, Miller's professional practice as an officer had been governed by a set of habits.

Nine years before, in 1924, the mysterious death of Rebecca May Anderson, and the subsequent investigation of her murder, had shared many similarities with the events unfolding in 1933. In Rebecca's case, police had also been unable to gather much evidence. The case had relied not on eyewitness accounts but on witnesses very close to the suspect. Miller had been the officer in charge, and he'd used a tactic that he would later try to use against Craig. In both cases, police had waited outside the suspect's place of residence, swooped in, and led them away for interrogation. In both cases, not just the suspect but the suspect's significant other had been subjected to intense interrogation. In the case of Iris Marriott's murder, Craig had cracked but his wife had not. In the Rebecca May Anderson murder case, it had been the other way around. During intense interrogation, a suspect's wife had claimed that her husband had confessed the crime to her. When the police couldn't then use this hearsay statement to pry a confession directly out of the suspect, the case had been abandoned.

In early 1933, Miller had already achieved more in the park murders case than he had in the Rebecca May Anderson case. He had a confession from Craig for one murder. Police also had the torch and cardigan, which they claimed had belonged to Gallard and been found at Craig's home. Miller now wanted similarly compelling evidence capable of securing a conviction for Bessie's murder. Police believed that when the killer had walked away from Bessie, he'd taken part of her with him: blood, pieces of fingernail, perhaps even shards of bone and brain. Blood had been washed out of the car, but it was almost impossible to wash out of a suit or a shirt or a tie. If police could locate a bloodstained piece of Eric Craig's clothing, they'd make it part of the case against him.

What police wanted was the suit – the one seen in the shady half-light on the night of Bessie's attack. The killer had worn this suit; there seemed to be consensus on this point, if no other. However, suits were a common form of attire in the early 1930s, and even working men usually in overalls could be seen sporting a suit after hours. What police really needed was a suit with incriminating evidence on it. Perhaps a smear of lipstick on the collar? But it had to be identified as a shade that Bessie would wear. Perhaps a handkerchief or other personal item of Bessie's? But it would have to be found in Craig's possession, or in his clothing.

A torn suit or a bloodstained shirt would be ideal because police could use them to paint a vivid picture of the crime and how it unfolded.

Police didn't return to Craig's apartment to search for more evidence, as the place had been thoroughly ransacked. Instead, they travelled to the home of the other woman who seemed to play a large role in Eric's life: his mother.

•

Police had already scheduled a raid of Mrs Craig's home to search for the missing suits; it seemed an ideal opportunity to question her.

When Miller walked up to Leah Craig's door in January 1933, he was searching for a literal stain. But he was also seeking to remove a stain – the metaphorical stain on his reputation as a senior officer in the NSW police force.

Miller knocked, flanked by two constables. It was a small, narrow terrace, typical of the housing in the east, just on the fringe of the city. There seemed to be no sound coming from inside. Just as Miller was about to knock again, the door opened in a very careful and controlled way. A tiny, neatly dressed and prim-and-proper older woman was still grasping the door handle. 'Yes? Can I help you?' she asked, sounding meek and fragile. Miller had interviewed hundreds of people in his time as an officer, and he knew the sound of someone wishing to give the impression of being frail and confused.

Police had done their homework on Mrs Leah Craig. She lived with her husband, Vivian, right around the corner from Eric and his wife, Mary-Caroline, and their two small children. Before that, Eric had lived in the same street as his mother, also just off Moore Park Road. And before that, he had lived with his mother.

Leah permitted the officers into her home, though in truth she was given little option. Her cardigan was neatly buttoned. Her stockings were straight and smooth. Her shoes were carefully polished. Her attire was reminiscent of Craig's outfit when he'd been arrested. Mary-Caroline had said that her mother-in-law still laundered Eric's clothing, and based on the immaculate dress of the woman standing before them, police didn't have a hard time believing this to be the case.

The more discoveries that police made about the life of Eric Craig, the more they realised that stain removal was something his mother had been doing her whole life.

Eric's real surname was Joseph, not Craig, and he was illegitimate. Police had made this discovery because he hadn't been able to produce the requisite birth certificate to prove his surname was Craig.

A country girl from the Victorian town of Ballarat who'd travelled to the city of Melbourne for better work opportunities in 1907, Leah found herself in one of the worst situations a woman might face at the turn of the twentieth century in Australia. She was alone, unmarried and pregnant. But she was also resourceful and determined.

Leah refused to have her child in an 'unwed mother's hospital', and she certainly couldn't afford to pay a doctor to have the child in secret. But she must have been persuasive, or at least persistent. She managed to be admitted to a hospital that, although ministering to the poor, fiercely defended its reputation as a respectable institution; a ladies' committee vetted patient candidates. The hospital relied on charitable donations from wealthy families who had no interest in being associated with an amoral institution. To be admitted, a patient had to prove significant financial hardship but also that they were of good moral character. As the Royal Women's Hospital today notes of the history of the organisation and the role it played for many poor women in the City of Melbourne: 'these were not people who wanted to be seen supporting an institution that assisted the morally lapsed. However this is precisely what happened.' Somehow, Leah managed to swerve past the moral guardians of the hospital and convince a doctor to support her admission. Leah had fought hard to see her son born with some chance of maintaining a good reputation. A good hospital was at least a start.

There is no father identified in Eric's birth records. The large cells in the birth-entry record table devoted to 'father' – name, surname, profession, age, birthplace, when and where married, father's parentage – are all blank.

The circumstances leading up to Leah's pregnancy can't ever be known. What is known is that at twenty-nine and unmarried, she would have defined the birth of a child as catastrophic because of the very real social and economic exclusion associated with illegitimacy at the time. She gave Eric her own surname at birth: Joseph. This was an important step in Leah's life because it set the tone for all that followed. The secrets surrounding Eric's birth were closely guarded by Leah for the rest of her days. With this one lie, a more morally acceptable narrative could be presented to the outside world: Leah had once been a wife but had been tragically widowed, and Joseph was her married name.

In the early years, Leah fought hard to give the impression that her son had been born in a respectable family situation. In truth she was aspirational, wanting a better lifestyle than she could afford. Living in Albert Park, she was caught fare dodging on a train travelling from St Kilda. She'd paid for a second-class fare but she and Eric were caught travelling in a first-class carriage. She was formally charged. When she appeared in South Melbourne Court to face the judge, she pleaded an unusual case – she blamed her six-year-old son. He was impulsive, she said; he'd leapt onto the train, and she had protectively followed in an effort to keep him safe. She was fined five shillings and received no further charge.

It would take ten years for Leah Craig to achieve the respectability that she desperately craved for herself, and her son. In 1916, with World War I well underway, 38-year-old Leah became swept up in a wartime romance. They married quickly before he was shipped off to fight in France.

Vivian Craig had enlisted in the AIF in October 1916. The paper trail surrounding this event highlights a man fully willing to step in and support both wife and child. In his enlistment papers, Vivian completed the forms as if Eric was his biological son. 'I further agree to allot not less than three-fifths of the pay payable to me from time to time during my service for the support of my wife and child,' he noted and signed at the bottom.

Leah no doubt prayed for the best but prepared for the cruel vagaries of war and the contingency that her husband might not return. Vivian nearly didn't.

Wounded in action while posted in France as a gunner and driver for the 13th Australian Field Artillery Brigade, he almost died three times. Deployed as part of a dangerous campaign often referred to as the 'battles of Bullecourt', from April to May 1917, along with other artillery men, he advanced and claimed French territory from the Germans. As farming areas were claimed and new posts were established, the brigades worked quickly to overhaul equipment, restock and gather local intelligence, while waiting to receive orders about where the troops should advance next. The war diaries report the difficulties and relentlessness of the campaign: communication was hard to maintain, the few tanks provided to assist the Australian troops were slow and underperformed, and a smokescreen of gunfire, wet weather and fog created almost constant challenges. As one field artillery report noted around the time of an attack that almost killed Vivian: 'more dead Germans than we have seen for some time'. It was a gruelling and ugly victory, and both sides suffered.

The area was gassed often in the month leading up to the attack that would maim Vivian. Men and horses got sick, or got lost and were simply never found. Animal and man rotted in the wet, cold field. It rained heavily on and off during the two months of the campaign, leaving many men with a debilitating condition called trench foot. Perpetually freezing conditions and the relentlessly wet weather caused widespread contamination and infection throughout the troops. Unable to ever completely dry boots in the muddy ground and the cold air, men rotted in their socks. Vivian would suffer with the echoes of the campaign for his entire life, with deep pain in his shins that couldn't ever fully be explained.

Artillery batteries were given plot points on a map to which they would advance. They were gassed and shelled, and in turn they gassed and shelled, as they attempted to gain ground. During a bold move by the Allies to push forward, Vivian was hit. He survived the near-miss of a gunshot, then almost died of the infected wound that maimed his hand. Weakened and depleted, Vivian had almost no immune system left. A bout of influenza, not a bullet, almost took him out the third time he faced death.

Vivian was sent to a field hospital in France, then the Australian auxiliary hospital in Harefield Park in England, and finally to the Duchess of Connaught Hospital in the village of Taplow. His poor health continued, and he was discharged and sent home after a prolonged period and multiple attempts by doctors to effect his recovery.

At the end of 1918, when Vivian returned home to his ready-made family, the three began to build their life together. Vivian didn't officially adopt Eric, but simply moved forward as if the past could be erased. Eric was expected to do the same. He was ten years old when his mother began signing her son's surname as Craig. Her name was officially changed when she married Vivian, though Eric's was not. His surname of Craig was incorporated into his life in ways least likely to arouse suspicion. When enrolled in a new school, he started fresh as Eric Craig.

The family was aided in their deception by many factors. The surname of Joseph turned out to be useful – if it ever appeared on official documentation, Eric could claim it was an error, that Joseph was simply an additional middle name. There were also thousands of families facing similar challenges. Many war widows eventually remarried, and the post–World War I period saw a forced acceptance and greater tolerance for blended families. Many assumed that any inconsistencies in documentation were due to a war tragedy or the loss of a parent or partner.

The lie of Eric's name was one that he maintained his entire life, across all official documentation. It was never discovered, unless he was forced to produce a copy of his birth certificate.

As Eric grew to adolescence, the family participated in a collective lie: Vivian was his biological father. The Craig family sought to rebuild their lives in the wake of the war, much like other families in the middle-class neighbourhood in which they lived, Albert Park. Vivian worked in the respectable job of clerk. The gunshot that had almost killed him left him with partial mobility to his hand and arm. Unlike many trades that relied on two working hands, clerk was considered a viable occupation for those with arm and hand injuries because it didn't require physical endurance, and it was possible to type one-handed.

Eric attended school as a Craig, not a Joseph. We know little of his relationship with his stepfather, but by all accounts Vivian had an imposing presence. He stood at five foot nine and a half inches, which was considered tall at the time; enlisted men during World War I averaged around five foot six. He had striking dark-brown hair and dark-brown eyes, and was solidly built. He was scarred significantly across his shoulders and legs, and he had a deep scar across his left cheek, which army records indicate he had before the war started.

Eric continued to live with his mother and stepfather after he completed schooling and entered the labour market. He worked for a short time at a stained-glass studio in Flinders Lane, East Melbourne. At eighteen he was working at Myer in the CBD; it was a good job and he was liked by his manager, who described him as an honest young man, 'regular and punctual'.

For reasons that aren't entirely clear, sometime around 1925 Vivian moved the family to Sydney. Although Eric had a job that might have facilitated his financial independence, he elected to follow his mother and stepfather. He got a job in the boys' mercery department at Lowe's, though it didn't last. At the urging of his stepfather, Eric enlisted as a soldier.

The move to Sydney completed the reinvention of Eric's life. As the family severed connections with Melbourne and made new friends in Sydney, the possibility of discovery that Eric might not be Vivian's son became even more remote. By the time Eric was nineteen, all of his employment documentation and army service records pertained to Eric Craig.

For Eric, much happened in a few short years. The army suited him, and he was promoted. In March 1927 he'd been enrolled for two years, and his lieutenant wrote of him: 'he has proved himself to be a very keen and enthusiastic NCO. I can also certify to his keenness, trustworthiness, and sobriety and I have always found him to be a good soldier.'

Little is known of Eric and Mary-Caroline's courtship. What is known is that they were married in 1929 when Eric was twenty-two. Mary-Caroline was still a teenager and had two children before she had turned nineteen. The couple built a life together under the watchful gaze of Eric's mother, who at the time lived in the same street in the eastern suburbs of Sydney.

Then Eric was kicked out of the army for stealing an officer's car. Under normal circumstances this would have been unfortunate, but given the economic climate at the time, it was disastrous. Eric found it almost impossible to get work, and this intensified his reliance on his mother for both emotional and financial support. Eric drove as a chauffeur for her neighbour – a job she arranged – though this job didn't endure either. He'd been employed as a driver for a wealthy man in Potts Point for three months in 1932, through to August, but that was the last work he'd been able to get.

When Miller knocked on Leah Craig's door, the detective would hardly have been expecting a warm welcome. We don't know much about what transpired between the little woman in the very smart day suit and her visitors from the police force. What we do know is that Miller and his team of officers left empty-handed.

If Miller was concerned about the lack of evidence to support his case, he didn't show it. His public statements were filled with bravado. A week after Craig's arrest for Iris Marriott's murder, *Truth* wrote:

> . . . after weeks of anxiety in the community when women and girls feared the footstep of a man behind them and shivered with premonition if a motor car came to a standstill near them; after weeks of ceaseless manhunting . . . the great search has almost ended . . . The police feel certain they know the murderer of Bessie O'Connor. Within the next few days there will be sensational developments and a charge of wilful and felonious murder expected to be laid against a good looking young man. Slowly a web of circumstantial evidence is being wound around the suspect. As cold and impassive as a scientist bisecting a rare specimen, Detective Inspector Miller is preparing for the big move he will make this week. 'I know that I will succeed,' he said.

•

The inquest into the death of Iris Marriott (aka May Miller) commenced on Friday, 20 January 1933. No doubt fuelled by newspaper reports about the crime, the inquest attracted a huge amount of public attention. Hundreds came – and while the vast majority didn't gain entry, the spectators didn't disperse after court officers turned them away. Instead, the crowds hung around the courtyard. If a person happened to leave, one of the many waiting would slip in to take their position. The photographs of the waiting crowds, published beside the news stories about the murdered women, reflect the scale of the challenge facing police. Physical profiles released about the killer may have been conflicted, but looking at the suspect walking into the courtroom did highlight one thing: the well-dressed man in dark suit, with a hat, could have been any one of the hundreds of men pictured outside the courtroom that day. From a distance, there was little to distinguish one man from another.

Very few women attended the inquest. Iris had two sisters but neither attended. Mary-Caroline was present. So too was Leah Craig.

When Leah entered the courtroom, all eyes turned towards her. She was hard to miss. Covered from head to toe in black, the woman moved through the room quite literally with her nose in the air. Her sleek black A-line fitted skirt finished at the knee. Her dark blouse matched her patterned black stockings. But it was what she wore on her head that attracted the attention of the entire courtroom: a thick, black, bird-cage veil that covered not only her face but her entire head. The mesh was so dark, it resembled that worn by a beekeeper. The netting was so tightly woven it allowed her to see out, but no one could see in.

First, one noticed the way Leah Craig dressed; next, one noticed the way Leah Craig walked. She moved with a sense of performance in every step. Crossing the floor, she strode over to the coroner's dais, not the public gallery. She stopped, pausing for a moment or two, then crouched down and prayed on the floor of the courtroom. She wept. She did not say a word; the performance was silent. But the message was communicated clearly and powerfully: *I am a mother. See me grieve for my lost son.* After her short prayer, Leah rose from the floor. She turned and seated herself right at the foot of the coroner, like a dutiful wife or a concubine who casts her eyes upward to the king. She then, and in a most extraordinary scene, crawled forward out of her seat, knelt on the ground and began praying again. This time she mumbled, 'I pray for my only son. I pray that all will tell the truth. I pray that none will falsely proclaim against my boy.' Being at the base of the coroner's dais, Leah was out of his line of sight but able to meet her son's eye, as he was required to stand in the area designated for the accused in the centre of the court.

In contrast, Mary-Caroline was close to invisible. She sat towards the back, doing all she could to maintain privacy. Her husband appeared to be looking for her, and their eyes met at one point. She smiled encouragingly at him. Then later, she stood inside the door of the court and twisted a handkerchief restlessly, wringing the tension in her hands out into it. Throughout the proceedings, she dabbed the corners of her eyes.

At one point, a young woman stood at the courtroom door, scanning the room for someone. When her eyes rested on Mary-Caroline she moved forward silently and whispered something into the woman's ear, so softly that no one could hear it. Mary-Caroline gasped and leapt from the bench. A court official attempted to stop her on her way out, for unseemly behaviour in court. 'My daughter's missing. She's run away. Get out of my way!' Mary-Caroline shrieked, all but pushing him away so she could exit. He stepped aside, and she tore off into the hall and was gone. Valma, her daughter, was found a few hours later, but Mary-Caroline didn't return to court.

While Eric's wife had momentarily attracted some attention, it was Leah who held the interest of those present. Unlike Mary-Caroline, who sought to sit at the back of the courtroom, away from the limelight, Leah seemed happy to assume centre stage. If it can be interpreted as a psychological strategy, it seems a brilliant one. To everyone assembled in the room, and to journalists reporting the story back to the wider public, it was a strong and undeniable demonstration of support for Eric Craig. For a man accused of heinous crimes against women, he still had the unfaltering support of two of them – and in this, his mother assumed a saintly repose. It also showed Eric that no matter where he went or what he'd done, his mother was right there with him. She had positioned herself at the coroner's bench so that every time Eric looked at the judge, he faced his mother as well.

It was Friday, so the inquest went into recess for the weekend, in preparation to resume the following Monday. It was normal for prisoners to be returned to Long Bay Gaol, particularly if a break in proceedings occurred over a weekend. This practice allowed Darlinghurst holding cells to maintain capacity for the daily pipeline of newly arrested prisoners needing short stays. In Craig's case, this protocol wasn't conformed to. On the Friday night, he was held over at Darlinghurst courthouse. He soon found out why.

On Saturday morning, without warning, Craig was called before a stipendiary magistrate, Mr Gibson, and found himself facing a new charge.

'For the murder of Bessie O'Connor,' read the officer of the court.

No one had seen it coming, least of all Craig's defence team. He was remanded and taken back to the cells, and one witness in the courtroom reported that he looked like a man 'walking in a trance'. The process from start to finish took less than three minutes, and because no one had expected the charge to be laid before the conclusion of Iris's inquest, fewer than ten people were in the room at the time.

It was a bold and unexpected move by law enforcement. As one newspaper reported, 'This was one of the most sensational police moves in the history of the state – the charging of a man with another murder while the coroner is inquiring into a previous killing. When the inquiry into the death of

May Miller/Iris Marriott is completed the police will ask the coroner to set down a date for the hearing respecting the death of Bessie O'Connor.'

When asked if he wished to apply for bail, Craig said 'no', softly.

On Monday the inquest proceedings continued. Leah Craig dutifully resumed her place at the front of the court, and Mary-Caroline at the back. A sea of suits surrounded the two women.

Craig didn't take the stand or proffer any evidence at the inquest. We can't know if his taking the stand would have made any difference to the outcome. What is known is that the coroner took a very certain position on the basis of the confession provided to him. While inquest findings were often phrased in a careful and circumspect way, preferring to leave the decision for the Supreme Court to determine, the coroner in this case didn't hold back. He ruled that Eric Craig 'feloniously and maliciously did murder the said Iris Marriott' and referred the matter to the Supreme Court for trial.

As Craig was being led away, Leah and Mary-Caroline flocked to him. Unconcerned about the threat posed by two tiny women, the officials showed a degree of compassion – less for the prisoner and more for the distressed women. Craig hugged Mary-Caroline around the waist and drew her to him. He kissed her on the lips. It was a long kiss, yet officials did nothing to stop the closeness between them. Craig's mother reached up to touch her son's hair and bald patch, while Eric continued to kiss his wife passionately. 'Be brave, my son.

Bear up,' Leah said. 'I am praying for you and everything will come out all right in the end.' Craig wept openly. He wiped his nose roughly with the back of his hand. His wide eyes were bloodshot and had the faraway look of someone gripped with terror. He spoke in the high pitch that signals the vocal cords are stretched tight, in a state of tension and distress. 'Why didn't you come and sit near me?' he asked. Mary-Caroline went to explain herself until she realised there was no point. Craig wasn't talking to her, but to his mother. 'My darling,' said Leah, patting the top of his hand, 'I was here all the time. I was in the court the whole time.'

10

WORST CRIME ON THE CALENDAR

The opening statement made by Crown Prosecutor L.J. McKean KC on 16 March 1933 set the tone for the trial. He was a stern man, known for precision. He communicated the air of this even as he sat carefully reading through the sheaf of papers before him, awaiting the commencement of proceedings. He stared intensely through the two small round discs of glass balanced on the end of his nose. His horsehair wig moved with him as he tilted his head back, as if it was a natural part of him. He pinched his black legal gown at the shoulders and adjusted it upwards, though no adjustment was really necessary. The Crown prosecutor gave every indication of being in total command.

Counsel representing Eric Craig included Mr Mack KC, Mr Goddard and assistant counsel Mr Woodward. All of the men were being paid at a heavily subsidised rate. Under the *Poor Persons Legal Remedies Act 1918*, judges could cap the fees that lawyers charged to represent disadvantaged clients. Under the act, a poor person was defined to be someone 'not worth fifty pounds (excluding his wearing apparel, tools of trade, and the subject-matter of the legal proceedings to which he is a party)'. It wasn't Eric Craig but Leah who had made a formal application to the state seeking financial support for legal representation.

Prosecutor McKean cleared his throat briefly, preparing himself for the monologue to follow. He tipped his head back again, in the manner of a person about to deliver inform-ation of immense gravity. 'The unfortunate woman was a follower of the oldest profession in the world,' he said.

A stillness and a silence fell across the courtroom.

Like the inquest, the Iris Marriott murder trial attracted record crowds. But it wasn't just the aggregate number who turned up that made the event noteworthy, it was the compos-ition of the crowds that was of interest too. Almost without exception, the attendees were men.

Leah Craig sat in the front row, this time as close to her son as the layout of the courtroom permitted. She was again dressed in black, her beekeeper's veil in place.

McKean foreshadowed the scandal and depravity that lay ahead. 'The Crown alleges that this murder was accompanied by circumstances that were particularly revolting.'

The words of the Crown prosecutor gripped the attention of all who were present in the courtroom that morning. Men squirmed in their seats, anticipating what might be said next.

But as quickly as McKean had gained the attention of the public gallery, he lost it. In an instant, all heads turned towards a low and repetitive knocking sound that approached from the hall outside. It was Mary-Caroline, and she was late. She was now attempting to cross the courtroom floor quietly – a task that her hard wooden heels seemed determined to thwart. She clumped inelegantly across the floor, despite her best efforts.

Mary-Caroline hadn't dressed to attract attention. With no make-up, a blue-grey crepe de chine frock and a fawn beret, she had dressed to sink into the background of the courtroom.

She was being led across the room by an older gentleman, who everyone assumed was her father. It was. Michael Patrick Tobin was an eastern suburbs local who had loyally supported his daughter since the ordeal with his son-in-law began. He escorted her all the way to the back of the witness reserve, then helped her to find a seat.

The first goal for the Crown was to establish the timeline of the evening of Iris's murder. To achieve this, McKean called Stanley McGroder, Iris's young lover, to the stand.

McGroder seemed disinterested, lackadaisical, perhaps even drunk. He had the ruddy complexion of one who either drinks too much or works too hard in the sun – journalists decided pretty much straightaway which one applied to McGroder.

Mr Mack, Craig's barrister, eyed McGroder with contempt during cross-examination. He mocked the man for not working, for failing to get a job, for having such a poor work ethic going on three years. This made McGroder look bad but did little to disrupt the Crown's goal in putting the man on the stand.

McGroder's testimony achieved two important things for the Crown's case. He verified the starting point for the events that unfolded on the evening of Iris's murder. She had eaten dinner with her lover before she left home to go to work – before 9 p.m.

'On that morning after doing some shopping and after staying at home for lunch . . . about 8 p.m. she got dressed and went out. I did not know where she was going at the time,' McGroder explained. There was little visible emotion in the man. 'The next time that I saw her was at the city morgue. I identified her body,' he said matter-of-factly. 'When she went out, she was in good health,' he added, almost as an afterthought, before he stepped down from the stand.

The prosecution had actually needed McGroder to look utterly hopeless on the stand, incapable of tying his shoes or even buttoning his shirt properly, and therefore unlikely to be a calculating and devious killer. The prosecution wanted to present Craig as the only likely suspect. In this regard, McGroder exceeded the Crown's expectations.

Detective Patrick Power took the stand. He described the naked body of the woman, the coral tree that had shaded her flesh from the moonlight, and the pools of blood surrounding her body. He also noted the number of bloodstains on the clothing collected at the scene and now exhibited as evidence. Power's testimony successfully described the carnage. Jurors could imagine the park, the dark, and the even darker discovery of what had occurred there.

Dr Arthur Palmer, government medical officer, confirmed that terrible violence had been levelled at the woman. Her head had been struck over and over again, and the wounds were triangular and deep. When Palmer noted the presence of brain spatter and powdered bone, some in the courtroom audibly gasped. A few men cleared their throats quietly, queasy at the evidence presented in the overly warm courtroom.

Palmer: 'On 10 December last, at about 11.30 a.m., I saw the body of this woman, May Miller (or Iris Marriott). As to her physique, she was a small woman. Her height was five foot one. I had no means of weighing her but just by feeling her and looking at her I would say she was about seven stone. A small woman.'

McKean and Mack sought to describe the violence of the assault in a way that benefited their respective cases. McKean wanted to emphasise that the tiny, vulnerable woman would have had little chance once she'd received a blow across the head, inflicted with the strength of an average adult male.

McKean: 'Do you mean small made?'

Palmer: 'Wiry, I should think. She was a small, wiry woman.' He then noted the cuts, how many, the length, and where they were positioned.

McKean: 'In your opinion would any one of those wounds be sufficient to cause death?'

Palmer: 'I would not like to say that.'

McKean had hoped that Palmer would run with the lead he had given him, but he did not. Instead, Palmer established something else entirely.

'It was difficult to say how much of the injury was due to any one wound. The skull was very much broken up. It was so much broken up that it could be removed with the fingers, sufficient to remove the brain . . . The skull was very much broken, I could remove it with my fingers without a saw . . .'

This, in McKean's view, was even better. He'd wanted to establish that an excessively brutal and cruel force had been used, and that the killer had clearly wanted to kill. Palmer had established this without being led.

McKean: 'So far as the brain was concerned, was there any brain protruding?'

Palmer: 'Yes there was brain in the hair, it was protruding into the hair. It was very much broken beneath those wounds, especially on the right side.'

McKean: 'And is it your opinion, doctor, that it would have required a great deal of force to cause those wounds?'

Palmer: 'Yes they would all have been hard blows.'

It was now Mack's turn to cross-examine. As Craig's defence counsel, he needed to show that Iris may have been small, but that she could still fight so wildly, so unpredictably, that this would have represented a threat to a man physically larger than her. Mack knew it was a big claim, given the condition of Iris's body. The mental image of a tiny woman dropping to the ground, limp and inanimate, as a man towered over her, bludgeoning her into the dirt, was definitely not what Mack wanted to conjure for the jury.

Mack sought to establish that not all the blows were the same. Perhaps one had been struck in self-defence, as the woman started the attack. Then, the defence suggested, the blow to the head may have created epileptic-like seizures due to changes in brain activity caused by physical trauma. Mack wanted to establish that any type of brain injury might make a person's behaviour erratic, unpredictable. It was a strategy that opened the door for a number of propositions to be made down the track. Mack needed to prepare a defence capable of providing an explanation for Craig's signed confession – he needed to provide a possible explanation for why the man had struck the woman in the first place.

Mack: 'What would happen immediately after that unconsciousness, you could not say?'

Palmer: 'No.'

Mack: 'I suppose you have known people to struggle after they were unconscious, to subconsciously struggle?'

Palmer: 'If you are unconscious, your movements could only be convulsive.'

Mack: 'But you have seen a fowl struggling after its head has been cut off, for instance?'

Palmer: 'Yes, it will run. I have not seen a human doing it.'

This to-and-fro between the defence lawyer and the medical expert continued for some time. Could she struggle? Palmer said this wasn't clear. Mack was determined to establish there was some fight left in the woman.

'You don't say that these wounds would produce unconsciousness completely?'

Palmer: 'I should imagine that each one of the three would knock a person down if they were standing and render them permanently unconscious. They might have a recovery later in the hospital under treatment.'

At this point the judge, Justice James, stepped into the conversation. His presence in the courtroom had been quiet up till now. He had listened. He had assessed. Now he weighed in with questions of his own, about the limits of human consciousness after an attack.

James: 'Take a skull injured like that, would a person recover from unconsciousness?'

Palmer: 'If the skull was crushed like that there would be no possibility at all. There would be no possibility of a head broken like this making any recovery.'

What followed this exchange was a parade of witnesses.

Gallard came first, the owner of the Essex that police believed had been used to pick up Iris. He presented confidently and was precise in his descriptions of the car and the items stolen from it. 'I did not give anybody authority to use it,' he noted of that evening. He then mentioned which of the missing items had been found.

Next on the stand was Mrs Mildred Gallard, his wife. She described the fawn cardigan that she had left in her

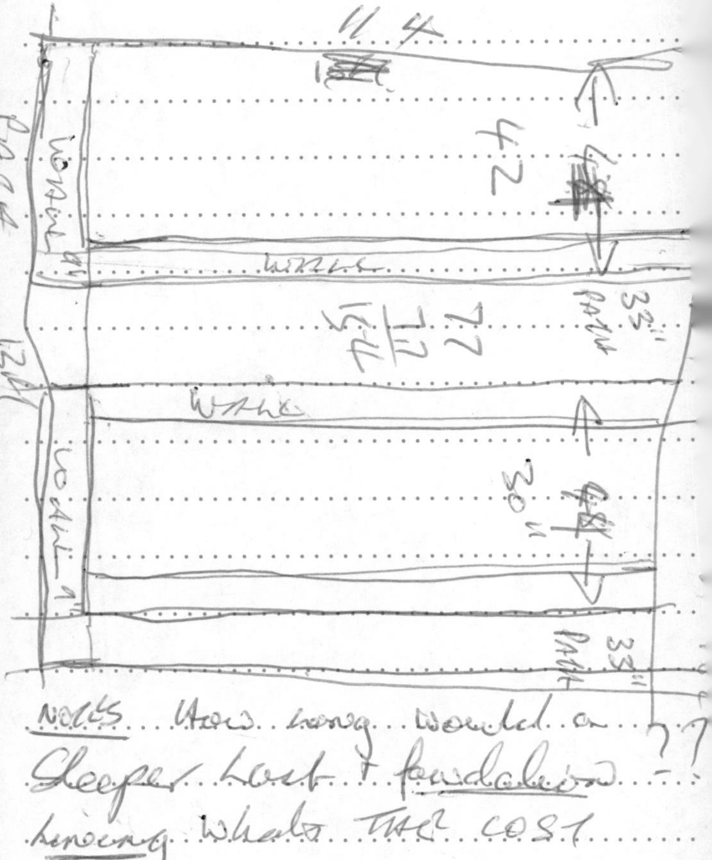

NOTES How long would a
Sleeper bed + foundation
lining What's the cost
Per
1st 90"

15 5

Path width 33" = 2ft 10 1/2

72
72
12
196

6½
6½

husband's car. 'The last witness is my husband,' she said. 'On 9 December last I put a cardigan jacket in his car – an Essex.'

Under the direction of McKean, an officer of the court stepped forward with a fawn cardigan. The item was handed to Mrs Gallard, so she might inspect it more closely. Her response wasn't as emphatic as McKean would have liked.

'It was similar to that,' she said. 'That is similar to the one I put in the car.'

Mack raised his body halfway out of his chair and said, 'No questions,' before dropping back down again.

Though Gallard had meticulously labelled many of the work items and tools in his car, the electric torch hadn't been one of them. And the torch, like the cardigan, could have been purchased in any department store. Gallard had bought his at Myer, and it was a common household item.

The cardigan that police claimed to have found in Craig's home was a lightweight sportswear-style jacket. Perhaps none of the men present in that courtroom were aware that it wasn't distinctive and had been an all-season trend. Natural tones had been particularly popular because they accompanied the surge of tweed patterns in skirts, vests and trousers in 1932 and 1933. Though greens and coppers had been trends, in addition to the traditional black, navy and red, the most common colour of all was brown. There were more shades of brown than anything else in women's cardigans – mid-brown, brown, beige and fawn. In fact, Mary-Caroline was sitting in court wearing a fawn beret that would have matched the cardigan used as evidence against her husband.

But although both items were generic in nature, almost impossible to identify as unique, Mack didn't point this out at trial.

To establish that it was Gallard's Essex motor car that had been stopped near Queens Park, bookmaker John James Mannix took the stand. He lived in Victoria Street, Waverley; his home overlooked Queens Park. When an exhibit – a photo of a parked motor car – was held aloft, Mannix said he'd been watering his front lawn around 9.15 p.m. when he'd seen the same make of car. It was the only one parked on the street. When he looked out through his curtained window later, the car was gone. 'Inspector Miller showed me a car similar to that. I did not see anybody in the car. I did not see the car go away. The latest that I saw it was about 9.15 on 9 December.'

Next, Leslie Egan, who'd been walking back though Centennial Park on his way home to Bronte, reported finding the odd objects in the centre of a local roadway near the island plantations of palms. It wasn't far from the crime scene. 'I found an envelope addressed to Mr Gallard in it. I rang him up. He came to my place and I gave him back his articles in the bag.'

Henry Naughten had found clothing in Cuthbert Street. The examiner confirmed that there was blood on the shoulders of the overcoat. Frank Benham, a motor mechanic, had seen the clothing under the tree as well.

With this sequence of witnesses, the prosecution seemed to successfully establish the plot points for the crime: a car had been stolen; that car had been used to drive Iris to her death; some things had been taken from that car and thrown away, while others had been kept. Detective Inspector Jake Miller took the stand. His testimony was vital because he gave the police perspective on the crime. Prosecutor McKean used a light touch with him. He knew there was power in letting a senior member of the police force simply tell the story, so he permitted Miller to lay it out, without interruption.

As Miller told that story, the crime-scene photographs of Iris's corpse were handed from jury member to jury member. Miller's narrative had a particularly powerful effect because it was accompanied by images of a woman left naked, beaten and debased. He described the vast quantity of blood on the ground, and the large slice across the top of the beret from a vicious blow.

'McRae said to Craig – the torch and the cardigan jacket were found in your place tonight and have been identified as having been in the car. And to this, I said to Craig, "We have reason to believe that that car was used in connection with the murder of Iris Marriott or Miller on the night of 9 December." I said, "I am going to ask you some questions regarding the matter. You need not answer unless you desire, but what you say may be given in evidence." He hesitated for a while and then he said, "I was mad. I did kill her. I must have been mad." He kept on repeating this.'

McKean: 'Did he say anything before that? You say that he hesitated for a moment?'

Miller: 'I don't remember it.'

Miller had characterised himself as so proficient an interrogator that Craig had simply offered up the information.

Miller: 'He wrote on the bottom of it, "I have read over this statement and it is true and correct, being made of my own free will, there has been no promise or threat or inducement made to me by Inspector Miller to make this statement." That is in his own handwriting.'

Judge: 'I suppose you put it to him that it was made voluntarily and of his own free will.'

Miller: 'He wrote it.'

Judge: 'Did you say what you wanted him to say?'

Miller: 'No. I said that if he liked he could write on the bottom, which he did. I did not word it for him.'

While the Crown had provided a close account of the timeline of that evening, they didn't detail the steps that had led to the front door of the Craig home. How had he come to be identified above other suspects? This wasn't outlined.

Justice James had questions for Miller – he wanted to know how the interrogation had unfolded.

Miller: 'Later on I saw Detective Sergeant McRae . . . that was about 11 p.m. About one o'clock in the morning of 7 January, together with McRae, I again saw the accused at the CIB.'

Judge: 'Why did you keep such hours? Were you in a hurry?'

Miller: 'No. The reason was that when the cardigan jacket and the torch were found there was some difficulty in the identification. I understand that Mr Gallard was not at home when the police took the articles there to be identified and that would cause the delay.'

In Miller's account, when confronted with the evidence of the cardigan and the torch, Craig had spontaneously confessed.

Miller claimed, 'Craig appeared relieved when he made the statement.' Miller further added, 'I didn't abuse Craig, I did not tell him that if the woman attacked him he would have a legal loophole of self-defence.'

Wiley and Swasbrick took the stand next. They assumed responsibility for what had occurred at Craig's home, as they had been the officers who had overseen the search conducted there. Wiley explained that 'in a suitcase under the cot was found a woman's cardigan jacket and electric torch.'

Wiley also corroborated Miller's account of the interrogation, and backed up his senior officer. He admitted that, yes, the interview had been long, but he argued that duress hadn't been involved. He gave his account of what he'd observed when he returned to police headquarters. 'On 7 January about 4.15 a.m. I saw Craig at the detective office and took him to the yard where we sat in a car. Craig said, "I am cold, can you give me a coat?" Two blankets were then given to him and Craig then said, "I am glad I told everything I have been nearly out of my mind and frightened to go out of the house. I went up the street a few days ago to do a bit of shopping for my wife and ran into a policeman and nearly collapsed. I went cold all over."'

Craig's defence team didn't challenge the broader police narrative about the crime and how it had taken place – they simply took issue with who'd been lined up as the main suspect.

From the very beginning of the trial, Mack had a big problem. Craig pleaded not guilty, but Mack couldn't strictly argue a case that Craig was innocent. There was the signed confession, and that was hard to explain. Mack had to deploy a tricky strategy: don't openly admit guilt, but offer the jury an explanation if they did think Craig was guilty.

Mack had some facts to draw on that could sway the jury towards mercy for Craig. For instance, Iris had been violent in her life. She had bitten someone in a previous attack. Mack suspected that police had told this story to Craig to give him an out. Mack implied that police had, in a boysy way, told Craig that they knew what Iris was like. They knew Craig had only been defending himself when she attacked him. If he would just admit it, he would avoid a murder charge. They already knew he'd killed her, and they only needed to walk into court and establish this, and he would get the death penalty. In effect, Craig had only one chance to save his life – admit he had killed Iris.

According to Detective McRae, who took the stand after Wiley, 'Craig said, "I killed her, she tried to kick me in the balls. She missed me and got me in the thigh."'

McRae was pushed by the defence team. 'Was the man on the verge of collapse? What was his emotional state, his physical state?' they asked over and over.

McRae stood firm, in order to protect both his own reputation but also to corroborate the account provided by police. 'At no time was he in a state of collapse. He was not trembling when he entered the car after daybreak and he did not drop the cigarette he was sucking ten times ... I questioned him about his heredity and about both sides of his family tree to see if there was any sign of insanity. I asked him if ever he had a certain disease also whether he had ever had tests taken of his blood. I was trying to ascertain why he should commit such a crime for my own information ... He acted like nothing other than a normal human being ... Craig was perfectly normal but his condition was one of genuine repentance.'

Mack took the opportunity to cross-examine the police witnesses. He had to establish that Craig had been pushed, that the stress the man had been under was so great that he had cracked. Craig's defence team needed to prove that his confession was false – but this was one of the most difficult things for a trial attorney to establish. It remains so today, but in 1933 it was particularly hard to refute a signed confession. The notions of duress and threat were rarely taken into account. It was generally believed that an innocent man would never confess to a crime he hadn't committed. Instead, Mack had to run arguments at somewhat contradictory trajectories. On one hand, he said the confession wasn't legitimate; on the other, he argued that if Craig had struck Iris, it was most likely in self-defence.

There were anomalies in the verbal recount of the crime that Craig had given to police. Mack pointed out these inconsistencies. Craig claimed to have wrapped the victim's clothes in paper, but none were ever found this way. Craig said he'd struck her with a piece of wood and then thrown the object into the gutter while making his getaway. But the weapon wasn't in the location where Craig claimed to have dropped it.

The protocols of trials being a little different to today, Mack referred to claims made by Craig that officers had badgered him, threatened him and intimidated him, in order to extract the confession. According to Craig, officers had said to him, 'You are either bloody well mad or the biggest liar I have ever met.' He also claimed that detectives had told him they had his fingerprints on the car.

McRae responded craftily to Mack, sidestepping the inference that this latter statement had been made to intimidate and scare Craig. 'No detective would make such a silly remark if he knew his work. If Craig's fingerprints had been found and they were known to have been in the possession of the department previously, they would have been identified within two minutes of his arrival at the detective office.'

Mack went in hard on Miller too, particularly on the matter of the confession. 'You prompted those words?'

Miller: 'No.'

Mack: '. . . the accused did not use the word "murder"?'

Miller: 'No, I think he said "killed".'

Mack: 'He did not use the word "murder"?'

Miller: 'No.'

Mack: 'You said nothing about it in the police court?'

Miller: 'If it is not in the depositions, no.'

Mack: 'Take the last paragraph of his statement, about no promise, threat or inducement being made. That was at your dictation?'

Miller: 'In this way, that I said to him, "Would you care to write on the bottom of that, that it is voluntary?" He said yes. That is what he wrote on it. I did not go word for word with him.'

Mack: 'Those are not his words?'

Miller: 'They are not mine.'

Mack: 'They look as if they were words that you used, technical words. Take the word "inducement". You know that is a technical word. He has no technical knowledge of the law?'

Miller: 'I could not say.'

For some time, the men verbally duelled over what constituted a technical word. They conjectured about whether a man like Craig might know legal terminology and which words the average man in the street might be likely to use.

Mack: 'I am going to suggest that if you say the word "inducement" did not come from you, people will not believe you.'

Miller: 'It could have come from somebody else in the room.'

Mack: 'It came from a police officer?'

Miller: 'I could not say definitely.'

Mack: 'There was nobody else except the police in the room.'

In addition to responding to the Crown's witnesses and their account, Mack presented the case for the defence. He didn't challenge the scientific evidence as presented. The woman had been struck violently by someone in that park. Someone had left their semen inside her body. All that Mack could do was reiterate how unlikely it was that Craig had been the one to do these vile things.

Mary-Caroline provided a statement saying that Eric had been home at the time the murder was estimated to have occurred. But a wife's alibi had little credibility.

Mack tendered character statements to prove that Eric Craig was a responsible, caring and sensitive man, and had no violent tendencies. Tessie Norman, a machinist working at a manufacturing company in Oxford Street, said she'd known him for two years. She described him 'as a very good tempered man'. Norman was cross-examined by Prosecutor McKean, but she wasn't rattled.

McKean: 'Would it alter your opinion if you knew that he illegally used a car and picked up a prostitute off the street, he being a married man with two children and living with his wife?'

Norman: 'I cannot believe that he would do such a thing.'

Amy Northrop, a widow from nearby Brown Street, Paddington, was called next. She had known Craig for three years. She was a close friend of Leah, and the family had lived at her property for a time.

Northrop: 'I have found him very calm and collected . . . I run a residential and he lived at my place for two years.

My experience was that he was a kind, decent man. He has never openly shown symptoms of indecency.'

Both of these character witnesses were women. Mack was sending a message.

Then came the locals from the neighbourhood of Waverley and Darlinghurst. The family greengrocer spoke on Craig's behalf. Charles Cottingham noted, 'I have known him as a very quiet and well-behaved man. I have seen him associating with other young men. He is not a quarrelsome young man.'

Edward John Sheedy, a contractor from Melbourne, had known the family through Leah for over twenty years. 'His habits were exemplary . . . He was an ordinary young man.'

McKean didn't bother responding to these claims. His case wasn't contingent on the jury assuming Craig to be a good man – McKean only needed to prove the man could lose his temper.

Then came A.M. Wonders, a local friend to Eric, Mary-Caroline and the children. 'I am a traveller living at Oxford Street, Paddington. I have known the accused for about three years. I found him to be gentleman right through. I have left him alone with my wife and my adopted daughter, Tessie Norman – who is twenty-one years of age . . . I heard no complaints none whatsoever.'

With that, the defence case rested. Court recessed.

•

After lunch, members of the public filed back in, along with the courtroom staff. Leah attempted to take a seat directly behind the bar table and opposite the dock so that she might have an unobstructed line of sight to her son. She'd only just taken her seat, and demurely crossed her legs low at the ankle, when an official swept up beside her, looming. She was moved to the witness reserve.

Mary-Caroline entered shortly afterwards and craned her neck forward, nodding at her husband encouragingly. Craig smiled.

The judge offered an opportunity for Craig to make a statement. He started strong: 'I didn't think I killed this woman.' But then the weight of it all overwhelmed the man, and he struggled to choke back sobs. 'I never saw her in my life before. She came at me like a fury.' He paused and sobbed further, then, perhaps in the absence of anything else to say, he concluded awkwardly with, 'That's all, gentlemen.' He buried his face in his hands, and collapsed, sobbing and shaking.

Mack's final statement to the jury seems clumsy, his words poorly chosen compared to what McKean then offered up. Mack said, 'It has been proved that he is not a man of violence or indecency. Here is a young man who has been brought up decently among decent people who the Crown say has committed a terrible murder. There must be some good reason for it. He must have been assaulted. Where is any other motive? There is none, and it was done in self-defence . . . She came at him like a fury and he was a lucky man she didn't kick him or bite his nose off.' In the end, Mack had chosen to hedge his bet both ways. He denied vehemently that Craig had done it. But if he had, it had certainly been an accident. 'The evidence is dead in his favour,' he said.

McKean was skilful and witty, and embedded a pop culture reference in his final words to the jury. A breakout hit movie screening around that time starred heartthrob Fredric March playing both Dr Jekyll and Mr Hyde. March had won an Oscar for his performance at the fifth Academy Awards, held only the month before Iris's murder.

McKean contended that it didn't matter what events had preceded the death – the viciousness with which the woman had been struck spoke to character. 'We don't know what was in the man's mind. It might have been another case of Dr Jekyll and Mr Hyde. A married man living with his wife and two children, virtually steals a car, picks up a woman and goes into the park with her. What kind of man is he? I doubt very much if any of you would like to have his character.'

In his final summing-up, His Honour Justice James provided some parameters to assist the jury with their deliberations:

> Gentlemen of the jury, the accused is here charged with murder. It has been put to you that it is the worst crime on the calendar. That ought not to affect your judgement at all. You will try this case the same as a case of simple robbery, you will look at all the facts and make up your mind on the facts, not considering the weight of this charge ... the Act says that murder shall be taken to have been committed where the set of the accused causing the death charged was done with reckless indifference to human life,

or the doing of an act obviously dangerous to human life. Where that takes place, where the act is done with reckless indifference to human life or with obvious danger of causing death, then in a case like that the jury will look at it in this way. The Crown may not be able to prove a motive but a man is presumed to intend the natural results of the acts that he commits. For instance, if a man fires a revolver point blank at another, what is the obvious intention? Is it not that he is going to kill him or hurt him very considerably? ... In this case you could if you wanted to, find a verdict of manslaughter. The next point put to you by Mr Mack is that it is justifiable or excusable homicide, that is that what was done was done in self-defence ... he must not kill a person unless he has retreated as far as he can so that he shall not have to do it. Take the case here. Here is a little woman without any weapon at all. A woman five foot one in height and seven stone in weight who according to him, attacks him. What is the obvious course for him to pursue? Is it to take up a piece of wood and hammer her over the head or should he get away from her? ... It is a matter entirely for you to say if he thought she was going to inflict grievous bodily harm upon him. If he did what he should not have done in order to protect himself, then the defence would fail. Now we come to the question of manslaughter. Mr Mack says that here there was sufficient provocation to cause you to reduce the charge in that way. Our law has dealt with the matter. Where on the trial of a person for murder it appears that the act causing death was induced by the use of grossly insulting language or gestures on the part of the deceased the jury may consider the provocation offered us in the case of provocation by a blow

. . . He had reasonable ground to believe that grievous bodily harm was going to be inflicted and that he could not protect himself except by killing the other person, he is entitled to be acquitted, just the same as if he thinks his life is in danger. I will leave the matter like that, if the jury find that he had reason to believe that he was going to be so seriously hurt that he had to kill the other person in order to save himself or if he thought that his life was in danger, under these circumstances he is entitled to take steps to protect himself even though it may result in killing.

The jury retired at 3.45 p.m. They deliberated for five hours, returning at 8.50 p.m.

Leah and Mary-Caroline, who hadn't sat together during the course of the inquests and this trial, came together as the verdict was read.

Craig stood silently. His chest rose and fell deeply, as if he was having trouble drawing breath.

An officer of the court read the jury's verdict from a small scrap of paper in front of him. 'Guilty of manslaughter.'

Shock fell across the face of the judge. Although Justice James had preserved a neutral tone throughout the proceedings, that changed the moment the verdict was read. He hadn't given any indication of his belief about the guilt or innocence of the accused before. Now it was clear James had been expecting to hear the words 'guilty of murder'.

Craig continued to stand. He seemed to be focused only on breathing. He had avoided the mandatory death penalty that would have come with being convicted of murder, but he still potentially faced a very long time in prison. His eyes remained closed as if he was desperately trying to imagine himself somewhere other than where he stood. He rocked back and forth on his feet like a child.

Justice James looked sternly at the now convicted man. 'In this case you have been found guilty of a very heinous crime indeed. I cannot quite see the facts the way the jury have found them.' The judge paused, staring at the piece of paper in front of him as if it held an explanation for the extraordinary events unfolding within his courtroom. He continued, 'But at the same time I am bound by their finding. Unfortunately I cannot consider the fact that you are a married man or that you have a wife and children. The punishment is for you and although they may suffer incidentally – they usually suffer just as much as anybody – it is a thing that should be considered before a person commits a crime . . .'

He assumed an even more serious tone, communicating his utter dissatisfaction with the verdict. 'Taking the best view I can of this matter, the fact is that you went there with a woman for some purpose or other which I only surmise, although probably the surmise would be fairly correct in regard to this matter. You took her there for some reason which I think is not the reason you gave. It seems absolutely inadequate altogether to say that you either feared that you were going to lose your life or that you feared you were going to suffer grievous bodily harm. No doubt there may have been a row between you, but to think that you did what you did merely because this little woman said that you should have a kick and because she kicked you in the thigh, to think that she was about to kill you or commit grievous bodily harm upon you does not appeal to my intelligence in any way whatever. However, this jury must have taken that view, I think. They have found you guilty of manslaughter. They may have done it on the ground of provocation. If so, what was the provocation?' Justice James looked over at the jury. If he'd shaken his head in displeasure, no one would have been surprised. But he did not. At all times, he remained composed.

Craig was called up for sentencing.

Woodward, assistant counsel to Mack and a member of Craig's team, then took the floor. 'The only point I want to remind Your Honour of, is that the accused is a married man. He has a young wife – twenty-two years of age. There are two children, one nine months and the other three years. I ask Your Honour to make the sentence as lenient as possible.'

Justice James then turned directly to Eric Craig, looked him dead in the eye and asked, 'Is there anything that you would like to say?'

A barely audible whisper of 'no' was the answer.

'I have to consider that when I come to consider the sentence. It seems to me that the provocation was quite inadequate. Under the circumstances I cannot do less than sentence you to twenty years' penal servitude as a result of this very bad action.' He looked again at Craig, who was now looking down. James commanded the prisoner's attention by saying, 'Look up, sir.' He wanted Craig to know that he was being judged. 'I sentence you to twenty years' penal servitude to be served in such gaol as the Comptroller-General of Prisons may direct.'

11

DEAD IN THE WATER

ERIC ROLAND CRAIG WAS PUT ON TRIAL FOR THE MURDER OF Bessie O'Connor on 29 March 1933. Official records describing this trial are limited. In the NSW state archives, stored in the large leather-bound volume of Supreme Court transcripts from that year, there is only a short summary pertaining to the March trial. The official record hasn't been destroyed, nor has it been lost: a full account was never collected at the time. For reasons that cannot ever be known, no documentation pertaining to the coronial inquest into Bessie O'Connor's death was retained either.

Some details regarding this trial can be confirmed. Craig's conviction in the manslaughter of Iris Marriott had occurred less than two weeks before. Legal proceedings associated with the murder of Bessie O'Connor had then commenced very promptly.

The process of jury selection occurred on the same morning as the trial and immediately prior to its commencement – just minutes before, in fact. Under the legal guidelines for jury selection in place at the time, an accused man was afforded the right to challenge twenty jurors. Craig vigorously exercised his legal right in this regard; he spent more time than most other accused men in deciding who should sit on the jury. On sight alone, and knowing nothing about the men other than the fact they shared some obvious physical characteristics – old, white and male – Craig rejected twenty jurors outright.

Some other details about this trial are known and not disputed. A quorum of thirteen people decided Craig's fate, comprising Judge Halse Rogers and a jury of twelve men. A record was also kept of the key personnel who participated in the trial. Of the many police officers involved in the 'sex slayer' investigation, Detective Sergeant McRae had been a key figure in progressing the Bessie O'Connor case. McRae played a pivotal role in managing the preparation of the police briefs of evidence, but it didn't end there. The detective continued to oversee what occurred in and around the court proceedings with great interest. He was there at every court appearance and at the inquests, and had orchestrated every line-up of Craig in the lead-up to the court proceedings. He was one of the officers flanking Craig as he was led into and out of police vehicles and court.

Craig entered a not guilty plea.

The murder trial proceedings had commenced on Wednesday, and by the afternoon of Friday, 31 March 1933, both the Crown and defence were delivering their final summations. The jury retired at 2.45 p.m. At about 5.10 p.m. the jury returned and requested that a section of evidence be re-read to them aloud. The jury then retired again. The court officers, responsible for caretaking and concierge of the jury, were surprised when the foreman knocked from the inside of the door indicating they wished to be released. It wasn't because they'd reached a decision, but because they said they could not. According to the law, if a jury reached stalemate, jurors were still legally required to deliberate for twelve hours at a minimum. For this reason, at about 8 p.m., the twelve men were locked in for the night.

The next morning, court officials arranged for the men to have breakfast and prepared the meeting room. We can't know what the men discussed that morning, nor how they derived their conclusions. But we do know what was going on in Sydney just beyond the courtroom walls.

On Saturday morning, 1 April 1933, another body was found, lying just beyond a perimeter of what police had defined to be the dark triangle of streets. The discovery resembled the others in many respects: the body was left exposed to the natural elements, in a public place, and there had been no attempt to cover up the crime. Indeed, there was almost a sense of exhibitionism to it all.

Passengers on a steamship ferry travelling from North Sydney to Circular Quay were the first to spot the body.

Floating facedown in the middle of the harbour, the figure was clothed in a heavy coat and their sex wasn't clear.

Water police were called. In the time it took them to arrive, word had spread and crowds had begun to gather. The ferries were still tracking back and forth across the harbour. As commuters disembarked at Circular Quay, they shared what they'd seen from the porthole in their short voyage over from the north shore. More and more onlookers gathered harbourside.

The body sat strangely flat atop the water, and it rocked and bobbed with the motion of the waves from the passing ships. The coat seemed to flutter in the water, giving the entire scene a dreamlike quality. One end of the figure particularly stood out against the backdrop of the deep-green sea – its head resembled the tip of a safety match, swollen and red. It was possible the victim had fallen overboard, but there appeared to be much more going on than a simple boating accident.

Police boat *Cambria* was launched and headed towards the crime scene. Spectators pointed, completely invested in the drama. The harbour was noisy, the onlookers continuing their fear-filled conversations with ever louder voices. Tantalised by what they could see, even from the shore, members of the public speculated about what had occurred.

A group of young women had gathered to gossip about the grim find. 'Has this one had her skull crushed? Like the others?' asked one girl. 'I bet there are others, that haven't yet been found,' another nodded knowingly.

A mother stopped with her teenage daughter. She seemed eager to use the event as an opportunity to teach her child a lesson: the city and strange men were dangerous, and women needed to be careful.

'It's the slayer! He's struck again!' shrieked one girl.

'Maybe he's still here somewhere, right now, watching!' shrieked another.

Competing with the ambient harbour noise of ferry horns, chugging engines and buffeting wind, the crowd was now at fever pitch. One question was on everyone's lips: How could there be another victim? Back in January police had proudly claimed to have captured the murderous menace who'd cruised the inner-city streets in search of vulnerable victims. Yet as April dawned, the evidence found in the harbour suggested that yet another woman had been mysteriously left for dead, in the dead of night. It is easy to imagine that some members of the public, and most certainly eastern suburbs locals, would not have forgotten that almost a year earlier, Hilda White had been murdered. If police had caught the man responsible for at least two of the 'sex slayings', and he was on trial at the courthouse, how on earth could this have happened?

Police were trying to disperse the crowd, but a defiant public simply refused to move. They wouldn't take their eyes off the activities of the water police. Across the NSW constabulary, the water patrols attracted special esteem. A number of events, over several years, had lifted the tide of public opinion on these officers in particular. Any kind of criminal incident on the water, even a small maritime traffic matter, seemed to attract the attention of the public more than land-based police work. Perhaps this was because bystanders could watch officers in action from any vantage point on the inner-harbour foreshore. One such incident had occurred only a few years before, and in 1933 the public were still talking about the heroic actions of the water police.

In 1927, a public transport ferry, *Greycliffe*, departed Circular Quay bound for Watsons Bay. It was the middle of the afternoon, the weather was clear and the boating conditions were calm. *Greycliffe* was crowded. It was a busy service because many schoolchildren used the 4.00 p.m. ferry to commute home. Indeed it was a busy time of the day in the harbour, as steamships like RMS *Tahiti* also arrived and departed then, carrying mail to places as far away as the United Kingdom and New Zealand.

No one expected what happened next. For reasons that to this day remain unclear, the slow-moving *Greycliffe* cut directly into the path of the fast-moving *Tahiti*. Inexplicably, the driver of the small transit ferry simply hadn't seen the beast of steamship steel even though it was about three times its size. Neither driver had time to steer defensively and there-fore nothing was done to counteract the horrendous impact. The ferry driver, completely oblivious, hadn't even had time to warn his passengers.

Tahiti hit *Greycliffe* with a force so great, it sliced the wooden ferry in half. Bodies of children flew through the air as they were tossed overboard.

There were forty casualties that day. The heroic efforts of police were reported far and wide by those who'd been eyewitness to the tragedy and by newspapers in detailed accounts. This heroism hadn't ended on the day of the collision. For days police had continued to deep dive to retrieve not just the bodies of children trapped beneath the wreckage, but their personal effects as well. Officers showed compassion and determination in their efforts to offer parents closure. If a child's body couldn't be returned, police did their best to return their waterlogged school satchels.

On that morning of 1 April 1933, Sydneysiders had crowded around the harbour to rubberneck, but they were also hopeful that the most noble of local police could step in to save them from a malevolent threat.

Cambria approached the floating body. It bobbed vigorously, bounced by the incoming waves that banged and popped against the rescue boat. An officer was poised with a grappling hook, waiting for the opportunity to swing it out wide into the open water. But a rolling series of waves came again, beating against the hull. No ships were nearby and the wind hadn't picked up, so police were somewhat mystified as to the source of the turbulence. They were waiting for a moment of calm that would permit them to retrieve the body. Then, with one large continuous roll of water that came suddenly and from nowhere, the body flipped over.

It was at this point that the officers realised how foolish they had been.

The body wasn't that of a woman. It wasn't that of a man either. Someone had plunged a large and very real stiletto dagger right into a very fake heart. The body was a shop-window mannequin refashioned to look like a murder victim. It had been nailed to a board and tethered to a buoy so it would remain within sight of the constant thoroughfare of ferries.

At first the prank seemed a vexatious, perhaps almost anarchic stunt, designed to undermine the authority and credibility of the water police. Or perhaps it was an attempt to undermine the trial of the slayer, the verdict from which was expected at any moment. But these theories were discounted as soon as police noticed the date. Someone was pranking for April Fools' Day, and they'd picked Sydney police as their target.

In an instant, an act of heroism was transformed into one of humiliation. Struggling as waves continued to roll against the boat, the officer swung the grappling hook out. It missed. They swung again. It missed again. The murdered mannequin was eventually hooked and dragged aboard with its sodden coat. The pranksters had even sought to re-create the look of a bashed victim, with red paint splashed across the brittle mannequin's skull.

Though April Fools' Day was generally considered an acceptable time for pranks, the water police struggled to see the levity in this one.

•

The police over at the Central Criminal Court were also having a tough time on 1 April. Eric Craig was brought in to stand in the dock. He faced the prospect of the death penalty, should he be found guilty.

Sometime after 8 a.m., the jury filed back in and took their seats. The foreman rose and was sworn in. He cleared his throat and shared the outcome of the deliberations between the twelve men. 'There is no possible chance of an agreement,' he said. 'We cannot agree,' he rephrased as if this might make the words land a little more diplomatically. Still, they hung in the air.

Judge Halse Rogers nodded gravely and said, 'I thank you, sirs, for your service.' He dismissed the twelve men.

This was a devastating blow for the police involved – they'd failed to bring Eric Craig to justice not once, but twice. He was convicted for manslaughter, but police had been seeking a murder conviction in the case of Iris Marriott's death. Now, the portfolio of evidence had proven inadequate in securing a conviction for the murder of Bessie O'Connor. The failure to convict could only have stung McRae and Miller, who'd been pivotal in shaping the narrative on which the prosecutors had based their case. As one newspaper noted on 2 April, McRae had only assembled puzzle fragments into a 'mosaic of circumstantial evidence'.

The state, however, hadn't finished with Eric Roland Craig. By 9 a.m., the judge ordered that he be remanded to stand trial for Bessie's murder again at the next available sitting at the Central Criminal Court. According to the court calendar, this was less than four weeks away. Craig's trial date was set for Wednesday, 26 April 1933.

Police had less than four weeks to strengthen their case. While the water police scavenged the scene for evidence so they might locate the people who had humiliated them, the officers assembled outside the courtroom contemplated a similar undertaking.

12

MOTHER-IN-LAW

ON WEDNESDAY, 26 APRIL 1933, ERIC ROLAND CRAIG FACED trial, for a second time, for the murder of Bessie O'Connor. It was a blustery day, though the weather didn't deter the crowds. At the Iris Marriott murder trial, hundreds of men and only a few women had queued for entry. This trial was different, and that was evident even before the doors to the courthouse opened.

The wind howled. Leaves spiralled in tall towers of air just beyond the courtroom door. Women clamped the hems of their skirts against their knees, and held tight to the brims of their hats. Men also braced themselves against the squall, their suit lapels popping up and down with each dirty gust of wind. With closed fists they held their coats closed, and with open palms they crushed the domes of their stiff felt hats against their skulls.

Inside the courtroom, officials braced themselves as well. Murder trials were places of drama and tragedy, and great emotion. A guilty verdict attracted a mandatory capital sentence, so the jury held life and death in their hands when they went to cast their vote for guilt or innocence.

The courthouse moaned. Windows rattled in their frames as a freezing wind swept through the corridors. But it wasn't the weather outside the court that staff were concerned about: a tempest of emotion was about to sweep through the room. This was to be one of the most unusual melodramas ever to unfold in a Sydney court.

The courthouse was filled with mothers. They had crowded the streets of Redfern for Bessie's funeral procession, and now they assembled here. More than eight decades later we can only conjecture on the reasons why this depth of sentiment surged both for Bessie and, perhaps even more so, for her mother.

Perhaps the women identified with Patience in a neighbourly way and had come out in force to show solidarity for her as a fellow Redfern local. One paper pointed out that Bessie and her champion diving brother Arthur had a host of friends, and that Redfern loyalty to the family was strong.

Perhaps some mothers of daughters felt called to the courthouse by the realisation that any one of their girls could have been taken in the way that Bessie had been.

Perhaps some of the women came not to sympathise but to judge. The female victims of sexual murder stood on conflicted moral ground in the early 1930s. If an unmarried woman was out with a man and looking for fun, on some level she was held responsible for whatever happened to her. If a woman was out soliciting and wound up dead, she still faced moral condemnation for her choice to engage in sex work in the first place.

Perhaps fear had driven some women to attend the courthouse that day. Months of news articles had affirmed that a predator had prowled the city. Perhaps mothers of the inner city had come to see the threat for themselves.

One thing was clear: Bessie O'Connor's murder had set the stage for the mother of all trials.

The Solicitor-General's and Attorney-General's departments had anticipated that heightened tensions might be associated with the second trial in particular. The Crown had already tried, and failed, to prove its case. The media, the legal establishment and the public now watched with an even closer interest.

For this reason, Justice Colin Davidson was appointed to preside over the case. Born in rural Mudgee, the son of the longest-practising solicitor in the state at the time (George Davidson, eighty-seven and still working), Davidson was an astute pick for Craig's trial. At forty-eight, he was the youngest-ever judge appointed to the Supreme Court bench. In 1928 he'd been the royal commissioner appointed to investigate bribery and corruption in the NSW Legislative Assembly – and he hadn't only been willing to look for corruption, he'd been willing to state that he had found it. In 1929 he'd been appointed chairman of the joint Commonwealth and State Royal Commission on the Coal Industry. By the end of 1932, he had overseen two recent royal commissions in less than three years. He was known for his well-reasoned and very measured rulings. He was also a lawyer with a reputation for great intelligence and a capability to explore new areas of his field. Davidson had worked in relatively untested areas of law, including workers' rights, and health and safety. He had a reputation for reliability and fairmindedness – his judgments were rarely, if ever, overturned on appeal.

Although Craig was far from the first person to have ever been tried twice for the same crime in New South Wales, it still wasn't a decision the state took lightly. Trials were expensive. They consumed a huge amount of state resources, including the time and commitment of the lawyers, their teams of professional staff, the judge and his support staff, the court officials, and the associated teams of supporting experts and consultants. Public commentators certainly debated the efficacy and economic cost of re-trying Craig. As a legal commentator for the *Sun* noted, '. . . the Crown has sometimes considered that a re-trial in light of probability does not justify the heavy expense entailed'.

Assigning a judge like Davidson to a high-profile trial like Craig's says much about the result that the state wanted: one that was above legal reproach. Every effort had been made by Attorney-General Henry Manning and Solicitor-General Cecil

Edward Weigall KC and his department to ensure an outcome. The second trial had been scheduled well after Easter and on the day after Anzac Day to ensure it could proceed without interruption.

There were also professional reputations to consider. Attorney-General Manning, Police Commissioner Childs, CIB Chief Pryor and Detective Inspector Miller all had a vested interest in securing a conviction for the man whom police claimed had terrorised Sydney as the 'sex slayer'. Ultimately, the attorney-general had made the final decision to proceed with the retrial, based on the recommendations of Crown Prosecutor McKean and the officers of the Solicitor-General's Department.

While these powerful men had taken April to calculate their chances of success and prepare for the second trial, so too had Craig. In April, he had changed lawyers. Mr Curtis KC would be the new counsel, supported by a team comprising Miss C. Jollie Smith and Solicitors, and the continued support of Woodward.

•

The unpredictable air currents that swept through Sydney on the first day of the trial seemed to carry right through to the courtroom. From the moment the trial opened, Justice Davidson was caught in eddies that he couldn't have anticipated and seemed barely able to control.

With the jury and judge assembled, and the trial officially opened, the judge made an announcement: someone had been sending him anonymous letters. The correspondent, claiming to know what had really happened to Bessie, urged the judge to 'do what they believed to be the just outcome'. Davidson issued a stern warning. He was confident in the belief that the person penning the letters was in court that day – and he put them on notice: 'I will hand these letters to the authority if this does not stop. It is a very improper thing to do and if any person has knowledge of any facts relating to this case, the proper thing to do is to give the information to police. It is for the police to decide if the information is proper to be put before a jury. If I receive even one more letter, the matter will be handed over to the police to formally investigate.'

Courtrooms are legal environments, but they are also sites of sorrow, loss, and emotional turbulence. Grieving family members come to seek retribution and to witness justice being meted out against those who they believed have wronged them. Families of the accused, experiencing a different type of grief, also come to seek justice and to vent their feelings. It was the judge's job to ensure that reason and balance prevailed.

Mary-Caroline Craig attended, though not every day. If she appeared to be in a daze or distracted, she may well have been. Her children were being cared for just outside the courthouse, and after her daughter Val's disappearance at the earlier inquest she was most concerned that they remain safe.

Leah Craig, in contrast, stayed for the duration of the trial. She was by now well known to everyone in court, and she dressed, always, in mourning attire. Her dark mesh veil made her instantly recognisable.

Patience O'Connor also attended the trial wearing black. She was younger than Leah but carried the same heavy look of grief as she entered the room and assumed her seat in the public gallery. Unlike Leah, however, Patience had actually lost her child.

As the two mothers assumed their seats, whispers could be heard across the public gallery. But it was not due to Patience nor Leah's entrance.

A scuffle had just occurred on the street outside the courthouse and now everyone inside was sharing gossip about it. A small, rotund older woman in a brightly coloured frock toddled, escorted by a tall, spindly and much younger man. They were headed towards the entrance of the courtroom. Everyone assumed they were mother and son.

She was supporting herself with an umbrella, which she used as a makeshift walking stick. But she also appeared to be supporting her son, who seemed to be less steady on his feet than his mother. He too cut a noticeable figure. He sported an oversized Homburg hat which was so large it hung loose and low over his eyes. Across his nose and mouth he had a scarf that he had knotted at the back in the style of a highwayman about to commit a robbery.

A photographer, eager to snap the bizarre couple as they awkwardly tried to negotiate the door, zoomed in with his camera on the mother and son. What he got was a prompt crack over the skull with an umbrella. 'He is my youngest child!' she snapped, shielding her son protectively as she struck out.

The skirmish now over, the couple shuffled into the courtroom. The vibrancy of the woman's dress seemed even more garish as the colours splashed inappropriately against the black and grey palette of the room. With her umbrella still in one hand and son in the other, the woman fussed as the odd couple assumed their seats in the public gallery with the other spectators. The young man politely removed his Homburg, smoothed down his hair fastidiously and placed his hat in his lap. Onlookers tried to avert their eyes, but many found it impossible to resist staring. The man may have removed his hat, but his mask remained in place.

The scene was observed by everyone in the courtroom, because it was simply impossible to ignore. A 1930s-styled Invisible Man had just entered, escorted by his very visible mother.

•

Prosecutor McKean began presenting the Crown's case. Every element of his argument hinged on identity. First, the identity of the car. Second, the identity of the male driver.

The police plotted the timeline of the car's movements. A blue Essex sedan was stolen from an unlocked garage attached to a residence just near Centennial Park. It was driven over to Redfern. Bessie O'Connor had been seen hopping into a royal-blue Essex sedan, driven by a man. The car had been parked just off Holden Street, near Redfern train station, close enough to Bessie's home that she could walk there but not right outside the residence. It was sometime after nine-thirty when they left Redfern on the evening of 14 December. No one on that street saw the driver. He then headed south along the Princes Highway.

The bridge near the entrance to Tom Uglys Point was a regular road stop for travellers, with an oyster saloon and a kiosk. The Essex stopped there. A young woman got out of the car, went inside and paid a shilling for sandwiches – two ham and one tomato. The proprietress who served the woman saw a man, but only in the distance, beyond the kiosk window. The car drove off shortly afterwards in a southerly direction.

The driver paid the toll to cross Tom Uglys Bridge. There is then a gap in the timeline.

Two people travelled across the bridge in a blue Essex.

Two hours passed.

Only one person returned.

After midnight, the suspected killer was then spotted by two others. He was alone.

Two men were taking a rest break at the roadside stop. They were parked in a convertible Dodge with the top down, which meant they were seated in the night air and had plenty of time to notice the man walking towards them, parallel to the Princes Highway. To the men in the Dodge the solitary figure gradually became bigger as he passed in and out of darkness, under the streetlights, one by one.

The mysterious man greeted the men politely, then they watched him go into the oyster saloon and come out again.

The proprietor of the oyster saloon, an older man called Watson, confirmed that a man had come in very late to ask for benzine (another name for petrol). The proprietor sent him away, telling him the shop was closed. The two men in the Dodge then watched the man flag down a bus driver.

Of all of the witnesses involved in these events, the prosecution relied most heavily on the bus driver, Percy Weekes, to provide a convincing account of what and whom he'd seen on the evening of 14 December 1932. It was this driver who'd managed to get the closest look at the man and spend the most time with him. He'd siphoned petrol from the bus and given it to the man in exchange for a ten-pound note – which the bus driver had politely refused, because the gesture was too generous. A man who happened to be at the same restaurant stop offered to drive the gentleman back to his car.

McKean's case for the prosecution sustained a number of losses early on, because the credibility of some of the witnesses was weak. They claimed to remember Craig after seeing him in the dim half-light but they hadn't consistently identified him at police line-ups – or it had taken several attempts for them to do so.

Curtis, Craig's new lawyer, provided a dramatic perform-ance for the jury. He badgered Detective Payne during his cross-examination, communicating his sense of disappoint-ment in Payne as an officer. The detective's methods, said Curtis, were akin to a 'third degree'. Curtis then explained this idiom to the jury. During the interrogation, according to Curtis, Payne had knowingly worn Craig down to a nub.

If Craig 'looked guilty', which was what officers claimed, it was because he'd been terrified and intimidated.

The trip to the murder site had also formed part of the psychological pressure placed on Craig, argued Curtis. The lawyer's voice was so loud that his words bounced back off the walls and could be heard echoing down the corridors. 'Then!' He barked this to ensure that everyone was listening. 'Then you took him out to the scene of the murder. You graphically described what had taken place there. You said to him, "This is where the pooooool of blood was . . . And here is where she was draaaaagggged through the sand."' All very dramatically, and loudly. The man had the look of thunder on his face. 'What was that done for, sir?'

'Just to show him,' said Payne.

The detective remained cool.

Curtis offered Justice Davidson and the jury an alternative view of the evening of Bessie's attack. It wasn't the bus driver, Weekes, who was important in identifying the suspect, but a man named Brown – a travelling salesman.

A court official stood and called 'Thomas Brown' to the witness box. The tall, spindly man rose slowly from his seat, and his mother dusted down his coat. A court official motioned to the man, gesturing that he should remove the covering from his face before taking the stand. Brown pulled the scarf off and shoved it into the front pocket of his suit. Much to the surprise of many in the courtroom, his features were regular; he hadn't been using the scarf to hide a deformity or affliction of some kind.

While Brown was being sworn in, Curtis shuffled the papers in front of him. He looked confident as he rose from the chair. 'I have called for and have had produced to me a statement taken from this witness at the Criminal Investigation Branch, Sydney . . . It is the one referred to in the evidence . . .' he said.

The judge motioned for Brown to introduce himself.

When the man spoke, his eyes were fixed on Curtis. 'My full name is Thomas Brown. I am a traveller, a boot traveller. I am not employed now. In December last I was employed at Willis Brothers, Newtown. I was employed as a traveller, a traveller for boots. I drove a car. I was driving a car on 14 December last. I can fix the date positively. I came from Kiama that day. I had been on business for the firm. About ten-thirty that night I got to Sutherland. When I got there I went into a restaurant and had a meal. I stayed there until about ten minutes to twelve. I left Sutherland at twelve midnight. I fixed the time by a clock striking. I don't know if the clock was in the restaurant or where it was. I heard some clock striking. Whether it was fast or slow or correct I don't know. After I had gone a certain distance I came across something. I noticed a sedan motor car. I had gone about a mile from Sutherland towards Sydney. I noticed a sedan car pulled up on the left of the road. It was a sedan car. It was a navy blue, a dark car. When I pulled up, I noticed it was an Essex car. When I saw the police subsequently I was able to remember a portion of the number of that car. I gave the number as 147. I could not remember the last three figures. I gave that number to the police as the car that was there. I could not remember the last portion of the number. I did not see in the back of the car at all. When I got there I noticed that the driver of the car had the bonnet open and he was at the front as I passed. As I passed I sang out. I almost pulled up. I said, "What is the trouble?" He said that the fanbelt had almost broken. I pulled up and went back and looked at the car. As I could not see in the engine of the car I turned my car so that my headlights shone on the car. I could see the fanbelt was almost broken. I asked the driver – did he have anything he could fix it with? He said he had not. I gave him some wire. He did not know how to start, so I fixed it for him with the wire. I tied the fanbelt together. I noticed something about the man at the time. I noticed that he had a couple of small scratches on his face and some blood on his shirt. I spoke to him about that. I enquired how he got the blood on his shirt. He said that he hit some ruts further back along the road and where he hit them he bumped his nose on the steering wheel. I got in my car and came on to Sydney.'

Curtis asked a number of questions to clarify the timeline Brown had presented. He also asked Brown to describe the man he'd seen.

'He was about twenty-five or twenty-six years of age, about five foot nine inches high. Very dark complexion, black hair parted in the centre, very broad and high forehead, very high cheekbones and his cheeks were sunken in. I did not notice anything particularly about his hair except that it was black and parted in the centre. I could not say if his hair was dry or what.'

Curtis seemed keen to move on, aware that the man's incessant repetition was likely to hinder and not help, because it could bore the jury. He prompted Brown to move forward with his story, and asked him about his return to Sydney in December.

'When I got to Sydney I did not remain in Sydney. I went away again. I arrived in Sydney about 2 a.m. It was about that time when I arrived when I got to where I was going to stay it was about 2 a.m. I left on the same day, and went as far as Armidale. I went away on the fifteenth and I was back in Sydney about 27 December. I got to Sydney between one and two o'clock and I went to the police at three o'clock . . . After that I did some work for the police. I was with them for about five days. I was paid by them.'

Curtis asked, 'What work were you doing?'

McKean called out, 'Objection!'

Curtis changed tack. 'You were in touch with the police for five days?'

'Yes. Subsequently I was taken to try and identify a man. That was on 7 January. That was at the Central Police Station. I went over the line-up and I looked at all the men and went back to the sergeant and told him that there was no man there that I should swear to that I saw that night. The sergeant said, "Do you see anybody that resembled the man?" I picked out another man. This man [the accused, Craig] was not the man I picked. The man I picked as resembling the man I saw that night was standing on the end of the line on the left hand of Craig. To my honest belief that was the man who most resembled the man I saw with the Essex car; he most resembled him. I was not at the coroner's inquest at all. I did not give evidence at the last trial. The first time that anybody connected with the defence got into touch with me was on Tuesday morning of this week, Anzac Day.'

McKean was then given the opportunity to cross-examine Brown. 'You are a boot traveller?'

'Yes.'

'I mean in the fullest sense of the word, a traveller selling boots and shoes on commission?'

'Yes.'

'And on behalf of your firm, Willis Brothers?'

'Yes.'

'The Crown calls Mr Willis into court.'

McKean raised his hand, motioning for Willis to stop before he moved close to the witness box. 'That will be fine, Mr Willis, if you could just pause there for a moment.' McKean turned to Brown again, and pointed his finger at Willis. 'Look at that gentleman, Mr Brown. Is that gentleman the principal of your firm?'

'That is one of them.'

'Who paid your wages?'

'Mr Willis.'

'Did the girl cashier give them to you?'

'Yes, at times.'

Curtis watched closely. He didn't like the direction of questioning, largely because he couldn't see why it was being pursued. This troubled him greatly because he'd entirely lost sight of the prosecutor's strategy.

McKean asked, 'There is a young lady employed there named Valda Nathan?'

'Yes,' said Brown, 'Miss Nathan.'

'The Crown calls Miss Nathan into court.' McKean held his palm out flat in the air, in the manner of a policeman stopping traffic. Miss Nathan was now standing next to Mr Willis. McKean, speaking again to Brown, asked, 'Look at that young lady. Is that the Miss Nathan in question?'

'Yes.'

'She keeps the wages book?'

'Yes, as far as I know.'

'Don't you sign the wages book?'

'No.'

'I put it to you that you were not out of the shop that day at all on 14 December?'

'Yes, I was. I was not there,' protested Brown.

'You were not at the shop on 14 December?' McKean spoke more firmly this time.

Brown seemed a little concerned but still answered firmly, 'No.'

'You did not receive your wages at the shop on 14 December?'

'No.'

McKean paused. He smiled. 'Just think before you answer. I ask you to pledge your oath. Were you not working in the shop on 14 December? Pause before you answer, sir.'

'No, I did not.'

McKean asked, 'Were you not working at the shop, in the factory on 6, 7, 9, 12, 13, 14, 15, 16 and 19 December? Just think, sir.'

'Read the dates again.'

McKean repeated the dates, reading them aloud again for the entire court to hear. He then pressed the witness for an answer.

'I don't think so,' responded Brown.

'Will you pledge your oath you were not?'

'Yes.'

McKean then paused again. He smiled smugly. 'Will you pledge your oath that you are a boot traveller?'

Brown's face fell. He began to look even more nervous, but there was a sense of surrender in his tone now. The confidence that had been present only a few minutes before had now completely dissipated. 'No,' he said.

'Why did you say you were?'

Brown was now scrambling. 'I was shielding someone else,' he said.

'I want to know who it was,' McKean said firmly.

'He is out of the country at the present time.'

'What do you mean shielding?'

'I wanted to save him. He saw it. I told it.'

'Are you aware that you are committing deliberate perjury?' McKean asked.

'I did not think there was any harm in it at the time.'

'I ask Your Honour for an order to commit this person for trial for perjury.'

Justice Davidson said, 'I will make no such order at present.'

'Mr Brown. You even went so far as to say this. This is the description you gave: twenty-five to twenty-six years, five foot nine inches, thin build, broad shouldered, well set up and erect carriage. Very dark complexion. Black hair parted down the centre. High forehead, very broad prominent cheekbones. Eyes deeply set in the head and cheeks sunken. Pointed chin. Hair had been oiled recently. Two scratches on the side of face extending from the cheekbone to the chin and blood on them not dry. Wearing a signet ring on little finger of left hand. Dark moustache under the nose, but might have been oil. On both sides of the shirt was blood. Might have been a businessman. Fingernails well kept and dressed in well-made navy blue suit. Cream fuji silk shirt. Hands soft, though there was grease on them. Collar to match shirt. No hat. Tan shoes, size eight, with square toes. Made by the Marshall shoe company, and you could see the welts all around and so on. And you gave all that description and it was all lies?'

'Yes.'

'All lies as far as you were concerned?'

'Yes.'

Now Curtis stepped back. He was shaken. He steadied his voice and tried to control his breathing. 'I will ask leave to cross-examine this witness.' The lawyer was obviously struggling to arrange his thoughts. 'This man, Craig,' he said to Brown, and pointed at the accused, 'he is a complete stranger to you?'

'Yes,' said Brown.

Curtis's face was turning red, but whether he was boiling with rage or embarrassment or both wasn't clear. 'I ask for permission to cross-examine this other man. He apparently knows something about it. I ask you to give me the name of the man you are shielding?'

Justice Davidson said, 'That's no part of this case. It's not relative to the case and not evidence.'

Curtis said, 'In a case like this where it is necessary to get to the truth. This man came to my office and told me this story. He's hostile to this case at this present time.'

'I don't think so,' said the judge. 'He's given evidence he said he would, and then it turns out the whole is untrue – that's your misfortune.'

Curtis turned to Brown again. Maybe the lawyer was embarrassed, but he was definitely livid. 'Is that your signature on each of the pages of this statement?'

'Yes.'

'I am going to suggest something and I want to be perfectly fair. When did you give the statement?'

'On Tuesday night.'

'And you saw me on the Wednesday night at my chambers?'

'Yes.'

Brown was dismissed from the stand. He made a break for the door. Brown's mother sat stiffly, poised and ready to act, but not moving an inch. Suddenly an attendant swooped in to block Brown's exit. He was shown, very politely, but firmly, to a chair. The attendant remained beside him, assuming the stance of a bodyguard.

As Brown sat there, Curtis unleashed an attack on the police and on the prosecution. He was humiliated, exposed and vulnerable. His voice cracked.

'It was a trick. I will say it was a trick. It was a blow. It was a great blow to me. One of the greatest blows I have ever had . . . I am sorry I have got to publicly attack the police . . . they had gone out of their way in methods which are a disgrace to British justice. The pick of the force has been called in to hound a man down. You have seen them – men of the highest calibre. They interrogated him till at least three o'clock in the morning. Why should they require this sort of third degree? I thought that we were proud that that system did not exist in New South Wales.'

Prosecutor McKean said, 'I will say nothing about it but to remark that I was amazed at my friend being taken in. How can notice be taken of the story by Thomas Brown that he was sheltering somebody? He is a moron! He has been to the pictures! He is seeking the limelight, or a reward, or God help the man he picked out! Fancy such a person being allowed loose to give a description of a man he never saw in his life! Would anybody be safe while this person is at large? In his chagrin my learned friend makes the police his butt. He knows this man wasn't called at the last hearing. He knew Brown was not called at the coroner's inquiry. Why was he called? It is obvious. The police are fair game. Sometimes by vilifying the police one can draw a red-herring across the trail and lead the jury off the scent. And it is a strange thing that the only attack comes from the bar table. There is no complaint from the accused or Mrs Craig. If it could be believed that a police officer high up in the service could play a trick on a man with a capital charge over his head, then God help the community!'

McKean's words only enraged Curtis more. The man was now utterly furious. The breeze which had been felt within the courtroom earlier had finally died down; Curtis's robes now fluttered from his own frenetic motions and gestures. He drew in a deep breath – but just as it became obvious that the man was gearing up to deliver another tirade, a groaning and spluttering could be heard from near the courtroom door.

It was Thomas Brown. His back arched, as if he was struck with a sudden and brittle paralysis. His body bowed and bent out of shape. His eyes then rolled back in his head, and he pushed his tongue out of his mouth on one side.

'I can't move! I can't move! I've been poisoned!' he screamed.

He grabbed at his throat, his thin fingers wrapping around his Adam's apple. He clawed at his neck, then at his heart, then at his stomach. Then he collapsed forward across the bench, as if he had passed out. His body writhed for a while. Lifting himself up again, he took a few steps sideways so he would clear the bench and drop onto the floor. He writhed wildly like a man possessed and then slumped, completely still and silent.

'Sir! Sir.' A court official slapped the man in rapid strokes across the face to try to revive him. Brown's mother, whose movements were slow, was rushing as fast as she could to her son's side. Unable to get the man to answer, court staff picked him up like a dead deer and carried him out of the courtroom. Brown's mother followed. He opened his eyes briefly as he was carried out but he said nothing.

The court staff had prepared for an emotional ordeal, but they couldn't have anticipated the source of the drama.

At about 3.30 p.m. on Friday, 28 April 1933, with both prosecution and defence having made their concluding statements, Justice Davidson summed up. The jury retired at 5.15 p.m. They returned briefly to court shortly after, to have sections of evidence read to them. It became very clear, within only a few hours, that the jury couldn't reach an agreement. Though they were locked away for the night, it did not bring them any closer to any agreement on Craig's guilt or innocence.

The next morning, Davidson issued instructions for a new trial.

As Eric Craig was led from the dock, he didn't hide his emotions. Tears rolled freely down his cheeks. He repeated six words loudly, over and over again: 'I did not kill Bessie O'Connor.'

Although the jury was discharged, Davidson's work wasn't over. A court official provided him with an update on Brown's status. The hospital had kept him overnight, for observation. 'He had rambled incoherently while in hospital, but doctors had tested him. His stomach was empty. There was no evidence of any poisoning. His heart rate had even shown no signs of distress. The hospital held him . . . but in the absence of any explanation and giving the man a clean bill of health, he was released into his mother's care.'

'Perhaps that is the best place for him,' was all Justice Davidson said.

13

RED GALALITH BEADS

THE THIRD TRIAL COMMENCED ON 6 JUNE 1933. JUSTICE MILNER
Stephen was appointed to preside. Curtis remained as Craig's
legal representative, and McKean continued as prosecutor for
the Crown. Both sides, frustrated with their previous attempts
to get a result, pushed forward more aggressively than they
had before, and explored new lines of argument.

Media coverage of the case continued, using fresh angles.
With just one photograph of Bessie available to them, the
papers began unashamedly altering it. In one touched-up
version, her hair has been darkened and her eyelids are shaded
to make them seem heavier. Her dress cuts away a little more
deeply, with a provocatively plunging neckline. Her image was
being used as sexual commodity. She was touched up with
a deep sultry stare, fuller, darker lips and a very powdery

white complexion. But the two-toned beads around her neck remain unaltered, the visual thread common to all the images of Bessie.

The trial process may have started, but the hunt for further evidence hadn't stopped. It was now over four months since Bessie had been discovered but search parties of police were still being dispatched to search the scrub around Farnell Avenue. Investigators' hopes were raised when clothing was found dumped nearby: a bundle of women's garments including a princess slip, a dress, a brassiere and bloomers, along with a strip of white cloth and a pair of men's torn underpants. Patience O'Connor identified the women's under-wear as having belonged to Bessie. But any hope that the discovery could strengthen the case against Craig was quickly dashed – the clothes couldn't be used to establish a connec-tion to him.

The Crown had now assembled a large collection of witnesses – twenty-six – who could attest in court to having seen Bessie O'Connor, and the car, and Eric Craig, on the road to Sutherland between 10 p.m. and midnight on 14 December. None offered a strong testimony on their own but the Crown had a plan. They were threading witnesses together, like beads on a choker. If their plan worked, the testimonies would fit snugly, like a noose around Craig's neck.

Craig's defence team was also trying to string facts together. Fact one: the crime had happened on a dark and overcast night so witness testimonies needed to be considered in the half-light in which they'd been cast. Fact two: all of the roadside stops along that route were popular, and it's likely that the face of the man in the blue suit was one in a sea of faces that proprietors would have encountered that night. Fact three: the presentation of photos in newspapers had weakened, not strengthened, the clarity of recollections.

While the previous two trials hadn't addressed the issue of Bessie's escorting, the third trial did, in a censored way. Dr Stanley William Milton King, microbiologist from the Department of Public Health, tendered his analysis. King identified the blood samples collected from the crime scene as human. He had also received smears taken from an internal examination of Bessie O'Connor. 'In the smears, that is semen. I could not offer any opinion as to how long it has been there in the vagina,' he added. This created the suggestion that Bessie may have had other sexual partners, and the liaisons had been recent. The mention of semen, openly in the court room, was a new development. The prosecution went in hard. The killer was depraved and there was no doubt sex had been at the core of this crime. No piece of bloodstained clothing gathered by police was wasted – it was all held aloft in court by the prosecution. The princess slip and brassiere had been torn off her body by the killer. Every time a new piece of clothing was produced for the inspection of the jury, Patience O'Connor broke down. 'My daughter!' she cried loudly. It was guttural and heart-rending. The baseline level of grief that surrounded Patience remained steady throughout the second trial but she was utterly shattered by the third. 'This is terrible,' she could be heard to say, as she sobbed to herself. The court waited in painful silence for her to regain her composure at several points throughout the day.

A Redfern local, Charles Lawrence, had created the first link in the chain of evidence presented by the Crown. He was an important witness for them because he was the only person whom police had located who was willing to say they'd seen a woman who resembled Bessie climb into a blue car, parked in a street near her home, on the night and around the time she had disappeared. This was a vital commencement point to the timeline that police were presenting to the jury about the night of her attack.

But when Lawrence turned up in court, he was drunk. It also looked like he'd been living rough. And the prosecution's problems hadn't begun with the cloud of methylated spirits that followed him as he walked through the courtroom. At the police line-up in the weeks preceding the trial, Lawrence had failed to pick out Craig among the men assembled.

When Lawrence was put on the stand, Craig's defence team quickly established the challenge of identification facing the Crown's case.

According to Lawrence: 'I went along the line and I said the man ain't there. He said, "Have another look along," and I said, "I'm sure he ain't there." I could pick him out of a million.'

Frederick Harvey was also a problematic witness for the Crown. His testimony was important because police believed his service station had been the first pit stop the killer had made. In the weeks preceding the third trial, Harvey had flatly refused to give evidence. He'd previously claimed he was unable to identify the young woman or the man. Yet now, at the third trial, his memory of the events seemed remarkable and crystal clear.

According to Harvey: 'An Essex sedan drove in from the direction of Sydney and drove in on the inner drive outside the office door and he asked me a question . . . There was a light in the office at the time. It throws a light outside. There was a light over where the car stopped. It is an overhead light. There is also a light on the pump. The light in the office is a hundred candlepower seventy-five watt. The man got out of the car. There was a girl sitting in the front seat of the car, on the left side.'

The only reason that Harvey had been working that night was because of a customer. The garage normally closed before the shop and the servo, but a customer needed some emergency repair work done on an ignition so that he could drive his car to Armidale the following day. Harvey had agreed to stay back late until the car was fixed. It wasn't until about quarter to ten that night, an unusually late hour for him to close, that Harvey began to pack up. He was out in the driveway stacking the displays, in the process of dragging a large rack of glass oil bottles back inside, when a car pulled up.

Harvey noticed the sedan's other occupant.

'She was a girl with a full face. She had rather bright eyes. She rather struck me as being a happy sort of girl, rather wide mouth. She had a long mouth, I would say. She gave me the impression that she was rather happy. She had that look. I should say she was about eighteen years of age. I have the impression that she was wearing some beads around her throat. I could not say what colour they were. The man got out of the car and spoke to me. He spoke to me first in the car and then he got out.'

When asked why it had taken so long for Harvey to become involved, he blamed the police – at the beginning of the investigation, they couldn't clarify what make of car they were looking for. Harvey said he'd wanted absolutely no involvement in the case, and used the apparent lack of clarity as an opportunity to sidestep his involvement. 'The police asked me about a tourer, the only kind of car I saw was a sedan . . . I did not want to be mixed up in a case which I thought had I nothing to do with . . . I could not see that the same man and the same girl could be in two different cars at the same moment,' said Harvey.

Just a week before the third trial opened, police had taken Harvey to Long Bay Gaol where he'd viewed a line-up. Police had got the answer they wanted, but it seemed barely credible. The man had picked out Craig – eventually. It took multiple attempts.

●

There was little in place at the time that formally governed police practice surrounding line-ups. These usually consisted of eight men, although more or less were used at a commanding officer's discretion. When a line-up was held at a gaol, prisoners and officers were typically sourced to stand in alongside the suspect, just because they were readily available. Little regard was given for whether the process was underpinned by fairness or likely to produce a biased result.

A vast and still developing body of science now informs the use of line-ups. It is now understood that if a prior description states that the suspect has a goatee, and only two people in the line-up have goatees, this biases the selection process towards those two.

These kinds of skewed results were common in the 1930s, as line-ups were often put together in ways that would produce the result police wanted. Locals were frequently used to stack the line-ups, and they often looked vastly different to the suspects whom they were standing beside. James Bassett, an electrical engineer who lived in Woollahra, reported that he was a regular stand-in at line-ups because a police station was so close to his home.

The conscious and unconscious signalling, gesturing and body language of anyone present at the time of a line-up is also important. Any officials present should ensure that a controlled environment is maintained, and all other factors should remain constant. It should certainly never appear that one person is being treated in any way differently to the others. This is far from what occurred with the line-up organised by police for the servo manager Harvey, who noted that he was persuaded and fed pieces of information that he needed to deliver before police would permit him to leave. In 1933, there was little awareness of the need to maintain constancy in the arrangements surrounding line-ups; indeed, some academics argue that in many jurisdictions of law and order the world over there remains little understanding of this need today.

Witness identification in a courtroom, it is now widely acknowledged, is the most unreliable type of all. 'Contrary to common intuition, however, courtroom statements of confidence are very poor predictors of accuracy,' notes one modern discussion of methodologically sound identification of a suspect by a witness.

•

When it was Curtis's turn to cross-examine Harvey, he tried to explain how misidentification might have happened in this case. Curtis also worked hard to remind Justice Stephen and the jury that Harvey was very likely recalling a photograph, not a person. The lawyer pressed Harvey on this issue in particular.

Harvey: 'I daresay I saw the photograph. I read the papers, and if it was in the paper I saw it.'

Curtis: 'You admitted last time that it was the photograph that you said you saw before you were taken out to pick Craig on 24 March.'

Harvey: 'Yes.'

Curtis: 'You said it was a sort of a photograph of Craig?'

Harvey: 'Yes.'

Curtis: 'Don't you think it is a good one?'

Harvey: 'No. He looks like a man of forty-nine years of age there.'

The tension within the room broke, just momentarily, as a few members of the public were heard to snigger quietly.

Curtis moved on without delay, capitalising on the shifted energy in the room and the renewed focus of those listening.

Curtis: 'You told me that the reason you did not go near the police was because the local constable told you it was an open car?'

Harvey: 'That is so.'

Curtis: 'There is no doubt about that?'

Harvey: 'No, that was the reason all right.'

Curtis: 'If you recognised the girl and knew that it was a blue closed sedan car, you knew it was a blue sedan car that was in the murder?'

Harvey: 'I did not want to get mixed up in the case.'

Curtis: 'There was a reward offered later?'

Harvey: 'I did not know until Mr Mack told me in this court, that is the only time I knew there was a reward offered.'

Curtis then moved to the process of how Harvey had been recruited as a key witness for the Crown.

Harvey: '[The police] came along asking for information practically every week.'

Curtis: 'Did you know that descriptions were circularised through the press with the account of the man believed to be in the car?'

Curtis put forward a methodical and skilful defence. He wanted to ensure the jury was aware of the amount of information the police had released to the press, and that this had prepped witnesses. Many interviewees had already known the broad timeline of events that police had been wishing to confirm. It was reasonable to argue that they'd tailored their statements accordingly. Indeed, there was even a reward for doing so.

The car had pulled out of Harvey's servo at Brighton-Le-Sands and driven twenty minutes further south. Next, police believed, the driver stopped at the Tom Uglys Point kiosk, and this was where Bessie purchased sandwiches.

Elizabeth Hamilton-Watts, proprietress of the kiosk, had earlier identified Craig in a line-up as the man she'd seen at her establishment on the night of 14 December 1932.

But Hamilton-Watts had also publicly stumbled when asked to identify Craig before, and Curtis set about reminding the jury of this.

Hamilton-Watts: 'I remember where I was at about ten o'clock on the night of 14 December last. It was a girl . . . She was served with some sandwiches. I placed them on the counter and I then walked outside. I saw somebody standing outside on the verandah . . . It was a man.'

At the inquest and previous two trials, Hamilton-Watts had variously described Craig as being five foot six or seven inches in height, and she'd said five foot ten inches in a police interview. In one witness statement, Craig was wearing a hat – in another, she couldn't recall if his head was bare. She had seen the man with Bessie, but only when she'd walked out on the verandah. It was a detail she had not emphasised before in prior statements about the night of Bessie's attack.

At the third trial, Hamilton-Watts claimed that the girl she'd seen in the kiosk was the same one she'd seen two days later. 'She was not alive then. I saw her at Redfern in Holden street at Mrs O'Connor's place. Her name was Bessie O'Connor. It was the same girl who, somewhere about ten o'clock or a little afterwards on the night of 14 December, was at my kiosk . . .'

Hamilton-Watts was a willowy woman with carefully combed hair, small round glasses, and a frail and husky voice. She bore an uncanny resemblance to Virginia Woolf. She claimed that she'd taken special notice of the young woman to whom she'd sold the sandwiches because the colour of the girl's hair resembled her sister's – a pretty shade of auburn, she said.

Before the third trial, Hamilton-Watts had been called on by police to pick Craig out as the man she had seen with Bessie O'Connor. She had done so, but the context in which that witness identification was made was important. Hamilton-Watts had confirmed a man as a criminal by walking across a courtroom and touching his shoulder while he stood in the spot where the accused was required to stand.

Curtis, Craig's lawyer, tried to undermine the credibility of the identification made by Hamilton-Watts. 'The tragedy was discovered on the morning of the Thursday. It would be in the paper on the Thursday night. You read it in the paper on the Thursday night?' Curtis pressed the woman for an answer.

'No, I did not. It was on the Friday at night-time after I identified the girl,' Hamilton-Watts said.

Curtis pressed the woman again. 'But somebody must have come to you in connection with the matter or you would not have been taken out to identify the girl.' Curtis was eager to remind the jury of the steps police had taken to secure the statements and witness confirmations they needed.

Police had gone to more effort with Hamilton-Watts than with any other witness. While many witnesses had claimed to have seen Bessie in person, Hamilton-Watts could with certainty state that she'd seen the girl – although Bessie hadn't been alive at the time. Officers had brought Hamilton-Watts to view the body, while Bessie was laid out at home, being prepared for her final journey to Rookwood Cemetery.

Judge: 'You first identified her when you saw her lying dead?'

Hamilton-Watts: 'Yes.'

The next stop on the Crown case timeline was the oyster saloon. The notion of a saloon might conjure images of a frontier pub or a Wild West–style bar – but oyster saloons were just the fish-and-chip shop of the early twentieth century and sold the equivalent of fast food. Due to their availability, Sydney rock oysters were a quick, easy and affordable meal for working families. Often called fish-and-oyster shops, or fish-and-oyster parlours, the saloons were particularly common in Sydney because the oysters could be caught and sold fresh, with salt, pepper or Worcestershire sauce. Although oyster saloons were often located near pubs, and local boys may have been employed to run pots between a saloon and a pub, the saloons didn't usually sell alcohol.

Watson senior, proprietor of the saloon, and Watson junior, son of the owner, were both present the night that the man in a blue suit and in a blue Essex stopped in, accompanied by a young woman. It had been about 12.30 a.m. on 15 December, they said, and the customer had asked for benzine. The man was having car trouble and he believed it was because he was out of petrol.

This seemed a compelling piece of witness testimony for the Crown – but there was just one problem. Craig had been brought in for a line-up while at Long Bay, and neither of the Watsons had picked him out as the man they'd seen. Later, Watson junior had claimed that Craig was the one, but only after several attempts at a line-up. At the third trial Craig's defence lawyer pressed Watson junior particularly under cross-examination – this muddied the witness testimony even further. It went on for hours and yielded little information. Justice Stephen shook his head in exasperation as he shared his frustration with the entire process. 'There have been so many trials,' he said, almost breathlessly.

In many ways Curtis's defence was ahead of its time. He foreshadowed a set of theories and discussions that wouldn't be recognised as credible until the end of the twentieth century.

Contemporary researchers in the field of neuroscience argue that witnesses' mistaken ideas about what they have seen can be reinforced over time. Memory isn't reliable, argue neuroscientists – it's highly prone to error, persuasion and corruption. As time passes, witnesses can gradually become more convinced of an untruth:

The phenomenon of confidence inflation which refers to the increased confidence expressed by a witness that occurs with the passage of time, surely reflects unconsciously prejudiced gathering of information to support identification. Witnesses talk to other witnesses, listen to media reports of their own actions and tell their stories to others who appear to believe them, all of which is reinforcing of the original identification ... a witness's repeated retrieval of the memory of having picked a particular face from a line-up serves to strengthen the memory of the selected face, which is likely, in turn, to increase the witness's confidence in the decision.

With reinforcement from the police and media, what began in the minds of witnesses as a fragmented set of shadowy images of a man in a blue suit with a young female companion developed into a vivid recollection of an encounter with Eric Craig and Bessie O'Connor.

Modern protocols surrounding eyewitness identification recommend an approach completely at odds to that taken by police in 1932. The US National Academy of Sciences, a significant contributor to the body of lore surrounding good practice in eyewitness testimony, notes that access to alternative sources of information about the potential suspect should really be limited before, during and after a line-up, because this is the only way to ensure that the witness account hasn't been contaminated or polluted by preconceived ideas, images or features about the suspect.

The more exposure that witnesses had to photographs of Eric Craig and Bessie O'Connor, the greater the likelihood for misidentification. Those photos had blurred with their original memories. The result is sometimes also described as a 'false certainty', because a witness can wholeheartedly believe that what they are reporting is true.

•

Along the chain of witnesses, the bus driver who'd encountered the man in the blue suit in the blue car was the last to be called by the Crown at the third trial. Percy Weekes had gone to great lengths to look smartly dressed for the trial. His hat was tipped on one side as he entered the courtroom, and he politely removed it to reveal hair slicked back carefully with cream. He was a compact man with narrow shoulders. His double-breasted light-grey suit was meticulously fitted. With a very thin and neatly clipped moustache and a generous gap between his two front teeth, he projected the air of someone playful and devilish.

Although Weekes looked like a card sharp, he presented as personable and convincing. Initially, at least, things looked good for the Crown. Weekes could attest he'd seen a man on the road that night whom he described as 'looking nervous'. He said the gentleman had tried to give him a ten-pound note in exchange for the petrol – Weekes had firmly refused to accept it. An old gallon petrol can had been confiscated by police and brought to court as a formal exhibit to give legitimacy to the story.

But there were problems. Weekes said the man who'd wanted the petrol had been wearing a dark plum-coloured suit and a hat. He hadn't picked Craig at the first line-up, nor the second one arranged for him. Weekes had finally picked Craig out when called to appear at the Bessie O'Connor inquest – then he had identified Craig as the man he'd seen. It was the most contaminated of identifications as Craig was sitting in the space reserved for the accused man.

Curtis made sure he reminded the court that Weekes's account could not be relied on. The many photographs of Craig that were circulated around the time of Iris Marriott's trial, and for the previous two trials pertaining to Bessie's murder, had clouded Weekes. Curtis pressed him. 'Now in the meantime you had seen Craig's photograph in the press?'

Weekes had to admit that his recollections of Craig had been assisted by the photographs he had seen. 'Well, I had seen something with Craig's name underneath,' he conceded.

The third trial quickly descended into a long series of legal debates about identification, line-ups, the use of photographs and the media. The jury was asked to leave the courtroom many times during the course of this trial while the admissibility of evidence and arguments were debated. Justice Stephen, the prosecution and defence freely debated matters of law and the prevailing protocols governing the science of identification.

Curtis appealed to Justice Stephen, his tone somewhat pleading.

Curtis: 'I submit that this is not sufficient evidence of identity.'

Judge: 'Not sufficient in itself. Coupled with other things, it may be an important link.'

Curtis: 'There is no fact in a connection with this case from start to finish, from the time the Essex car was stolen until this unfortunate tragedy occurred which identifies the accused with the act as so set or any act in connection with it except identity. That is the issue. It is not a case where identity could be corroborated by a document or an instrument from which an inference might be inferred. There is no circumstantial evidence from which an inference could be inferred.'

Judge: 'Except evidence given by various people of things happening in a setting.'

Curtis: 'I am not disputing that the car was stolen or that the girl was in it or that the girl was murdered in the car. The whole question is the identification of the accused. There is no fact in this case which points to Craig as the person in the car except the identity of these particular places . . . The only evidence connecting that man with the accused is the evidence of one man who, apart from his identity in the dock, has failed to identify him. Since the case has come on, this man has been placarded and given much publicity. I submit the court would not allow a possible miscarriage of justice. It should be recognised that if a person is brought into the box and asked if this is the man, that this is not identity which should be allowed to go to a jury.'

Judge: 'Not in itself, no.'

Curtis made compelling arguments. The jury wasn't present to witness any of them because Justice Stephen considered these issues matters of law, pertaining to the admissibility of evidence, and therefore not matters considered suitable for open discussion in front of them.

Mary-Caroline was the only one who could corroborate Craig's story that he'd been home on the night of Bessie O'Connor's attack. She said he'd been home until 8.10 p.m., had left for two hours or so, then returned at 10.15 p.m.

Prosecutor McKean's strategy was straightforward and uncomplicated: undermine everything about her. His line of questioning did little to progress the substantive claims about timeline or details of the crime, but instead focused on derailing the faith that Mary-Caroline had in her husband – while also rattling the faith the jury might have in the honesty of a suspected criminal's wife.

Each day of the trial, Mary-Caroline had moved slowly and calmly. She left and returned to the courtroom often, each time gliding almost gracefully across the floor. After so many months of learning how to walk across the courtroom without making a sound, it offered a misleading impression of her state of mind. Up close Mary-Caroline presented as anything but calm.

Her abject fear became evident when she took the stand. She spun and massaged a piece of cloth in her hands restlessly, constantly. She seemed unable to comprehend the enormity of the situation in which she found herself.

McKean: 'I suppose you were happy with your husband?'

Mary-Caroline: 'Yes.'

McKean: 'Why did you delay before answering the question?'

Mary-Caroline: 'I was happy with my husband.'

McKean: 'Then why delay?'

The defence objected to the question. The judge permitted it.

McKean: 'Why did you delay in answering me as to whether or not you were happy?'

Mary-Caroline: 'It was an unexpected question.'

McKean: 'It needed a thought to answer then?'

Mary-Caroline: 'No.'

McKean: 'It needed more time to answer?'

Mary-Caroline: 'No.'

McKean: 'Surely even if the question was unexpected, if you were happy it would be easy to say yes or not at once?'

Mary-Caroline: 'Yes.'

McKean: 'Why was the delay?'

Mary-Caroline: 'I was not thinking. Our circumstances were very happy.'

McKean: 'What circumstances – do you mean your financial circumstances?'

Mary-Caroline: 'Yes.'

McKean: 'That was an easy one to answer. Are they the only circumstances as you refer to?'

Mary-Caroline: 'Yes.'

McKean then asked a very direct question. 'It is not disputed that your husband was arrested on the sixth. Did you have any knowledge or know they were coming?'

Mary-Caroline: 'No.'

McKean: 'Did you ask for a reference as to your husband's mechanical ability and saw that it would assist him very much in trial?'

Mary-Caroline: 'Yes.'

McKean: 'You didn't tell Sergeant McRae that you didn't know where your husband was at night-time?'

Mary-Caroline: 'No.'

McKean: 'Did you do any washing on the night of 14 December? Other than your children's things?'

Mary-Caroline: 'No, and my mother-in-law didn't take away any clothing either.'

She also noted that, much like her husband's dancing, motoring wasn't an activity she shared with him. She had seen him drive a car but had never been driving with him.

McKean asked a series of other questions too, about the period of time that Craig had already spent in prison. Mary-Caroline claimed she'd never been left alone with her husband when visiting him – a warden or constable had always been at her shoulder. She had remained on one side of the gaol cell door, he on the other, so she'd spoken through a hole in the door.

Mary-Caroline left the witness stand and returned to her seat. A woman seated behind her, a complete stranger, felt so moved by the young wife's predicament that she leaned forward and touched her on the arm. 'Hope, hope,' she whispered into her ear.

Utterly broken, and feeling utterly invaded, Mary-Caroline turned and snapped, 'Hope? He's my husband!'

Given the unusual circumstances of the case, and the fact that so much speculation surrounded what the witnesses had seen on a dark night, an excursion was arranged. One night the jury were taken by bus to visit the many sites along the road to Sutherland.

Much of the final day was taken up with Justice Stephen's summation.

At 2.17 p.m., the jury retired.

Leah whispered through the bars of the dock, though no one could hear what she said before Craig was led out. Journalists commented that the court had never seen anything quite like the openness of the display between mother and son.

At 7.40 p.m. the jury returned.

Guilty.

Curtis said, 'The accused will now make a statement, Your Honour.'

Craig rose from the hard wooden bench, rested his hands on the dock rail and gripped tightly. He looked directly at the jury. 'Your Honour and gentlemen of the jury. I did not murder Bessie O'Connor and I did not even know the girl. I have never been out with her. Gentlemen, the statement that I have given to the police of my movements that night is absolutely correct. I have been out of work over eighteen months. I had no money on me that night other than the shilling my wife gave me before I left home. That was all I had in my possession. I shaved before leaving the house. I served an apprenticeship in the motor firm of Dodge Brothers and

Kellow, Faulkners and at various times have acted as a chauffeur. I do know something about cars.'

Justice Stephen handed down what was then the mandatory sentence for murder: capital punishment. In June 1933, Craig entered death row.

Mary-Caroline, and Leah too, ran to Craig in the dock as soon as the announcement was made. Fearful of getting in trouble, Mary-Caroline did not reach in towards him. Instead, she leant her head down. His fingers were still curled around the dock rail, and she brushed her cheek against the back of his hand.

14

CLEANSKINS AND DIRTY MINDS

In August 1933, Craig's life hung in the balance on death row at Long Bay. His cell was only metres away and within clear line of sight of where he could be put to death. The imposing iron girder, specially constructed to be a weight-bearing beam for the gallows, and the trapdoor beneath it, were located right outside death-row cells forty-seven and forty-eight.

Craig lodged an appeal to the High Court seeking the right to a further trial. His wait was an anxious one. He passed the time quietly.

It was common for prisoners on death row to receive religious counsel, and the gaol was generally lenient in permitting them to do this. Some on death row were even known to request a special audience with the officers responsible for their arrest; this was considered part of the process of seeking redemption and atonement leading up to execution. There is no record of Craig making any requests of this kind. He didn't agitate for special treatment. He was provided with a Bible for study and reflection. He received counselling from a priest, but no more than any other man. Instead, he drew comfort from two people in particular: Mary-Caroline, who continued to visit him, and Leah, who visited him even more.

Craig had good reason to feel nervous. The public nature of the killings, the intense manhunt that had preceded his capture and the time that the legal system had invested in his conviction meant that he was considered one of the most notorious criminals in the state. The inquests and his four trials had been widely publicised and watched closely by the public. His case had been observed every step of the way, and his name had been consistently in the news in the eight months leading up to August.

But Craig was in a precarious situation for other reasons that lay beyond media attention. His case hadn't been the only one of its kind in the decade or so before his arrest. Indeed, the crimes of which he'd been convicted fell into a category of criminal activity in which there was significant academic and legal interest. Mandatory death sentences for murder convictions didn't always lead to executions – but they could. It all came down to how the system assessed the quality and capability of the man.

For a period of just over twenty years, from 1917 to 1939, Long Bay Gaol was the site where executions were conducted in New South Wales. Death sentences could be issued for a wide range of crimes, including armed robbery, rape or murder. Of the nine men executed during this period, some common themes emerge in a case-study examination of their crimes. The circumstances of the individual crimes varied greatly, but they all involved a murder conviction. James Wilson and James Massey were executed for armed robbery and murder; William Simpson killed one man and attempted to kill a police officer in the aftermath of a robbery; Edward Williams slit the throats of his children to spare them from poverty. The other five executions were associated with crimes involving what was then known as 'sexual murder'.

Craig had been convicted of crimes carried out in public places. This set them apart from the vast majority of criminal activity at the time. If a murder occurred in the home, in the domestic sphere, as a result of organised crime or because of drug or alcohol use, this event had a context that offered an explanation. The public could understand an argument between family members at home that got out of hand. They could also dismiss murders between criminals over drug money or illegal activity. But when members of the public were found dead in public parks, this was more difficult to dismiss.

•

When someone is killed in a public park, in the dead of night, it sends a signal that the city is dangerous – that lawlessness not lawfulness rules the metropolis. In this regard, Craig's convictions bear a number of similarities to those of William Cyril Moxley. Each man was accused of two murders. Moxley was convicted in August 1932, and only a year later Craig found himself in a similar predicament. He could only have reflected on these parallels with absolute horror, as public outrage over Moxley's crimes had resulted in swift action by the state.

Like many working men in 1932, at the peak of the Depression, Moxley had hit hard times. He'd been seen by locals in the west and south-west of Sydney driving his rattling work truck along dirt tracks, through forest adjacent to burgeoning suburbs. He set up camp, lived rough, felled trees and chopped wood to sell. One of the places where Moxley had been sighted was the forest at the back of the Strathfield golf links.

Dorothy Ruth Denzel and Frank Wilkinson were a couple in their twenties. One night in April 1932, they had been enjoying an evening alone in a suburban park in Strathfield. It was an area popular with young lovers. Police argued that sometime before midnight, Moxley stumbled upon the couple by accident.

No one knows exactly what happened that night in April 1932. Moxley claimed he asked the couple for money, while police suggested that he held them up. Moxley claimed that their deaths occurred only because a 'situation had got out of hand'. Dorothy handed over money, he said, but Wilkinson lunged at him. A fight ensued, and Moxley overpowered the strapping Wilkinson. Sometime later that same night, the two young lovers were buried in shallow graves at Holsworthy. A post-mortem examination of Frank's body determined that he'd been shot through the back of the head. The explosion of pellets had blown out his face. A post-mortem of Dorothy's body determined that she'd been raped and killed – though in what order was beyond the ability of forensics at the time to determine.

At trial, police stated that Moxley had driven the couple about twenty kilometres south to Holsworthy. Dorothy had been bound and gagged, locked inside the cabin of the car with Moxley as he drove. Frank, with hands and feet tied, had been forced to ride in the 'dicky seat', sometimes called the 'mother-in-law' seat: a small space located roughly where the boot of a modern car is.

Moxley pleaded insanity. He had brain damage, he said, and this condition culminated in memory loss that created a lack of empathy; he retained no memory of the trauma he'd inflicted on people. He also claimed to suffer from blackouts and migraines – and syphilis, but lab testing found he wasn't a carrier of any known venereal disease. Moxley had a long criminal record, and these claims didn't help his defence. They suggested a pattern of behaviour that would be difficult to rehabilitate and a character resistant to change. The jury returned a guilty verdict.

Although Moxley fought hard for mercy, he represented himself awkwardly and incompetently at an appeals trial, and his attempts to have the death sentence commuted failed.

Newspapers provide some insight into the paradoxical ways in which 'sexual murders' were viewed. On one hand, the papers painted a scene of dark and deadly delights harvested by someone bent on hellish pleasures: 'the devil roamed one night', wrote one article of Moxley. On the other hand, and with no hint of irony whatsoever, reporters wrote of the tragic loss of a man still trying to seek redemption and be a good father: 'Moxley prays: reads bible', said another article.

During his last days on death row, Moxley relied heavily on the prison chaplain, a Salvation Army lieutenant colonel called Pennell. And on the eve of his execution, the prison permitted Moxley to have one last visit with his thirteen-year-old son. There's evidence that gaol staff made a vast effort to preserve the last meeting between father and son as a dignified experience, untarnished by the humiliation of gaol. Some witnesses reported that the staff maintained a charade that it wasn't a gaol but a hospital ward, and this is what they told Moxley's son. Staff had even gone to the effort of decking out the block and cell in a way that created a more convincing illusion.

While standing on the gallows, Moxley waived his right to utter any last words or to make a final statement. He was, however, permitted to keep a diary about his final days. 'Death is sweet . . . Pennell and I have spent a happy night together. We looked for my star. It appeared at 5.25 a.m. We gazed at it together. It is my guiding light. I feel quite calm . . . I have said goodbye to my friends and relatives for this earth. I know I shall be with my mother by 9 o'clock today. I shall know the great secret.'

Only a year before, in August 1932, Moxley had walked from the same section of cells where Craig was now located. It was six steps from the cell door to the trapdoor. The specially prepared executioner's rope, expertly knotted to break his neck, not strangle him, was slipped into place. A white cap was then dropped over his head. The lever was released, and so too the trapdoor beneath his feet. His body fell through the hole and dangled between the two floors of the prison. Witnesses claimed that within ten seconds of leaving his cell, he was dead. As required by execution protocols, Moxley's body was left to hang for twenty minutes before being pulled down.

The execution provided the state with an opportunity to analyse the physical characteristics of a man, and the brain of a man, capable of committing such a vile crime. It was a legal requirement that a post-mortem and coronial inquest follow any execution, and the state took special interest in cases like Moxley's. X-ray examinations of his skull and a supporting medical report show foreign matter (bits of metal) in the right temporal region. These were most likely bullet fragments remaining from a shot to his head much earlier in life. To some extent this confirmed, far too late, what Moxley had claimed: he had indeed been brain damaged, and perhaps it had altered his behaviour.

Moxley was, according to the thinking at the time, a man with a dirty mind. And he wasn't considered to be unique. Alfred Patrick Ball was captured for the brutal murder in

March 1932 of Katherine Sims in inner-city Erskineville. Ball's defence team submitted evidence to suggest an insanity plea based on a fallible mind. He had lost consciousness and reason at the time he was committing the murder, or so it was claimed. In this case the plea was accepted, and Ball was found not guilty on the grounds of insanity. The Crown was furious over the verdict. Justice Halse Rogers, who would later preside over Craig's second trial, issued a grave warning about the great danger associated with defences of what he called 'automatism', or the displacement of sanity because of a build-up of a kinetic sexual disturbance in the system.

But Moxley's fate, still being discussed in the prison a year later, would have formed a terrifying backdrop against which Craig could contemplate his prospects. Once the state had deemed you to be irredeemable, your captors might show you the odd kindness, but death was inevitable.

Craig's case for appeal could be interpreted in a very limited number of ways, and these would be deeply informed by medical understandings. Two prevailing theories governed understandings of sexual violence at the time. In one scenario, the perpetrator was perceived to be diseased, infected with obsessions and impulses that could be traced to a physical cause such as a head injury, brain damage, or perhaps a defect in the family line. Someone with a 'dirty mind' was afflicted, and was perhaps worthy of special consideration when accused of committing a crime.

The alternative theory was that so-called 'sexual murderers' or 'sex slayers' were more accurately described as cleanskins. If this was true, such a murder could be committed by a much wider range of people. A cleanskin blended into the community because they didn't have a criminal record and didn't exhibit a pathological tendency for illegal behaviour. After having committed the act, they simply returned to their normal lives. This perhaps made them the most difficult criminals of all for police to catch – a cleanskin could remain hidden in plain sight, potentially for years.

The notion of a cleanskin was markedly different to the modern-day archetype of a serial killer. Since the 1970s, a strong mythology has emerged around the classification of serial killers. They are often believed to be highly intelligent, cunning, and driven relentlessly by an abnormal desire for personal and sexual gratification. They are also considered to be exceptionally rare, with far less than 1 per cent of the human population considered capable of conforming to the behavioural profile currently used to describe and classify them.

At the beginning of the twenty-first century we may reflect on the notion of the serial killer as something akin to a monster in the dark, but take comfort in the belief they are rare creatures. The idea of a cleanskin posits a far more frightening theory: the capability to kill may lie within many men. The suggestion that a sex crime could be explained by a momentary lapse of judgement made good copy at the time. *Smith's Weekly* described them as 'momentary killers' and printed a hand-sketched cartoon to accompany an article: a hunched and hairy figure dressed in caveman-style animal skin drags an oversized club along the ground with one hand and with the other he drags a woman by her hair. The message was clear: rape and murder were connected to evolution. Sex crimes were so deeply part of being male, they went back to the Stone Age.

Craig's conviction occurred at a time when sexual crimes, in particular, were being reassessed in light of new medical evidence. While no one wanted to be seen approving of such criminals, there was a recognition, on some level, that the antecedents of these crimes were more complex than once thought. In 1922, the University of Sydney created its first chair in the discipline of psychiatry. Professor John Macpherson was consulted formally by the state attorney-general's and prisons departments to assist in the determination of mental acuity and the predisposition to commit certain types of sexual crime. William Siegfried Dawson, who in 1927 followed as head of psychiatry at the university for a seven-year term, was a high-profile and vocal participant in discussions about the criminal mind. Dawson maintained his private practice so that he might continue to experiment in the development of techniques to treat unique sexual disorders. Sexual crimes, of all different varieties, were a matter of significant research interest to him.

The Department of Health expanded its analytical branch throughout this time. Assessments of men identified to be dangerous represented a new priority for the state. Trials of

those considered to be the most dangerous were to be identified and 'expedited'.

In the mid-1920s, around the time of Rebecca May
Anderson's murder, an article published in the *Labor Daily*
highlights how sexual crime was perceived to be an enduring
challenge for society, one that might best be overcome by a
unique partnership between scientific technique and legal
redress.

> There arises from this hideous act – as indeed from all other
> outbreaks of a sexually related nature – one of the greatest
> problems of life today. The entire ambit of criminality arising
> from or resulting in sex lawlessness or sex-horror must be
> investigated, not by the detectives but by the scientists. The
> function of the former is to bring the individual pervert to
> trial and conviction. The passion of the latter is to help us
> to an understanding of a solution of the grave menace of
> abnormality which, issuing from our social order, threatens
> its fabric . . . the time has surely gone by for prudish evasion.
> Government and people alike must seriously reflect on the
> number of crimes which are constantly occurring against
> sex or related to sex. The need for a scientific study of the
> psycho-pathological field of this branch of criminology is
> imperative . . . Criminal statistics prove the sad fact that
> sexual crimes are progressing in our modern civilisation.

In 1928, a special council of Dr Dawson; the Inspector
General for the Insane, Dr Hogg; key members of the CIB;
and visiting detective experts from Scotland Yard and the
Parisian Sûreté, in conjunction with the state attorney-general

and health minister, convened a conference to consider the appropriateness of special punishments for sex criminals in New South Wales.

In early twentieth-century Australia, new ways of thinking about crime emerged from the burgeoning and increasingly influential field of psychiatry. With this came new tools in the measurement and treatment of sexual crimes, which were only just beginning to be incorporated into criminal justice and prison reform.

The definitive medical text on sexual psychopathy had been published in Europe in the 1880s, but it had taken twenty years to be translated, and even longer to be absorbed by the antipodean colonies. Written by Austro-German psychiatrist Richard Freiherr von Krafft-Ebing, *Psychopathia Sexualis: A Medico-Forensic Study* remained influential in the realm of criminal justice practice in New South Wales well into the 1930s. In 'Chapter 5: Pathological Psychology in its Legal Aspects', Krafft-Ebing noted, 'criminal statistics prove the sad fact that sexual crimes are progressing in our modern civilisation'. Due to the spate of such crimes in Sydney from the early 1920s onwards, the message resonated powerfully with criminal justice officials.

'Mania, satyriasis [an excessive sexual desire in a man] and epilepsy' – all were considered conditions derived from a common physical source. And it was through this that psychiatrists developed a taxonomy of criminal acts. The category of 'lust-murder', for example, was seen to occur because 'the crime of rape may be followed by the murder of the victim. There may be unintentional murder, murder to destroy the only witness of the crime, or murder out of lust. Only for cases of the latter kind should the term lust-murder be used.'

The 1930s saw further experimentation with medical inter-ventions intended to correct a predilection for sexual crime. In 1937 Frederick Enston, a 32-year-old mechanic in Sydney, was sentenced to six months' gaol after behaving indecently towards schoolgirls. If Enston would agree to an examination with the gaol surgeon, and if a defect could be found, the judge said he would be prepared to allow the man to be issued with a licence. This involved similar conditions to parole: living in the community, under scrutiny. If Enston agreed, he'd be released post-surgery. Lionel Davis, a labourer convicted of a sexual offence against a six-year-old girl, underwent a psychiatric assessment. He claimed to have been kicked in the head by a horse when he was four, and since then he'd experienced sexual impulses that he could not quench. He too agreed to be sterilised. By the end of the 1930s, certain types of offenders were offered leniency if they agreed to undergo sterilisation – sometimes euphemistically referred to as 'cure by surgeon'.

Clinical case studies of those who'd suffered brain damage and then gone on to commit sadistic acts of sexual violence were used to develop psychiatric theories. One such case included the detailed study of Swiss stable boys, twenty-four and nineteen years of age. Both were afflicted with imbecility; in the case of one, it was attributed to childhood meningitis.

One subject confessed to sexual arousal when milking the cows. He experienced concurrent 'violent erections and sensations of fear'.

A range of what were perceived to be involuntary sexual impulses were increasingly being attributed to brain disorders throughout the twenties and thirties in Sydney. 'Much more important are the numerous cases in literature in which epileptics who, during intervals, present no signs of active sexual impulse, but manifest it in connection with epileptic attacks ... they deserve careful study. In this way certain cases of violence and rape would be understood and legal murders prevented ... In no domain of criminal law is cooperation of judge and medical expert so much to be desired as in that of sexual delinquencies.' The field of sexual psychiatry was developing a range of terms for the afflictions of sex-brain dysfunction. 'The individual afflicted with satyriasis is forever exposed to the peril of committing rape, thus becoming a common danger to all persons of the opposite sex ... Luckily satyriasis is a rare disease.' Mild satyriasis was possible, in which men were 'the slaves of insatiable libido'. The term 'sexual satyr' entered the vernacular of Australian journalism, and it was used to describe the park murderer of 1932 on more than one occasion.

The *Psychopathia Sexualis* noted that the potential for depravity existed in many men, it just came down to whether a single man had enough of the active ingredient for dysfunction. Craig was now firmly considered to be on the spectrum of sexual dysfunction. From the state's standpoint, the only question pertained to where he sat along this spectrum. Would Craig be considered a cleanskin – a man prone to sexual misfires but one capable of treatment and redemption – like Alfred Ball? Or would Craig be considered beyond rehabilitation and end up like Moxley?

15

THE INTERVIEWS

BY THE TIME SPRING ARRIVED IN 1933, EVERY FIGHT THAT COULD have been fought by Eric Craig was lost.

His appeal to the High Court, seeking a new trial, failed.

This dismissal of Craig's appeal says more about the need to preserve the reputation of law and order than it does about fairness or justice. Two judges voted for an appeal to be granted, and two against. 'It would be dangerous indeed subversive of the whole administration of criminal justice if this court intervened and gave leave to appeal from the decision reached in such circumstances,' notes the High Court ruling.

One newspaper highlighted the continuing and perhaps intensifying ambiguity surrounding Craig's guilt. 'They were in apparently as much disagreement concerning Eric Roland Craig and his complicity in the Bessie O'Connor murder as the first two criminal juries which tried him. So ended another chapter in the historic Craig case. Even the High Court could not come to a definite and unanimous decision as to what should be done. What happens to Craig now?'

Though Craig's battle was over, others took up the fight. The flagship anti-death penalty organisation, the Howard Prison Reform League NSW, campaigned on his behalf. Only one option remained: an appeal to the Executive Council to seek commutation of the death sentence. It was custom, though not a legal requirement, that death sentences wouldn't be carried out unless unanimous agreement be attained from the Executive Council. Craig's only option was to throw himself on the mercy of the state of New South Wales.

The Howard Prison Reform League agitated hard in Craig's defence. They paid for advertisements in newspapers urging members of the public to attend what they described as 'a monster public meeting' at St James Hall in Phillip Street. The league wanted as many people as possible to attend, including regular working folks, so an evening rally was organised: 8 p.m., Monday 18 September, right near a city train station.

It is not possible to know how many turned up to show their support for Craig. What is known is that the league wrote to the Minister of Justice directly on Craig's behalf.

Minister of Justice

Dear Sir

. . . I am to convey to you the following resolution duly adopted:

That this meeting of the Howard Prison Reform reaffirms its opposition to Capital Punishment and therefore does earnestly request the Government of NSW to commute the Death Sentence passed upon Eric Roland Craig to imprisonment for life for the following reasons:

(a) That as two juries disagreed as to Craig's guilt and two High Court Judges in their considered opinions believed Craig should be granted a new trial there is a grave element of doubt, a punishment that is not irrevocable should be inflicted. Capital Punishment is irreparable.

(b) Capital punishment is not necessary and does not act as a deterrent ...

Honorary Secretary
Mr Norman Sachisthal

A special meeting of the Executive Council was organised at Parliament House on Macquarie Street for 18 September. What discussions occurred within the council chambers weren't recorded, though the prevailing medical opinion of the day would certainly have been sought and considered as part of these deliberations. The meeting lasted several hours.

Only the final decision remains. It's less than one page long.

Craig's sentence was changed from death to 'for the term of his natural life'. But the high-profile nature of his case clearly warranted some additional wording, so it was amended to include 'never to be released'. This official decision was published in all of the major newspapers.

A range of interpretations might be brought to bear on this ruling. Did the state feel the need to reassure the public that their safety could be protected after all? Women had been killed and discarded, but the police were capable – Craig's capture attested to this. Or, given the challenges that the Crown had experienced with securing a trial verdict, was there less than full confidence in the man's guilt?

Media interest in Craig's story hadn't waned. The Executive Council announcement represented an opportunity for one last front-page exposé. The morning after the decision, the *Daily Telegraph* conducted two interviews simultaneously in two Sydney homes. The paper wanted to compare two accounts of the next chapter in the story of Eric Craig.

•

Her rent still unpaid, Patience O'Connor had been evicted from the terrace off Eveleigh Street where she'd lived with Bessie and her sons. She'd moved to the other side of Redfern. It was quieter, further from the rail yard and train station, but was considered rougher. Perhaps without being aware of it, Patience had drawn closer to the dark triangle of streets that had tragically shaped the course of her life. Her home was now just near the place where Iris Marriott had been taken and not far from where she had been killed. It was also very near the sites of Hilda White's and Rebecca May Anderson's murders.

Patience lived only a few streets from Mary-Caroline. In their own ways, both of these women were trapped by the social and economic forces of the dark triangle.

Mary-Caroline sat in the front room of the small apartment she'd once shared with her husband. Her hair sat flat, smoothed down carefully atop her ears and framing her small face. She sipped tea, the china cup cradled in both hands, in the manner of a child sipping soup. The *Daily Telegraph* journalist couldn't help but notice that the scene radiated a soft and tender sense of motherhood: a quiet toddler playing on the floor; the gently curled form of a sleeping baby in a cot; a watchful mother.

Mary-Caroline sat angled in the upholstery, her legs neatly crossed at the ankle, knees tilted to one side, hands resting in her lap. She assumed the posture of an adult, but in the oversized and stuffed lounge she seemed small and childlike.

The journalist sat in the chair opposite, his leg kicked out like a lectern to prop up the notebook while he scratched his pencil across the paper. 'Your husband's appeal has now failed, you made a very public outcry when that appeal was lost – do you want to talk about that?'

Just like she had in court, Mary-Caroline didn't answer straightaway. She pursed her lips thoughtfully. It was the kind of pause that could have meant she was holding back tears. Or she could have been wading through the mire of many deep thoughts and was simply taking extra care in ensuring that the right one floated to the surface.

The journalist waited a while, but still no answer came. He prompted again. What was she doing now? How did she pass the time?

'I realised I had to get back again into the custom of working to keep myself. I work part-time as a waitress in Circular Quay.'

Mary-Caroline was working at a café and indoor refreshment room called Sargents. It was a dining hall that seated hundreds, iconic in Sydney at the time. Sargents offered simple food for the working man, for families, and for travellers. They specialised in pots of tea, sandwiches and baked goods. By World War I, Sargents had outlets all over the city and ran a large-scale catering business. They specialised in affordable meat pies and apple charlottes, and came almost to define the Australian tradition of a pie with peas, potato and gravy.

In an economy that wasn't hiring, the Sargents dining hall was one of the few places where Mary-Caroline could get work. At twenty, with two children and little employment experience, she'd adjusted her expectations to the role that she'd thought she would play her entire life: a housewife. Then, in the few months before September 1933, she'd had to readjust her expectations: she was a wife without a husband, a single parent, and a woman head of a household. In 1933, these were all atypical roles to play.

'I am virtually a widow with two children,' she said. 'How does one be courageous? How does one set about the task of living while your husband faces his own lifetime in prison?' She posed the question to the journalist, though it was directed at herself. 'I was a waitress at Kings Cross when I met Eric, and he used to come in from the garage where he worked. That's all I can do, I suppose. I suppose I'll keep on being a waitress again. There are the children to be thought of.' She paused for a long time.

The only sound in the room was the scratching of the journalist's pencil.

When she spoke again, she picked up the same line of thought. 'If it were not for the children, I could go back and start practically where I began. I could wipe off, except say in my mind, everything that has happened. But there are always the two babies. Later I will get another job, somewhere where nobody is likely to know me.'

The journalist had settled into the rhythm of conversation and, sensing that Mary-Caroline was more at ease, he pressed with a harder line of questioning. She had described herself as a widow – he wanted to ask if she wished for the unthinkable. Then he thought better of it, and rephrased. 'Do you sometimes feel this has all been a terrible mistake? That if you could change it you would?'

Mary-Caroline's answer was measured but seemed honest, largely because she answered with hesitation, not bluster. 'Of course. But I'm glad I married Eric.' Then, perhaps feeling the need to explain what must have seemed a strange response under the circumstances, she added, 'If he had not met me he might have met and married some woman who would not have stuck to him through all this. And if it had been some other woman who stuck to him – well, I would not like any other woman ever to go through what I have been through. I am a prisoner too. No one seems to realise that. They have put him in the gaol for the rest of his life. They don't realise that they have put me in gaol too for the rest of my life.'

'And now the news that your husband's sentence has been commuted to the term of his natural life, by the highest levels of power in the state – the state cabinet – you must be relieved.'

'When he was sentenced, I never fainted or howled or screamed. But at night, when I fell asleep, I woke up screaming the house down. I had visions – saw things. But I had to keep control of myself all the time for months. Even when I went to see Eric, and he was despondent, sometimes I had to make light of things and then I was afraid he might think I was callous. I think if I had not had other things to worry about I might have given in, but there were money matters and the babies.' She stopped suddenly, as if mid-sentence. The journalist was about to ask another question when she resumed her chain of thought. 'During the coroner's inquest my little girl left home and was lost for hours. They told me about it and I was worrying about that. You see, Eric was quite safe at the moment. He wasn't in danger of getting lost. The thing at the time was to find the baby, and perhaps things like that took my mind off the worse danger their father was in.'

Mary-Caroline paused again before adding 'It's gaol for me too'. She wasn't shrewd enough to be calculating in the selection of her words. She spoke earnestly, perhaps more so than was wise given the profession of her conversation partner.

'But I do think all this will make me a better woman somehow than I would have been. There are the children and perhaps I can look after them so that they will not suffer. I feel old and well, I haven't even got the vote yet . . . I think of all the people who have money and for want of a little money, we may have to let things stay as they are. But nobody's interested in him but me, I suppose.' Mary-Caroline hadn't mentioned Eric's mother – then she corrected herself. 'But nobody could have been more splendid than Mr Curtis and Mr Woodward though, and Miss C. Jollie Smith and Solicitors. Nobody could have been more wonderful than she and her staff. Now it's only just a matter of carrying on living and keeping my mind on the happy things that have happened. I can't bear to think of the unhappy things.' She paused again, and the journalist waited for tears to fall. 'Some day, something may happen that will make everything turn out all right,' she said, with all the conviction of wanting the statement to be true.

Meanwhile, just a short distance away, a *Daily Telegraph* journalist knocked on the wooden door of a small terrace in Kepos Street, Redfern.

Patience O'Connor asked him to take a seat. She, too, served tea, conforming to all of the formalities of an afternoon visit – teacups with saucers and small spoons, a pot of sugar. She passed a napkin to the journalist. It was polite and ordered, and the afternoon sun streamed through the window with an early spring warmth. But there was an unmistakably dense and heavy emptiness in the house.

This journalist went straight to the heart of the matter. 'The Cabinet decision, Mrs O'Connor, how does it make you feel to hear such a thing? Do you want to make a statement about it?'

Patience's voice was thin as she spoke around the lump of pain in her throat. A waterline of tears rose in her eyes. 'They have seen fit to show mercy to Craig. I can never feel that he deserved it,' she said. Her reaction was raw, uncontained. Her voice quivered.

The journalist, unflinching, proceeded with the intensity of an interrogator. 'Mrs O'Connor, the Howard Prison Reform League has come out publicly to applaud the decision to commute Craig's sentence.' He waited a moment for that fact to sink in. 'Do you have any statement about that? What would you say to them?'

Her eyes filled again with tears, but this time her voice was steady and strong. 'I would say to the Prison Reform League, it is not just that a man who has committed such foul crimes should escape the full punishment. He murdered a woman of the streets. And then he went on to murder my innocent little girl.' Patience had turned from devastated to incredulous to angry. 'Cruel?!' She snorted dismissively. Then she breathed deeply, and changed tack so she might make her point more convincingly. 'Much money has been spent on his trials,' she said firmly, shaking her head in disbelief. 'Yet, I can't get enough to pay a fare to my daughter's grave at Botany. It is three months since I was there. My own mother suffered a stroke soon after poor Bessie was murdered. She may live only a few weeks longer. They discharged her from Sydney hospital as incurable.' The burning anger of her words subsided, and in its wake was what Patience believed she'd been left with for eternity: 'A broken heart.' The words were like an epitaph. She looked briefly out the window. 'A broken heart. That is what I am suffering from.'

The *Daily Telegraph* piece published the following day, 19 September 1933, was titled 'Two women on Craig's reprieve'. It was far from the only article published on the Craig case that day. Every major paper picked up the story, and the regional news media provided extensive copy on it too.

Some articles focused on the precise wording of the Cabinet decision. While his sentence had been commuted and Craig wouldn't hang, the intention of the government was clear: he posed a threat to society so great, he shouldn't ever be paroled. Though, as the *Daily Telegraph* noted with some alarm, it 'does not actually bind future governments . . . it is still within the prerogative of the Governor to release Craig and the phrase is used to indicate to future governments the opinion of the present cabinet'.

While newspapers had sought to map the great distance between the adversarial sides of the justice experience between the victim and the villain, when it came to the experience of the women who formed the family backdrop to the crime, the gulf was not quite as great as journalists had portrayed it. 'To two women it carried two meanings, worlds apart,' was the editorial conclusion drawn by the *Daily Telegraph* article. What journalists didn't recognise was how close the worlds and how similar the heartache of those two women had become.

With Eric Craig now locked up, newspapers lost interest in the story. There were no articles affirming victory for the police. No journalists made the proclamation that the women of Sydney could rest easy because the streets were now safe. Which was just as well.

Eight years after Bessie's murder, there would be another. And then another. And then another.

16

OVERTURE TO DEATH

FOR THE NEXT FEW YEARS, CRAIG FOCUSED ON ACCLIMATISING to life in prison. His wife and his mother also sought to adjust to their new lives. There's no evidence that the women grew closer as a result of their grief – indeed, the evidence points to them drifting further apart. Mary-Caroline moved away from Leah and leant more heavily on her own father for support. Both women tried to keep low profiles. For a time, Mary-Caroline used an alias.

Leah visited Eric often and was an enthusiastic correspondent with the department. Her letters to officials read like personal petitions. She advocated for her son: the prison conditions were not acceptable; she worried about her son's nerves; the prison was too far away and the travel was a strain for her. Leah also wrote a lot about herself: her husband's ailments, the sad circumstances of her life, and her loss as a mother whose son was taken from her. The letters are often prefaced or concluded with a plea for secrecy: 'If there is an answer to my letter please send in a plain envelope as I have to be so careful . . .' or 'PS . . . please do not write to me I am afraid of someone getting my letter'.

It's worth noting that in the many pieces of correspondence that Leah sent to the Attorney-General's department and the Comptroller-General of Prisons, at no point did she protest her son's innocence.

Both Leah and Mary-Caroline found it difficult to travel to the prison. Eric spent time at Goulburn and Bathurst, both of which were several hours away by train. The state authorities provided one-trip-only rail passes from Central to the prison stations. But these passes weren't simply issued – the family had to prove significant financial hardship and the application process was an ordeal. Every time a family member sought a complimentary ticket, their financial situation was invest-igated. Police surveilled the women and made surprise visits to their homes. They even interviewed Leah's landlord, and they visited the residential clinic where her husband lived as a long-stay tuberculosis patient.

Mary-Caroline asked the department to respect her right to privacy and anonymity. She pleaded. She phoned the police administration and begged them not to interfere and asked them to stop inquiring as to her circumstances. Every time police came asking questions, it alienated her from her neigh-bours. This had made it difficult for her to stay in one place, she said. It made it difficult for her children, she said. Letters exchanged between the Department of Attorney-General and Justice and the police provide insight into how difficult Mary-Caroline's life was becoming. It is clear that she felt harassed by police. It is also clear that the harassment persisted long enough for her to make complaints about them. She had no financial resources to mount legal action against the department and she had no political influence, so the department, for the most part, ignored her. Interestingly, government officials gave her claims some credibility by writing a letter to the police department. It admitted nothing, but implied police should back off. 'Mrs Craig stated that she did not wish enquiries to be made by the Darlinghurst police as to her circumstances, as she is now living under an assumed name, and did not wish the position to be known.' Mary-Caroline named Detective Sergeant McRae and Detective Wylie as particular culprits. Both officers denied these accusations.

Mary-Caroline persisted in this way for five more years, until she could bear it no more. The last piece of correspondence that she wrote regarding her husband is from late 1938: she applied to the Department of Prisons, the agency responsible for family liaison and co-ordinating and managing the affairs of prisoners. She applied for a free rail pass, pleading financial hardship. At the time she was living under an assumed name and still working as a cashier at Sargents. She hadn't seen her husband in four years. The letter gives some indication of the struggles experienced by the woman in seeking to support herself and her two children.

'I respectfully apply for the issue to me of a Railway Pass to enable me to visit my husband. It will not be possible for me to pay a visit at Christmas time and the only opportunity will be during the present Eight-hour weekend.' Mary-Caroline was taking the public holiday provided by the Labour Day weekend because she simply had no other way of getting time off from work.

Shortly after, the governor at Long Bay received a letter that was then referred to Craig. It wasn't from Mary-Caroline, but from her lawyer. Mary-Caroline was petitioning for a divorce. 'Prison separation' was one of the few grounds for divorce that the legal administration didn't ever contest. Craig had no option but to accept it.

It was not the first piece of unusual correspondence the Long Bay governor had received about Craig that year. The governor received one other letter regarding him. It reminded prison authorities that in the wider community nagging doubts remained about Craig's guilt.

To the Governor, at Long Bay penitentiary.
18 March 1938. Carnation Avenue, Bankstown.

Dear Sir
I was at Coogee aquarium Ladies swimming carnival early in I forget the date 10th Nov or 10th December. Just before Bessie O'Connor was murdered at National Park. I came out the ladies swimming carnival before the last events sat in tram. Empty tram another empty tram

in front with a few tram drivers and conductors. A man came out with a girl in a dark overcoat. My description of man – good speaker, strong voice, about 5.8 or 5.9, reddish complexion.

A pleasant girl.

Man said 'good night digger, seems all right'. The girl laughed. All of a sudden he got a bit wild. Locked back door of motor car with a key. I forget colour. I think greenish. He said I am going to murder this girl in the car. I asked or beckoned her to get out as I had about 5/- on me to get in tram. No she said. A short man flicked a flashlight on radiator part

[the rest of the letter is so damaged, it is unreadable]

From TE Davis, the one legged soldier

The letter was referred to the Comptroller-General of Prisons, who referred it to the Undersecretary of Justice, and a copy was eventually provided to the CIB. It bounced around for close to eighteen months, until it was filed away. It wasn't taken seriously. The administration remained confident that they had the right man behind bars

And then another murder occurred.

•

On the morning of 9 March 1940, a woman's partially naked body was found on a beautiful corridor of bushland called Chowder Head in Sydney. She had been beaten and strangled. Though the discovery was made in the heart of the residential area broadly known as Mosman, the body lay in a pocket of wild and untamed beachside reserve called Clifton Gardens. This was a popular weekend retreat for Sydneysiders because it offered that unique foreshore experience of beach, bush and the exquisite beauty of the water.

Like many of the other women discovered since the early 1920s, she was found on a Saturday. And as with the other victims, someone had dealt her a vicious blow to the head. Her attacker had torn at her suspenders so violently, her garters had snapped. There was a stocking around her neck, slipknot fashion. It had been pulled to her ear and tightened there. Because the attacker had clubbed and choked the woman, it was difficult for the medical examiner to determine what had killed her. The post-mortem ultimately identified the cause of death to be strangulation. Based on the insect activity around the body, she hadn't been exposed for long – clearly she'd been attacked and murdered only the night before her body was discovered.

Police inspected the scene and began to piece together a theory about what had occurred, based on the fragments of evidence left behind. A handbag was found, as if thrown, about twenty-five feet from the body. The attacker had struck while the woman was out walking, police surmised. They conjectured that the knot used on her throat was one that might be known by a sailor.

The woman was quickly identified as 23-year-old Betty van Tonder, a South African nursemaid working for a wealthy family who lived locally. Betty was quiet, had little in the way of a social life and had no enemies who would wish her harm. If the murder itself baffled the city, the police response to it and the conclusions ultimately drawn seem equally baffling as we look back on them today.

An investigation into Betty's life and a study of her personal effects led police to draw a number of surprising conclusions about the circumstances that might have led to her death. Their conclusions were derived from a set of understandings about Betty as a woman and appear to have had very little to do with the crime itself. Police and public perceptions of the earlier murders had been shaped by the fact that so many of the women had been prostitutes and therefore held some culpability for the way in which they died. In 1940 police exhibited similar biases, as this investigation was informed by some spurious assumptions too.

Investigators looked closely at Betty's hobbies. She was an avid reader. At the time in Australia, and for close to twenty years, book sales had been dominated by mystery and 'whodunnit' fiction. Deeply influenced by British tastes and fashions, Australian readers had an appetite for the vast quantity of British crime writing being produced. A police search of Betty's room found a stockpile of detective books. The 1920s and 30s are often described as the golden age of crime fiction, and Betty, like many young readers, had purchased bestselling popular novels. But police read much more into this.

Betty's book collection included many popular women crime writers. English authors Agatha Christie and Dorothy L. Sayers

sold extremely well in Australia. Christie had recently introduced a female crime-fighting hero in the form of Miss Marple,
a homely and sharp-witted woman who was fascinated by
the machinations of murder. But of all the crime fiction that
Betty had purchased, police concluded that she was a fan
of one writer in particular, New Zealander Ngaio Marsh.
Betty had been reading Marsh's latest novel, and police came
to believe this was significant – the title *Overture to Death*
seemed eerily to foreshadow her fate.

Interviews with Betty's friends and family contributed to
the police perception of her as someone with morbid fascin-
ations. She'd also been known to send somewhat forlorn
letters home to her sister in South Africa. The young woman,
isolated and living a long way from family, was prone to
loneliness, and she had talked about suicide in one letter. This
further entrenched the assumptions forming in the minds of
investigators: the woman had been of frail mind, they said.

According to police, while the physical evidence and
circumstances of her death suggested murder, her consump-
tion of crime novels, combined with her desperate loneliness,
had led her to dangerous experimentations. Betty had cleverly
engineered her own strangulation. How she had achieved this
feat, why she might tear off her own suspenders, and why she
might leave herself half-naked and exposed near the harbour
were all secondary concerns to investigators.

Police prepared a thorough briefing for the coroner
outlining their theory: 1) Betty had left home, handbag on
her forearm. 2) Betty had promptly marched herself to a public

space with a sense of deadly purpose. 3) She had strangled herself in the open air. Police argued that Betty had become fixated by a seductive death wish: a desire to be immortalised like one of the victims in her thrillers. *Truth*, a newspaper known for its unvarnished and sometimes savage commentaries on public figures including the police, dismissed the case as daft. It was 'far-fetched', the paper noted, and built on 'flimsy suppositions'.

The coroner agreed with the news outlet, rejecting the theory posed by police as utterly absurd. The case was thrown out.

Truth didn't let the issue go. In July it published an article assembling a timeline of police incompetence. This wasn't just about Betty's case, the editorial noted, but about a pattern of inaction and downright poor policing when it came to investigating sexual murders and public disposals of women across the city's green spaces. The paper's criticism was scathing, particularly so because it had resurrected critiques of prior crimes against women. *Truth* accused the police of inefficiency, laziness and nepotism. The result? Sexual murderers continued to stalk the city: 'the murders of the past . . . are still unsolved, while the blood-stained culprits roam at large . . .' The paper also argued, with a heavy degree of cynicism, that the theory about suicide by strangling had been self-serving: if police could have a mysterious death ruled a suicide the number of unsolved cases recorded for that year was reduced.

The article reminded the public of Hilda White's murder, which had never been fully investigated when the initial police case had fallen short. 'In this case – unlike the affair of Betty van Tonder – it was NOT suggested that she strangled herself. It was very clear from all the circumstances that the girl had been lured into the park and then had been savagely assaulted and murdered. No solution!'

The paper also discussed a more recent event that suggested the pattern of serial killings of women that had occurred in the previous decade was repeating itself. Just near Hyde Park, and dead centre of the dark triangle that had featured in the murder cases eight years before, a woman had gone missing. But unlike the park murder victims, Lucy Brown Craig wasn't a prostitute. Employed as a secretary in the prestigious Macquarie Street medical precinct, Lucy had left work on Friday afternoon, 12 April 1940. She was never seen again.

Witnesses claimed they'd seen Lucy briefly on Darlinghurst Road early on Friday evening. She'd been with a man in a grey suit and with what was described as a 'toothbrush moustache'. This was the last reported sighting.

Lucy's father, Dr Brown Craig, vehemently rejected any suggestion his daughter had run away. And his public statements echoed those he'd made to police: 'her life and upbringing and her nature and outlook were such that she would be unlikely to find any attraction in some capricious adventure'. Police interviews conducted during the investigation certainly confirmed this profile of Lucy, and so too did the evidence. If she had willingly left, she'd also left behind every single possession aside from the clothes she was wearing and her handbag. According to one newspaper, 'She was well educated, she was doing work that occupied her pleasantly, she was happy at home, she was immersed in the round of "doings" of her younger set circle.'

There could only be one conclusion, said *Truth* in July: Lucy had been 'preyed upon'. 'Lucy Craig's case joins the list of mysteries . . . The strange case of this vanished girl is a grave indictment of the effective operations of the Criminal Investigation Branch which now makes the clear admission that it cannot even find a missing girl, cannot trace her, cannot provide any theory other than the one that she is probably dead.'

While no one used the term 'daisy chain', and it was not a label employed by anyone at the time, there was a chain of sexual murders which seemed chillingly similar. As *Truth* newspaper noted at the time, 'the murders of the past . . . are still unsolved, while the blood-stained culprits roam at large . . .' Eric Craig's incarceration had not stopped the threat of sexual murder.

A further set of eerie similarities surround these two events in 1940. Betty van Tonder and Lucy Brown Craig both went missing on a Friday night. Betty was twenty-three and Lucy was twenty. Both sported the same bobbed hairstyle, which perhaps can be chalked up to the popular fashion for chin-length bobs. What is more disturbing is the uncanny resemblance the women shared in physique and aesthetic. This becomes obvious when images of the women are compared side by side – they could have passed for sisters.

Although we cannot be certain that Lucy Brown Craig was murdered, her disappearance remains unsolved to this day.

For six years the public spaces of Sydney lay fallow of corpses. Then, in June 1946, a brutally assaulted female body was discovered in a derelict cemetery at Camperdown in Newtown. Like Betty van Tonder, the victim had been strangled as well as bashed. Her body was left on a patch of overgrown grass between two gravestones.

It would have been impossible for police to posit a suicide-by-strangling theory this time. The body was covered in bite marks, and bruises and cuts covered almost every limb and were present across the torso. The rape had been so violent that the clothing had been torn apart and was bunched under the body in a bloody mess.

At the scene, police were shocked not just by the violent features of the criminal act but by the features of the victim as well – the body was not that of a woman in her twenties or thirties, but of a child. Police immediately issued a public warning: 'She was murdered by a sex maniac . . . parents are to keep their children off the streets after nightfall until after he has been found.'

It didn't take long to identify the victim. Elizabeth Norris had reported her eleven-year-old daughter, Joan Norma Ginn, missing on Wednesday night, 12 June 1946.

It was late in the afternoon when Elizabeth had sent Joan to fetch a loaf of bread from the local store on King Street. Finding the bakery sold out, Joan returned empty-handed. Her mother sent her out again, but this time to see if a family friend might have some bread. Joan had to travel further away this time, by tram. When her daughter hadn't returned several hours later, Elizabeth contacted the police. They began looking for the lost child almost immediately. Around twenty-four hours after her disappearance, they found her.

Joan was still wearing the short blue socks and the little black shoes she'd had on when she left home. Her soft lemon-coloured cardigan had been skilfully used by her attacker, in the manner of a straitjacket, to pin her arms and prevent her from fighting back. Joan had been raped repeatedly and strangled with strips of her own singlet.

Interviews with friends and local families were used to build an understanding about the victim and her movements. Joan had been spotted near King Street while it was still light, 'walking hand in hand' with a tall, bearded figure who 'had his hat pulled down over his eyes'. Another witness account placed Joan – a little later in the day – closer to her home, on a dark street, again with an unidentified male. The witness claimed to have overheard the man say, 'We'll go down this way,' to which Joan was heard to reply, 'I don't want to go down to the park.' The girl had also been spotted catching a tram, and witnesses placed her at several points along its route.

There were other stories about Joan as well. The inferences that had often been made in association with crimes against women – that the victims were somehow responsible for being attacked – had even pervaded the commentaries surrounding the attack on a child. Joan had, according to neighbours, a history of loitering in the street and asking passing men if they had any pennies to spare.

Police followed hundreds of potential leads: tip-offs about local men whom neighbours had always viewed suspiciously. Officers boarded suburban trains and trams scouting for suspects. The investigation descended into a manhunt for the archetype of an urban sexual pervert: a dirty old man in an oversized flasher's coat.

The case quickly became unwieldy, ungovernable, expanding into a series of facts that police struggled to connect. A search of the graveyard uncovered a bundle of clothing: socks, a frock and a pair of men's underpants, along with a blouse and cardigan. But police couldn't be certain if this package had anything to do with Joan Ginn's murder.

There were too many suspects and too many phone calls with too many tips. Police, poorly prepared for the scale of this challenge, had to sift through over two thousand calls from members of the public, in addition to over two hundred letters.

Investigators released information about the stash of clothes to the public. This only unleashed a flood of hoaxes. One anonymous caller claimed to be the murderer and said that during the crime they'd dressed in women's clothing and had assumed a female voice.

Then Joan's mother began receiving anonymous letters. The writer claimed to be the man responsible for killing Joan. He also claimed to have committed the murders dressed as a woman – he said that Joan hadn't known she was in the company of a man, nor the fate that awaited her, until the very end. Cruel pranksters also sent death threats to Joan's family. The writer claimed they had killed Joan, and that Joan's mother would be next.

The hoaxes even crossed the state borders. In Adelaide, a man faced charges for impersonating a police officer – he'd swindled a member of the public by claiming that he was investigating the Joan Ginn murder case in Sydney. He'd assumed it was simply too far away for him to be caught.

Police pursued every archetype of predator. A man in a military greatcoat had been spotted near King Street, in an area where Joan was known to stand, on the afternoon of her disappearance. A local airman, just returned from the war, was interviewed. But so too were old men, young men, tall men, short men, working men, homeless men. One witness claimed to have seen Joan in the company of a man 'in want of a shave' and '27–28 years of age'. By mid-June, over four hundred men had been hauled in for interview, and thirty were on the suspect watch list.

Police transcribed three full confessions to Joan Ginn's murder, and all proved to be bogus. Investigators persisted with the case for years, but no one was ever formally charged. To this day, the case remains unsolved.

•

In November of the same year, a woman's body was discarded in a public reserve, Cooper Park, in the city's east. The location was familiar: about two kilometres north of Centennial

Park and Moore Park, where the bodies of Hilda and Iris had been discovered, and close to the sites where those of Rebecca May Anderson and Daisy Maude Kearney had been found. This was rugged landscape retained as a place for exploration by the wealthy local residents, with bush trails, cliff-side paths and dramatic sandstone formations. The terrain lent itself perfectly to the disposal of a body. The park was close to the road, but not visible from it. The body had been found hidden beneath one of the many large, flat stone overhangs that occurred naturally across the path; this too had helped to obscure it from anyone wandering along the main trails.

The woman had received heavy blows to the head, and there were bruises and abrasions all over her body. It also appeared that she'd been strangled. What were described by police as her 'scanties' had been folded and put beneath her head, in the form of a pillow. Like all of the other victims, this woman, too, was naked, but remained accessorised with jewellery and other adornments. Despite having been stripped, and clearly having endured a violent attack, the woman was still wearing her shoes and short white cotton gloves on her hands.

Police paced out the crime scene, carefully counting the steps from the park entrance to the location of the body. There were fifty-eight steep stone steps leading to the large, flat stone where she'd been found. This meant the woman had walked to the place where someone had murdered her. She hadn't been driven there. She hadn't been dragged there.

In the absence of any other information, with nothing found through fingerprinting, police doorknocked locally in hopes of identifying the woman. Slowly, investigators began to assemble a picture of an eastern suburbs woman whom residents hadn't seen for a few days, and whom more than a few people had observed to be odd.

Eventually she was identified as 45-year-old local woman Ada Amelia Lambert. She lived in a boarding house on Edgecliff Road, Woollahra, which was walking distance from Cooper Park. Ada was married, but her husband was in his mid-seventies and lived permanently in a psychiatric hospital. Three of her four children were in state care. Ada was employed as a laundress at the Women's Hospital on Crown Street, Surry Hills.

Ada's face was slackened with the distinctive collapsed jawline and shrunken mouth of one who has no teeth. Like many people who grew up in the first half of the twentieth century, Ada had suffered tooth loss, and her upper and lower dentures were missing.

No one was willing to confirm that they were Ada's friend. But plenty of people were willing to serve up their cold and somewhat distant judgement of her as a lonely and meek misfit. She had lived with many people in the boarding house, yet none said they'd been close to her. Her neighbours hadn't talked to her, though they observed that she talked to herself. Her workmates were also less than flattering when sharing anecdotes about Ada. Fellow hospital workers called her 'Bunny', but the nickname wasn't derived from any affection for the woman: Ada was perceived to be like a rabbit because she was slow-witted and scared easily.

Ada's husband wasn't deemed mentally competent to identify a body, which made her nineteen-year-old son, John, the closest thing to a next-of-kin adult. He'd been living independently and away from his mother for some time, working as an apprentice bookbinder in the city. When police finally tracked him down, his commentaries brought yet another level of sadness to the death of the woman. John didn't recognise his mother, and even a recent photograph didn't jog his memory. 'I haven't seen her for over three years, and I don't really remember what she looks like,' he said.

Ada's handbag was found nearby. Some music albums and exercise books, with a denture plate on top, were found later, neatly stacked on steps leading down to the park. The other part of her dentures turned up later that week – local children had found the curious object on a seat just outside the public school.

Her piano teacher, Mrs Agnes McKenna, seemed to be the only person who could muster a kind word about Ada. 'I have never seen a woman with nicer or smaller hands,' she said, 'they were always like velvet.' She added, 'I feared something would happen on Saturday when a black moth flew round the house while Mrs Lambert was here. I said to my husband, "That means a death in the house."'

Detectives saw similarities between Ada's and Joan's murders because the killer had struck and gouged both victims, though investigators didn't consider the murders to be linked.

A sharp stick, from one of the many eucalypts in Cooper Park, was said to be 'protruding from [Ada's] body'. The language used to describe the location of the stick is censored, even in official documentation.

As the investigation progressed, more locals were interviewed, all of whom provided similar information. Men hung around Cooper Park – men who spent their working lives in cars, trucks and delivery vehicles. They often stopped nearby to drink thermos coffee and eat lunch from a sandwich pail. Based on the statements of two teenagers, who identified Ada's handbag as the one they'd seen her holding while talking to a man, police narrowed their search to a local truck driver: Clifford Kennedy.

Police followed Clifford Kennedy and took him into custody at Bondi Junction. He'd been taking his mother on an outing to the cinema.

During the interrogation, police said that Kennedy confessed. He also offered an explanation for what had occurred, they said. 'The reason I went to the park with the woman is quite obvious, but at no time did I intend to harm her or injure her in any way and I can only bitterly regret that it was through my drinking that day that this tragedy took place.' In his own words, 'drinking made [him] sexy'. Kennedy claimed he had gone to the park with Ada, he had persuaded her to have sex, but 'she eventually and quite willingly did'. According to her murderer, she kept loudly saying, 'I love you I love you I love you', and wouldn't be quiet – Kennedy claimed it was this that caused him to put his hands around her throat. Ada 'struggled and then went limp. And I went home and went to bed,' Kennedy said. He added that he hadn't turned himself in during the three-week manhunt only because this would have hurt his mother, and he was trying to spare her that disappointment and shame.

At trial, the isolation and poverty of Ada's life was discussed in detail. In the courtroom, an officer held up the blue dress she had worn to piano lessons. It was thin and threadbare, but it had also been torn to shreds by the attack. The jury could imagine precisely what had occurred: the killer had grasped the front of the dress at the neckline and, in one motion, torn it right off Ada's body.

The dog-eared exercise book that Ada had used to learn piano theory was then passed around for the jury to inspect. Agnes McKenna, her music teacher, was the only one close enough to Ada to feel the intense sadness of the moment. She openly broke down.

Journalists present at the trial described the events as they unfolded in court. 'At no time did the personality of Mrs Lambert ... emerge in clear outline. She remained elusive – a shadowy little woman in a dim, blue dress, with a soft voice and diffident ways ... something wistful and fugitive in her manner.' And this, according to the story told by the defence, had contributed to the crime.

One common thread was woven through the commentaries on Ada: it was dangerous to be a lonely woman.

What unfolded at trial was a solid and consistently maintained narrative about the crime – a didactic on women, and their behaviour. There was no doubt that Ada Lambert had faced sad travails during the course of her life, but police derived many conclusions from this. Police began building a portrait of Ada. She was a wife without a husband, a mother without children. This led to loaded presumptions about the way in which the crime against her had escalated: that sadness and loneliness make women desperate – not just for human companionship, but for the company and attention of men. The story told at trial was a tale of two people. A core narrative about men versus a core narrative about women. On one hand – a normal man with normal impulses that had gone momentarily awry. On the other hand – a person of unstable character who was decidedly abnormal in desire. Kennedy, although still characterised as brutal, and one who had demonstrated a shockingly poor lack of control, was still, quite simply, in the eyes of those examining the case, a man.

While acknowledging the 'sadism' of the crime against Ada, the jury managed to draw an astonishing conclusion. They acquitted Kennedy of murder, convicting him of manslaughter instead. Justice Owen, in passing sentence of twelve years' imprisonment, stated, 'I think the jury has taken a merciful view of the charge against you, I hope the sorrow you have brought to your mother will be some punishment to you.'

Almost twenty-five years had passed since the murder of Daisy, but not much had changed in the way Sydney police dealt with crimes against women. When they were the victims of horrible sexual crimes, they were treated as though they shared some responsibility in these acts. If they were engaged in sex work, their immorality was to blame. If they were out after dark, and were 'too trusting' of men, this was their problem too. Even reading crime novels was seen as an unsavoury pastime for women. Loneliness and desperation for human companionship had driven the women to poor choices and risky titillations, and this had been their downfall, or so it was argued.

At the end of 1946, *Smith's Weekly* threaded together some, if not all, of the murders that had taken place since 1932. It was a sensationalist column written by 'The Man in the Mask', an anonymous avatar that permitted the paper to publish provocative commentaries on social issues. When they saw the headline 'Park murders' splashed across their city's papers, Sydneysiders may have been shocked that their home had become such a brutal place to live.

But perhaps they shouldn't have been. That same headline had appeared way back in 1932.

17

NEVER TO BE RELEASED

In the late afternoon of 30 July 1950, in a flat in Glebe Street in the eastern suburb of Randwick, Mary-Caroline busied herself in a small kitchenette. She stacked teacups and placed them back inside a cabinet. She straightened the pastel bakelite canisters on the countertop so they stood in a straight line from biggest to smallest. She neatly folded three large towels. Mary-Caroline swept and mopped the floor. She closed the internal doors on either side of the kitchenette – one leading to the sitting room, the other to a bedroom. The room seemed smaller and a little warmer now. It was a cold July day, and closing doors immediately prevented a cold draught from being able to pass right through the flat. Taking two towels from the counter, she rolled each of them into long tube shapes and dropped them at her feet. She nudged the snake-shaped rolls across the floor and pushed them into the gaps between the door and the floor. Jamming the towels firmly into place with the pointed toe of her slipper, the draught that could be felt through the flat immediately dropped away. The two doors stopped rattling. With the floor clean and the room now warm and cosy, Mary-Caroline opened the oven door and fiddled with the gas valve, just as one might in making dinner preparations. But she did not clatter trays in the kitchen, nor chop vegetables. She leant down to closely inspect the oven and sized up the oven rack. However, it wasn't a tray she placed inside the oven, but a folded towel. She carefully positioned it just inside the oven so that it rested on the hinges and held the door open. She flicked on the gas. Bending down on her knees she laid herself gently on the floor of the kitchenette, just as one might climb into bed. She made herself comfortable by tucking her knees a little closer to her chest, and then curled her body into a foetal position. Mary-Caroline placed her head upon the neatly folded towel. With the oven door as her pillow, she closed her eyes and waited for sleep.

When Mary-Caroline's father, Michael Patrick Tobin, arrived at the flat about twenty-four hours later, he found his daughter lying in a curled position on the freshly mopped kitchen floor, with her head in the oven. It was a remarkably efficient way to die. She was posed as if sleeping. Half of her body was streaked with bright pink.

The gas supplied to households in 1950 was different to the natural gas we use today. Illuminating gas, as it was called, had a particularly deadly active ingredient: carbon monoxide. It saturates the blood quickly. The body loses consciousness rapidly, some say within seconds, as the brain is starved of oxygen. Within minutes, Mary-Caroline would have been dead.

And perhaps when death arrived it felt strangely familiar to Mary-Caroline. Death had formed a macabre backdrop to her life for close to twenty years. The deaths of Iris Marriott and Bessie O'Connor had shaped the course of Mary-Caroline's entire adult life. In death, she followed these other women by taking the same rite of passage through the legal system that they had eighteen years before. Since she had died suddenly and unexpectedly, the state required that a cause be determined. The discoveries of their bodies had prompted coronial inquests. So too would the discovery of hers.

While it was very clear what had happened, and no officer who attended the scene that day suspected foul play, in accordance with legal process the matter was fully investigated by police. It was one of the most straightforward legal proceedings to take place that year. The inquest was held on 18 August 1950 and was officially described using the legal title of 'A Magisterial Inquiry Touching the Death of Mary-Caroline Mann'. At first glance, the turn of phrase seems awkward, and somehow inappropriate in the context of the clinical matters being considered. Considered from another angle, this title reflects the realities of the work done by the medical examiner undertaking the very tactile task of inspecting a cadaver. Dr Clarence Ernest Percy did indeed touch the death of the woman, physically examining her corpse in order to make his determinations, though it is important to point out that he read the body too.

When bodies aren't discovered for a few hours, post-mortem lividity becomes an important tool in defining toxicities that may have played a role in death. The colour of the body changes like that of a mood ring. For those with the technical capability to interpret them, these colours have meaning.

After death occurs, processes of circulation gradually cease. The blood starts to slow and stop, settling under the skin in accordance with the forces of gravity. If a body is lying facedown, the front will fill with blood, and become dark and discoloured; the back will also not remain the colour that it was while the person was alive, but will appear cooler and paler as the blood drains away. If a body is lying on one side, the blood pools on the lower side, and colouring will reflect pressure points where the body was experiencing contact with an object.

Different chemical reactions within the body affect the colours of post-mortem lividity. Blue with a little pink indicates that the death has not come about because of an overdose to the system by poison or a toxic chemical. If the same body lies there for long enough, the colour will slowly become more purple. The presence of hydrogen sulphide poisoning in a body will present as blue–green, and phosphorus turns a body a deep brown. Where an overdose of opiates has occurred, the lividity presents as black.

The medical examiner read Mary-Caroline's mood. The loops and knots of thread on the surface of the towel dappled the surface of one side of her face almost prettily with pink. Her lower body, too, was a cherry colour, much like one side had been dipped in brightly coloured wax. In the official words of the medical examiner, this 'widespread bright pink post mortem staining' confirmed that she had died of carbon monoxide poisoning.

At the inquest, only two exhibits were produced: a medical examiner's report and a note.

Deaths at home by carbon monoxide poisoning weren't uncommon in the mid-twentieth century. Piped into many homes in Sydney for heating and cooking, the gas was almost completely undetectable to the human senses. While gas now has additives that give it an odour, seventy years ago it did not. If a leak occurred in a home, or a valve was accidentally left on, poisoning occurred quickly, often without the victim even realising they were in danger. Indeed, it was so common it was sometimes referred to as the silent or quiet killer.

Mary-Caroline's death, of course, was not discounted as an accident. There was the position of her body and the towel in the oven to consider. In addition, the flat had been firmly sealed to ensure the gas could not be released. Sergeant Arthur Spithill of Randwick police had searched the flat she'd shared with her father and found 'no defect of the gas supply'. The same sergeant had found a note left by Mary-Caroline.

She'd tried earnestly to make a new life for herself and her children, but her life seemed to remain defined by a pattern of loss. She remarried, then left her husband two years later. Mary-Caroline's two children – twenty-year-old Valma and eighteen-year-old Robert Eric – didn't live with her. In the lead-up to her death, Mary-Caroline had been particularly distressed because she'd believed Valma had gone missing and she'd been unable to get in contact with her. Her father had been away for a night, and this had given Mary-Caroline the opportunity to kill herself without interference.

In his formal statement to the police, Kenneth Lionel Mann, her second husband, described Mary-Caroline's state of mind. 'For the past two years she was in ill health suffering from nerves. She would not go to a doctor. I had heard her express an intention of taking her own life, more than once. She was depressed at times. Her father was living there. He is seventy-six and is feeble . . . The note shown to me is my wife's handwriting.'

Mary-Caroline's father also attested to his daughter's state of mind at the time of her death, and he noted that she had tried to support herself by working at Connie's Tailor. 'I last saw my daughter alive on 30 July 1950. It was about 3 p.m. She complained of her nerves then. She was worried. She had never gone to a doctor over her condition.'

If the colours and patterns of lividity can be read like a mood ring, so too can Mary-Caroline's note. Strangely, it hadn't been written just before she died, but four months earlier in March 1950. Mary-Caroline had clearly been considering her options for some time. There is an unevenness to the words; they spill down the page irregularly, congealing in some places in clumps, while in others they seem to scatter into specks.

Just in Case   7 March 1950
Anything untoward should
happen to me
M Mann

The past has been enough and I think the
Future will be too much.
My sister Elsie I give my clothes and what ever jewerly I
may have, in
Particular my watch
To my Son My furniture and Insurance policy No 7990834
To my Daughter my Sewing Machine and
Insurance Policy No 07995833

Such money I may have in the bank
To my Husband with Love
M Mann

In her interview with a journalist in 1933 Mary-Caroline talked about the nightmares that plagued her in the wake of Eric's incarceration. Perhaps the method she had chosen for her death reflected a desperate need for sleep – a long sleep which was peaceful and without nightmares. In one way, Mary-Caroline's death in 1950 added to the daisy chain of victims in the inner east. She died quietly, and very differently to the other victims. While it was not a murderous instinct that took her life, it was still a predatory one. Police, in their relentless determination to hunt and find someone who could be identified as the murderer, had targeted and stalked a man until they achieved a conviction. Eric Roland Craig may have been tried and convicted for the deaths of Iris Marriott and Bessie O'Connor, but some might argue that it was his wife who received the death sentence.

18
RELEASED

MARY-CAROLINE MADE AN INDESCRIBABLY SAD CHOICE WHILE standing in that kitchen in Randwick in 1950. However, the pre-dated note that she left behind suggests that she had been contemplating the decision for a long time prior to that fateful winter day. Eric Craig would also reflect on his release from his sentence, long before it would actually happen. His journey from prison to freedom, however, would be a far more circuitous one than being carried quickly and silently away by monoxide. Eric Roland Craig's first exit from prison took meticulous planning. The infrastructure needed to support his release had been adequately identified, the exit strategy was well coordinated, and provision had been made for the man beyond the gaol's walls. There was just one small problem: prison officials were the last ones to know that Craig was about to be free. At about 2 p.m. on Sunday, 26 October 1941, and after two years of planning, he escaped.

Prison guards only realised there was a problem when, at 4 p.m., Craig wasn't present for mandatory rollcall. Sunday afternoons were the one time in the week when prisoners were afforded a little freedom. Between 2 and 4 p.m., they were permitted time for socialising and interacting, and most gathered in the B-wing recreational yard to do so. While some chose to play chess or cards, Craig elected to go to the chapel alone.

The prison guards didn't know it at the time, but when Craig left the chapel that afternoon with his head bowed meditatively and assuming the quiet shuffle of a monk, it wasn't prayer he had on his mind. He was more occupied with the twenty-foot hemp rope he'd shoved under his prison uniform, and the grappling hook dangling perilously on the inside leg of his trousers.

From there, and no one is entirely sure how, Craig managed to make his way to a location where he could scale a high wall unseen. He swung the hook up the wall, then pulled himself up hand over hand. It's believed he scaled three walls this way, one of them twenty feet high. Once on the rooftop, he ran across the fernery just near the governor's house and dropped freefall directly into the vegetable plot. On reaching the ground he flung himself over an iron fence and ran off.

It was bold, especially considering he escaped in broad daylight.

Craig had thoroughly accounted for everything. He'd even looked beyond the prison timetable to maximise his opportunity to flee. That day was the Feast of Christ the King, which only occurred once a year. Held on the last Sunday in October, it was a popular day out for Catholics in the town of Bathurst. Children dressed in their communion garments, worshippers held up banners, and all assembled at the end of the holy walk for a benediction. The Eucharistic procession was scheduled to occur at 3 p.m. that day; it meant most of the town would be assembled at St Vincent's Hospital Park. Each year, thousands of people came to witness the procession. It was perfect for someone who wanted to slip quietly into the back of a crowd.

Local police and prison wardens mounted a search. Close to a hundred officers were called, including those from neighbouring districts and those who were off duty. The governor of Bathurst Gaol called the police commissioner for extra reinforcements. Two special agents were dispatched to assist: German shepherd tracker dogs Zoe and Disraeli. Along with their detective handlers they made the three-hour road trip to Bathurst. The whole state, it seemed, was once again on a manhunt for Eric Roland Craig.

Officials conjectured on Craig's possible escape plan. Australia was at war, so it was possible the prisoner planned to enlist for service and be sent abroad. Police provided enlistment offices with a description of Craig.

The ground search was extensive. Police set up roadblocks in case Craig managed to steal a car. Officials began to panic.

As the hours rolled on, Bathurst Gaol faced grave warnings from the Comptroller-General of Prisons: the problem went beyond a prisoner-management issue. An embarrassment of this magnitude could affect the reputation of the government. One of the state's most dangerous criminals – as the newspapers dubbed him – wasn't only loose but had – without much effort, it seemed – climbed his way out of what was believed to be one of the most secure prisons in the country.

It turned dark. The search continued. While the human officers broke their way through dense patches of scrub in heavy protective work boots, canine officers Zoe and Disraeli scrambled over logs, and crawled under hedges and through drains. But at about 2.30 a.m. the entire operation ground to a halt. With Craig now missing close to twelve hours, the officers had pressed on, unaware the dogs were severely injured. Both were now lame, at least temporarily, from the razor-like and sticky thorns of the tiger pear cactus that grew wild in the area. Without dogs to pick up Craig's scent, humans could do little tracking in the dim moonlight. The search was called off until daybreak.

An official description of Craig was shared across police radio, and officers were told to look out. The words and phrases brought Craig to life, but not in a way that provided officers in the field any real guidance on what they were looking for. Craig was described as having 'large starey or glassy eyes' and a 'scar on the forehead', and being 'agitated in demeanour'. The description bordered on caricature, as though Craig was a cartoon criminal.

News reports provided more misinformation than genuine insight about the man. He was known as the stocking strangler but the crimes for which Craig had been convicted hadn't involved stockings or strangling. Craig had a fetishistic knowledge of knots, said newspapers – other than his brief work experience as a tie salesman, there was no evidence this was the case either. The *Sydney Morning Herald* article was perhaps the most inaccurate, with a headline that labelled Craig a 'cunning and desperate criminal'. When he was captured at six on Monday morning, less than fifteen hours after his escape, he seemed anything but cunning.

Just near the Macquarie River, about half a mile from Rock Forest Road and about ten miles out of Bathurst, a police constable approached the man with his revolver drawn. The constable needn't have bothered. Craig turned and put his hands up. 'No need for the gun. I am Craig. I don't want to give any trouble,' he said. When he raised his palms in the air they were covered in dried blood, slashed from the barbed wire he'd wrestled with in order to make his escape.

As police walked him to their truck, Craig seemed very agreeable. He told them, 'I wasn't able to light a fire last night, I was too scared of being caught.' Police handcuffed him and threw him into the back of the van. He asked for a blanket.

•

In the weeks following, when officials were certain that Craig was now securely in solitary confinement, an investigation began.

When captured, Craig wasn't wearing prison garb but civilian trousers and a brown sweater. He'd also somehow acquired a cap and sports coat that fitted him perfectly. When asked directly, he told police he'd got the clothing from 'sources he would not reveal'. Wardens were suspicious. The clothes weren't from inside the prison, and it appeared that as soon as Craig had escaped he hadn't hung around town to steal but had headed for the road out of town. So where had he got the clothing from? Prison officials reflected on the week that had led up to the escape. On the Thursday morning, three days before Craig got out, he'd received a visit from 'a woman who claimed to be his mother', noted one prison official.

This raised many questions. Had someone posed as Leah Craig in order to smuggle in the contraband of civilian clothes? Or was it possible Craig's real mother had conspired to assist her son? Prison officials had many suspicions, partly because of the unusually close relationship the two seemed to share, but in the end nothing could be proved.

Craig claimed he'd hand stitched his pants from khaki fabric stolen in the prison workshop. Investigators, comprising a mix of prison personnel and police, noted that the pants bore an uncanny resemblance to military breeches, a style of riding jodhpur that had formed the basis of the AIF uniform in World War I. It would have been familiar to Craig, as his stepfather, Vivian, had worn the uniform proudly.

The survivalist kit that Craig had assembled also troubled prison officials. When captured, he'd had in his possession a knife, tobacco, two razors, and matches. He'd even fashioned a catapult with which to catch rabbits and birds.

Though Craig wouldn't reveal where he had acquired most of his clothing, he did fess up to the origins of some other items. While in prison he'd slowly sourced and stashed stolen wire, a heavy piece of lead, and a hook from the workshop. He further admitted that much of the planning had taken two years. He'd made the rope himself, he said. But how had he managed to acquire enough fibres to make twenty feet of rope?

The answer to this was also found inside the prison walls – attached to them, in fact. A large hemp net had been installed within the prison complex about two years before, fixed to stretch tightly between the top floors of two blocks of cells. Unofficially called 'the suicide net', the structure had been put in place to stop prisoners from scrambling over railings and leaping off high points of the building.

Craig had planned his escape for a long time. He had squirrelled away sections of hemp left over from the install-ation of the net. He'd been patiently winding himself a rope over a solid two years of work.

What wardens had observed to be religious fanaticism in the months leading up to his escape appears to have been a ruse. While Craig had been praying, reading the Bible and enthusiastically honing his skills as an organist, he'd also been using the chapel organ to stash his escape supplies. The escape rope had been coiled inside the instrument for months.

•

While Craig had worked hard, in secret, to orchestrate his release, he couldn't have known that wheels were being set in motion across the justice system to consider the official release of men like him.

In order to understand how a man whose file had been stamped with the words 'never to be released' could then be considered for release, it is important to understand what was going on both within and without New South Wales at the time.

Six years after Craig was imprisoned, in September 1939, Australia had officially entered World War II. As an enthusiastic supporter of Britain and the Allied forces, Australia made a significant contribution to munitions and labour. Fiscal cutbacks occurred across all areas of service provision as the government sought to make savings. The prisons, like every other public service department in every state, had their budgets cut. With the war well underway, in June 1940 the NSW Premier Alexander Mair issued a decree to every department across the state: reduce spending and divert all available labour to the war effort. 'Give what you can. Give until it hurts,' he implored, in a lengthy memorandum entitled 'Premier's Appeal to Public Servants'. 'Australia can contribute her proper share in this gigantic effort only if she marshals her resources of money and materials and directs them in the right channels. The task of those at home therefore is to provide the sinews of war.' Keeping prisoners was expensive, so the department began to review where and how they might reduce prison populations.

The reach of the police and the military extended during this time, and this would also indirectly impact the prison system. The *National Security Act 1939* was introduced by the Commonwealth government during World War II with a view to securing public safety and defence on the home front. The Act expanded the powers of the state in its surveillance of anyone residing in Australia. Under this legislation, the government tightened their control over 'enemy aliens' in the interests of maintaining national security. 'Threats to national security' were broadly interpreted – residential homes or places of trade were all confiscated by the state. Many migrant families were turfed out of their homes and relocated to prison compounds. German or Italian names were considered suspect because Australia was officially at war with these nations. As the war progressed, Japanese families were also targeted.

The Act led to tens of thousands of people being displaced from the homes where they'd raised children, the businesses they'd built, and the farms they'd owned and worked. They were led away and not permitted to mix with other members of the Australian community. Their right to live freely in society had been revoked by the state, much like that of convicted criminals. And as with criminals, the state needed somewhere to place them. The ideal place, authorities decided, was a prison. Public fears about criminals like Eric Craig hadn't gone away, but in wartime the public's focus shifted to people perceived to be much worse: foreigners.

In the early years of the war, prison-management strategies changed to accommodate an influx of a new category of prisoners: enemy aliens. While vast purpose-built facilities would eventually be built at Liverpool, Cowra, Orange and Hay, at first the government needed secure accommodation to house those identified as potentially dangerous insurgents. This was an onerous undertaking, largely because of the scale of the detention places needed. The internment camp that would eventually be built at Liverpool was estimated to accommodate about seven thousand alone. Until these special facilities were built, the state needed to improvise by using prisons they already had – authorities just needed to work out what to do with the current tenants.

At around the same time, an independent committee was assembled to consider what constituted 'life imprisonment'. It comprised ex-judges, medical experts, prison comptrollers and legal experts. In 1941, former State Attorney-General and Minister for Justice D. R. Hall noted that 'the practice of sentencing people to life imprisonment with the provision never to be released had built up a legion of hopelessness in NSW'. That same year, the tally of prisoners never to be released in the state had blown out to a number higher than anyone had expected. By 1941, forty prisoners had faced the executive stamp of 'never to be released'.

When the war ended, discussions regarding prison reform continued. In 1950 the Crown Solicitor and the Assistant Law

Officer King's Counsel (roles which had responsibility for both advice on and management of legal affairs in the state) made formal recommendations that prisoners who had served twenty years should be released, since this reasonably constituted a 'life sentence'. Solicitor-General Cecil Edward Weigall KC campaigned on behalf of this recommendation, arguing it served the interests of a good economy and a progressive society. As he was the most senior legal adviser in the state who held a non-political position, his views had legal legitimacy and carried weight. Men who were released sooner, it was argued, could make a proper contribution to society and thereby reduce the burden on the state associated with meeting the costs of lifelong accommodation.

In 1950, the Attorney-General's Department sought advice about who might be moved from the maximum-security to the low-security prisons. With the growing population during the post-war baby boom, it was projected that thousands more prisoners would need to be accommodated eventually – therefore, the system needed a way to become less labour and capital intensive. At the end of the 1940s, Craig's file was pushed forward for consideration with a group of others.

•

To understand how a man deemed one of the worst criminals in the state might be considered for parole, it is necessary to consider what kind of man Craig was.

Eric Roland Craig was a model prisoner. It seems hard to believe, given the dim view that law and order officials take of prison breaks today. Nevertheless, this is how Craig was viewed. As part of a work prison programme he became a proficient French polisher. He worked in the tailor shop. Indeed, one of only few negative comments about Craig on his prison record sheet was that he smoked in the tailor shop, against the rules.

Just after the war, prison reform became an important area of policy for the state. The state needed workers, and it also needed to reduce the costs associated with maintaining incarcerated inmates. In 1946, Premier William McKell appointed a committee of experts to report on the prison system in New South Wales, and following on from this the Attorney-General developed a scaffold on which a new prison system might be built. It was one of the most comprehensive examinations of prison life ever undertaken and looked at everything from prisoner treatment, punishment and psychology to diet, rostering and training. Both of these initiatives sought to examine more closely the classification of prisoners and to better understand how rehabilitation might form part of the prison experience.

The prisoner rehabilitation experiment launched in New South Wales placed great emphasis on education and, in particular, training provided by the State Prisons Department. Much of the state's rehabilitation work was conducted at a low-security prison facility called the Emu Plains Prison Farm. While publicly the farm was described as a place that housed the young, so they would be kept away from hardened criminals, in reality the farm preferred compliant and hard-working inmates of any age.

Because of Craig's exemplary conduct record and his work ethic, he was sent to the low-security farm. Within a short time, he was promoted to a management role. As one behaviour record, reported by a prison staff member, noted of Craig at the time: 'The Superintendent has allotted Craig superior ratings.' Within only a few years, Craig became the leading hand of a major work programme for the prison system. His official title was 'head poultry man'. At the farm he was known as an accomplished killer and a good dresser – but only of chickens.

Craig's case was considered by the parole board every four years. Every time, he was knocked back. It wasn't his record inside prison but, rather, his reputation outside that had prison officials concerned. While prison officials saw one side of Craig, he still had a loathsome reputation amongst those members of the public who remembered the crimes for which he had been sent to prison. While the activities of the rehabilitation committee were kept firmly out of the public eye, information was occasionally leaked. One letter, sent by a concerned citizen, highlights the perception of Craig that remained twenty years after his imprisonment.

To the Minister of Justice

There are not many of the older generation who have not repulsive memories of the evidence brought out at

the trials of this monster . . . Craig's papers were marked
'Never to be released' and says that every woman and
particularly every woman who is a mother of a daughter,
will walk in terror if this sex slayer is set free.

Our committee desires to know if it is true that the
Government intends to release this savage beast, and if so
on what grounds . . .

Labor Women's Central Organising Committee
Edna Roper

•

For the next five years, Craig worked diligently and quietly.

In 1952, the Prisons Department appointed a psychiatrist
to work closely with prisoners. The goal was to reduce anti-
social behaviour using a thoroughly modern psychological
approach, influenced by developments overseas, particularly
in the United States. Prison psychiatrist Dr John McGeorge
assessed men and women, after arrest and before trial, while
in gaol and before release. He advocated for a more progressive
system, and believed in rehabilitation if prisoners were offered
the proper mental health interventions and supports.

McGeorge was there to make a professional assessment
of claims for an insanity defence. But he was also there to
assess the men, to classify them based on their level of sexual
deviance. If a man was convicted of a sex offence with another
man, consensual or not, the state took a dim view of this. One
judge sums up the attitude towards sexual activity between

men at the time by saying that the men were irredeemable in rehabilitative terms: 'Once a sexual offender, always a sexual offender,' he noted in a ruling.

In late 1956 Craig faced what he believed would be a major setback. He believed it would sever any possibility of him ever being released.

One of Craig's daily responsibilities was to ensure that the large refrigerator units were kept clean and closed. It was essential that the poultry was stored at a controlled temperature, reducing the risk of contamination.

In the lead-up to Christmas, a delegation of official visitors was expected. Kitchen staff would be required to serve an impressive meal. Craig had cleaned and sanitised the coolroom shelf so that he might store the freshly dressed poultry. When he returned to find that other food had been placed on the shelf, tempers flared, and it got physical. During an altercation with a fellow prisoner, Craig struck a man in the face. The heated argument happened, somewhat ironically, in the coolroom.

The official conduct report from the prison notes, 'The Comptroller-General personally saw Craig and informed him that having regard to the length of time he had served and other circumstances the greatest possible consideration would be extended on this occasion. Craig expressed regret and gave a promise to behave in an exemplary manner in future and finally apologised to the other prisoner who was quite prepared to let the matter rest ... Craig has taken a keen interest in his work. Since his unsatisfactory behaviour in December last there have not been any occurrences of misconduct and he appears to be have settled down again satisfactorily.'

Prison authorities sought the advice of John McGeorge. Craig had never pleaded insanity, but he needed to be properly assessed given his label as a violent offender. His prison record was excellent, and wardens and welfare personnel who worked closely with him believed he was ready for release. In March 1957, Craig was scheduled for a comprehensive psychiatric assessment and referred to McGeorge.

The psychiatrist conducted his assessment of Craig alone, based on a question-and-answer conversation about Craig's attitudes, values and personal reflections.

He continues to deny his guilt on the second charge although admitting everything in the first case. He is unable to explain his action saying it was the time of the depression, he was out of work and was in an unsettled frame of mind. He claims that his victim was a consenting party and there was an argument over payment during which she kicked him where it hurt most. He lost his temper and struck her with a piece of wood. He is quiet and respectful in manner and there is no evidence of any psychiatric disorder. He gives a reasonable and rational account of himself. There is nothing to suggest that he is not capable of exercising complete control. He proposes if released to place himself completely in the hands of the St Vincent de Paul society and to carry out fully any instructions given him. He expresses appreciation of the treatment received from the Prisons Department, which is tactful if nothing else. It does not appear that there is any likelihood of a repetition of his offence.

Craig fell into a category of prisoner that, from a psychiatric standpoint, was deemed to be low risk. McGeorge argued that violence was, to some extent, natural; the circumstances in which the violence occurred were what mattered. In his professional opinion, there needed to be a distinction drawn between 'violent' versus 'habitual' criminals. In his opinion, 'the man who was put in gaol for a violent crime often made up the best type of prisoner'. This view assisted Craig's campaign for release.

This campaign was successful on 24 July 1957.

Eric Craig was considered one of the prison system's great success stories. In recognition of this, the Comptroller-General of Prisons wrote several letters, personally, to each member of Craig's parole team. 'I had great pleasure in conveying to the Minister advice of the great part which you had played in Craig's successful rehabilitation ... The Minister has asked me to convey to you his grateful appreciation of your work in this difficult and often unrewarding field. I should like to add my personal thanks,' the Comptroller-General wrote in one. In another he stated, 'Undoubtedly this case underlines the extreme value to the community as well as to the individuals of the work of both the Departmental staff and the voluntary assistants through Civil Rehabilitation Committees.'

The prison system was proud to lay claim to the achievement of having rehabilitated a particularly dangerous class of criminal: a killer. A perhaps more cynical interpretation is to state that they'd indeed achieved the impossible: they had successfully rehabilitated a man for crimes he may not have committed. What is known for sure is that the deaths of Daisy, Rebecca, Vera, Hilda, Iris, Bessie, Betty, Lucy, Joan and Ada were not properly investigated. Bad police work, inconsistent witness statements and gendered assumptions plagued all of these investigations. Though we cannot ever know for certain, it is also possible that a single serial killer was active from 1922 to 1946. The killings were similar, and in some cases startingly so. Justice has not been served for these victims so much as preserved. Like perennials gathered from the pretty parks and gardens of Sydney they were picked, then plucked. They remain, to this day, pressed like flowers between the heavy pages of dusty police tomes.

Though the state never made any formal admission that they might have arrested and convicted the wrong man, after twenty-four years Eric Roland Craig walked out of prison a free man.

19

KEEPING WATCH

FOR THE NEXT FIVE YEARS, ERIC CRAIG WAS WATCHED CLOSELY by the state. His movements were monitored by his probation officer, and he was put on what was called a prison licence. He couldn't leave the state without permission. Probation officers audited his personal life, and his places of work were monitored too.

Craig was supported on the outside by a working group of church and welfare organisations; employers (the Chamber of Manufactures of NSW) and the Labor Council. The Prisons Department continued to have a strong and influential voice too. The support organisations provided significant financial assistance and donated clothing, domestic appliances and furniture, and also supplied an important network of connections to potential employers. With the help of a parole and welfare officer from St Vincent de Paul, Ted Plowman, Craig secured employment and accommodation.

After the formation of the Civil Rehabilitation Committee in 1951, statistics published on the first five years of its operation indicate that about 1200 released prisoners were referred to the committee. Employment was found for only about half (six hundred), and for those who couldn't return to live with family, accommodation was found for only about one quarter (three hundred). Craig was indeed a success story. He had gained employment, found accommodation and appeared to be thriving.

Craig commenced work immediately as a clerk at Drug Houses of Australia. He stayed in that role for only a month – newspaper journalists had discovered where he was living. Once again, the name of Eric Roland Craig was splashed across Sydney's broadsheets. One article included a detailed account of the crimes for which he'd been convicted, along with his employment details – and, most damaging of all, a photograph.

Craig left the position. With the assistance of Plowman, he found another job as a clerk in a manufacturing plant for auto parts. To earn extra money, he worked on weekends and at night as a private investigator. He advertised in the paper. Most of his work came from unhappy wives and husbands. Craig gathered evidence of infidelity to support divorce petitions. He staked out apartments where he knew clandestine affairs were being carried out; he tracked cheating husbands and wives, and banged on motel doors at 3 a.m. As far as his probation officer was concerned, he worked part time as an 'insurance agent'.

Craig did everything he could to sever his connections with the past. There's no evidence he ever saw his children again. And for the first time in his life, he seemed to be building a life without the involvement of his mother.

Just as he had once before, Craig reinvented himself by changing his name. In 1917, Eric Roland Joseph had transformed into Eric Roland Craig. Forty years later, in 1957, Eric Roland Craig became Anthony Campbell. His parole officer agreed this was a good idea and, given the problems he'd experienced with the media, it was all part of making a fresh start.

Sometime not long after Eric was released, he met Deirdre Williams, a divorcee with a daughter. He believed that in order for this relationship to work, he had to keep everything about his prior life a secret. He told Deirdre he was forty, although he was closer to fifty. He told her his biological father was Vivian Henry. He told her that his work as a private investigator was dangerous, so protecting his identity was necessary. Eric even convinced his probation officer, Plowman, to participate in the deception. Deirdre believed that Eric and Plowman were best friends.

Deirdre and Eric married, and began building a house together. The name of the suburb was perhaps interpreted by Eric as an omen, a promise of the good life that now lay ahead for him and his wife. The couple settled in Merrylands.

Eric continued to be closely monitored by the parole administration. A report highlights the level of continued confidence the board maintained in his ability to reintegrate. The principal parole officer provided a glowing report on Craig's progress: '. . . excellent prospects this man faces in the future. There are still several danger spots, one of which is Craig's marriage, where his wife, to my knowledge, is unaware of his background. It is Mr Plowman's opinion however, that at this stage a disclosure of the past would not really affect Craig's marriage. Nevertheless, this aspect together with Craig's quick temper, could cause trouble. However, with Mr Plowman's help and the support of this office, I feel reasonably certain that Craig will continue to make good.'

In the final stages of his probation, Craig wrote personally to the principal parole officer.

Dear Sir
As I am in the period of my last weeks of my 'licence',
I thought you might like to know just how things have
gone with me over the last five years. As you know I am
now happily married and have now been promoted to
second-in-charge of my department in the same firm of
which Ted Plowman and yourself went out together in
September 1957, since then I have got myself another part
time position which in terms of money all add to greater
comfort in the home that I am now building.
    It is easy to see that I have no worries nor do I anti-
cipate ever running into strife again. The story in fact is
not as easy as it sounds. Every fellow coming back to the
free world has a pile of worries ahead of him which in
my own case can easily help him to come undone. In fact
once would need someone to whom you can turn at any
moment of day or night . . . Without trying to sound as if
I am endeavouring to build up Ted Plowman might I say

that only for his help I would not be where I am today. He has been my friend in every sense of the word, who I have seen at least once or twice a week since my return home ... There will be a lot of mugs who will always fill the newspapers with their criticism and have a lash at fellows who are trying to do the right thing. This sort of business affects the chances of a lot of men who are inside looking forward to the day of their release. If you have people who can find time and the personal friendship such as given by Ted you won't have much trouble. It is the personal touch that is needed coupled with the understanding and guidance of your own parole officers.

In writing this letter to you it is something I feel is good and right and from here on I will always remember what has been done for me and wish you every success in your effort to help others on the way.

Yours sincerely
E R Craig

In 1963, Craig was completely released from the obligations of his prison licence. The probationary officers eased their scrutiny of his life. With his change of name, it was also much harder for newspapers or even police to locate him. Which was just as well.

About twelve months after he completed probation, a discovery was made only six kilometres from Eric and Deirdre's new brick home in Merrylands. This discovery might have led police, and a journalist or two, directly to Craig's front door – if they'd known where to find him.

•

It was in the early morning at the end of January 1964 when a teenage girl was found nude, facedown, with deep wounds to the top of her head. Her body had been dumped on a public reserve near Cabramatta, along the Georges River watercourse, in a local inlet known as Prospect Creek. Her shoulder-length hair, which had been waved and coloured, now lay floating in the dirty water with the reeds. Her face was caked with mud.

The media quickly picked up the story. Within twenty-four hours of the discovery, Sydney newspapers were splashed with the types of headlines that had appeared so many times in the forty years before: the nude girl murder, the river body, the river murder, the hitchhiker murder and the park killer.

The police quickly pursued an investigation. Barbara Judith Makin, a seventeen-year-old from Granville, had been reported missing. The body found matched her description. Autopsy results described the dreadful death that had unfolded for Barbara: she'd been beaten so violently that her throat was broken.

Police quickly drew conclusions. Given the location of the body, a vehicle had been involved. They also quickly discovered that Barbara had been known to hitchhike. The official report of the Police Commissioner of New South Wales for 1964 notes the presence of a disturbing new trend: 'A number of attacks on females in the Metropolitan Area of Sydney, including several serious cases of rape and indecent assault, gave rise to grave concern.' Police believed it was time to approach the problem differently. A task force of special mobile patrols was raised. Men in motor vehicles, it seemed, were prowling the streets looking for women victims – in response, police in patrol cars would prowl the streets to stop them.

While officers on patrol kept watch over the city streets, constables continued their exhaustive search of the park and peat where Barbara was found. At Prospect Creek, the officers scoured the scene for any physical evidence of the crime that might assist in the identification of a suspect. Constables combed the area on foot in search of a murder weapon too. The first searches yielded nothing.

Though it wasn't found during the initial searches, a tyre lever was eventually discovered at the scene. Local van, cab, delivery and truck drivers were interviewed. Charles Doherty, a 26-year-old truck driver from Fairfield, was one of them. He lived only four kilometres away, and was known to pick up hitchhikers.

Back at Prospect Creek, and just in time, police finally found what they'd been looking for. Near to where the body had been located, a constable happened upon something unexpectedly. He saw a metallic glimmer, out of place in the muddy reeds. It was a man's chrome watch. The wristband had been snapped in what had surely been a violent struggle.

Doherty was said to own a gold-coloured watch.

He gave a statement to police. He was taken to the murder scene. He did not confess. 'Everything seems to be blank. I do not even remember picking the girl up in my truck. I have no recollection of anything and certainly had no intention of injuring or even touching the girl,' he said.

At trial, Doherty said he suffered from dizzy spells because of a car accident three years before. His mother, Jean, said his memory loss was on account of the fits he'd had as a child.

With Doherty's conviction, NSW police were able to report to the state parliament that they'd achieved a strong clearance rate. Of the sixty-seven murders reported in 1964, only two remained open at the end of that year. In the absence of a confession from the accused, the physical evidence had been the keystone of the police case. When the constable had found a man's watch on the banks of Prospect Creek, he'd struck gold.

But how close had the constable come, in the dense and overgrown wilds of the Georges River parkland, to over-looking the little broken thing? If not for the chrome wristband reflecting the morning sun, he wouldn't have seen it.

That day, as he'd stood beside the creek, the constable had stopped for a moment to consider the significance of his discovery. He dug his fingers into the sticky grey soil to retrieve it. He laid the object flat in the palm of his hand. The face was caked with mud. He inspected the shattered band, like broken metal wings dangling from either side of the dial. He wiped it clean. The arms weren't moving, and the watch appeared to be dead. All the same, he instinctively leant down and brought the dial to his ear to listen for any sign of life.

The clock was still ticking.

ACKNOWLEDGEMENTS

I WOULD LIKE TO THANK THE FOLLOWING FOR THEIR ASSISTANCE in the writing and production of *The Killing Streets*.

The archivists at the NSW State Archives, Kingswood, Sydney and the National Film and Sound Archive, Canberra. The National Library of Australia's 'Trove' online portal.

Thank you sincerely to my publisher Sophie Hamley, and the team at Hachette: Fiona Hazard, Karen Ward, Jenny Topham, Daniel Pilkington, Chris Sims, Anna Egelstaff, Bella Lloyd, Christa Moffitt and Deonie Fiford.

AUTHOR'S NOTE

A RANGE OF PRIMARY SOURCES HAS BEEN DRAWN ON TO WRITE this book, including: inquest papers; NSW Central Criminal Court transcripts; High Court rulings; Department of Attorney-General and Justice files; gaol records; correspondence held by Department of Prisons and Comptroller General's Office; and newspaper articles. Direct quotes cited throughout the book have been drawn from original court transcripts held at the NSW State Archives, Kingswood. It must be noted that due to the passage of time, some original records (particularly pertaining to the oldest cases) have been lost or destroyed. Where there are gaps in the records, reasonable extrapolations have been made based on the only evidence available.

The author makes special note of the process used to identify horticulturalist/arborist David Frame in this story.

There is no way of confirming that David Frame was present at the discovery of Iris Marriott's body, but he was most certainly important in the discovery of Hilda White's body and provided a number of important insights to police in assisting their investigation. David Frame's presence at the park on the morning of Iris Marriott's discovery is an assumption based on many known facts. Frame worked the early morning shifts and he had an important role in managing the tree stock in the area at the time. Frame's testimony has been drawn on to create a compelling account for the reader. There is no evidence at all to suggest that Frame was involved in the murders of the women described herein, and neither should his inclusion in this story be taken as tacit implication that he had any involvement.

ENDNOTES

CHAPTER 1: WHITE IRIS

p. 6, 'By 1932 the CIB in Sydney': 'Our fingers sign for us', *Smith's Weekly*, 26 August 1939, p. 17.

p. 13, 'The medical examiner said': 'Social outcast battered to death', *Truth*, 11 December 1932, p. 18.

p. 15, 'Though O'Keeffe's work was not exhibited':A. Kreymborg, 'Secrets of real beauty', *Daily Telegraph*, 20 September 1930, p. 9.

p. 16, 'Digit by digit': 'Identification of criminals', *Brisbane Courier*, 20 December 1902, p. 5.

p. 17, 'Jardine was now well known': 'Jewel index for police', *Daily Telegraph*, 6 October 1932, p. 1.

p. 18, 'offensive behaviour charges were laid against people': 'Offensive behaviour', *Illawarra Mercury*, 2 February 1934, p. 6; 'Offensive behaviour', *Queanbeyan-Canberra Advocate*, 22 January 1925, p. 3; 'Offensive behaviour', *Sydney Morning Herald*, 3 January 1925, p. 10; 'Offensive!', *Goulburn Evening Penny Post*, 8 June 1932, p. 2.

CHAPTER 2: WHITE, HILDA

p. 20, 'a Centennial Park worker walking behind the kiosk': 'NSW unsolved crime no. 3', *Truth*, 18 August 1940, p. 17.

p. 21, 'Hilda had been thirty-three years old': 'Woman murdered in Centennial Park', *The Sun*, 27 July 1932, p. 13.

p. 21, 'At the time, Centennial Park': 'Centennial Park', *The Land*, 10 September 1937, p. 18.

p. 21, 'Iris, in particular': 'Dramatic incidents in May Miller murder', *New Call*, 9 February 1933, p. 19.

p. 22, 'Iris lived with her lover': 'Mother's sobs in corner; Wife smiles to the accused man', *Daily Telegraph*, 21 January 1933, p. 7.

p. 23, 'A newspaper article printed at the time': 'Young woman lured to death: ghastly park murder', *Truth*, 31 July 1932, p. 15.

p. 23, 'Another newspaper printed indiscreet details': 'Many men seen', *The Sun*, 28 July 1932, p. 15.

p. 24, 'The crime bears a curious resemblance': 'Social outcast battered to death', *Truth*, 11 December 1932, p. 18.

p. 25, 'with a closed fist': 'Park murder', *National Advocate*, 28 July 1932, p. 2; 'Woman strangled. Signs of desperate struggle', *West Australian*, 28 July 1932, p. 13.

p. 25, 'She had writhed and struggled': 'Park murder', *National Advocate*, 28 July 1932, p. 2.

p. 26, 'the struggle seemed to have continued': 'Woman strangled. Signs of desperate struggle', *West Australian*, 28 July 1932, p. 13.

p. 26, 'Police speculated about how this had led': 'Many men seen', *The Sun*, 28 July 1932, p. 15.

p. 28, 'He returned an open verdict.': 'NSW unsolved crime no. 3', *Truth*, 18 August 1940, p. 17; 'Woman strangled', *Brisbane Courier*, 26 August 1932, p. 20.

p. 28, 'mockingly declared April to be the month': 'Fatal end to orgy', *News*, 27 April 1932, p. 5.

p. 29, 'William Pryor had been appointed': 'Police changes: meteoric Mackay', *Goulburn Evening Penny Post*, 30 March 1932, p. 3; 'Mac. the Mystery', *Truth*, 14 April 1929, p. 1; 'Big jobs for new chief', *Daily Telegraph*, 27 April 1932, p. 7; 'Inspector Pryor chief of CIB', *Newcastle Sun*, 2 April 1932, p. 1.

p. 29, 'According to the *Labor Daily*': 'Say killer of woman now dead', *Labor Daily*, 26 March 1932, p. 1.

p. 30, 'Dorothy Denzel and Frank Wilkinson': 'Police recover Dorothy Denzel's body', *Maitland Daily Mercury*, 13 April 1932, p. 1.

p. 31, 'A report in the *Telegraph*': 'Foreigner may have murdered Saywell', *Daily Telegraph*, 17 September 1932, p. 6.

p. 31, 'The leather pouch in which he carried his change': 'Footprint of slayer', *Daily Telegraph*, 27 April 1932, p. 7.

p. 31, 'After weeks and weeks of frustrating travel': 'Carried on his murdered master's business', *Truth*, 5 June 1932, p. 14.

p. 32, 'A sleeping woman was spooning the corpse': 'Fatal end to orgy', *The News*, 27 April 1932, p. 5.

p. 33, 'Police couldn't forensically match a bullet casing': 'Bullet is found', *Daily Telegraph*, 28 April 1932, p. 6.

CHAPTER 3: DAISY CHAIN

p. 35, 'The first in the sequence was in May 1921': 'Moore Park murder', *Muswellbrook Chronicle*, 17 October 1922, p. 3.

p. 36, 'At the time, this parkland included': Moore Park heritage analysis 2016 prepared for Moore Park 2040 Future Directions report, CAB Consulting Pty Ltd Heritage Urban Design Landscape and Architecture, Church Point; 'Moore park murder', *Goulburn Evening Penny Post*, 31 October 1922, p. 2.

p. 36, 'A "dirty old man doing a dirty trick" ': See *Truth*, 30 August 1903, p. 3; *The Sun*, 29 March 1911, p. 8; *Chronicle*, 3 May 1924.

p. 37, 'The impact of these behaviours': 'Wicked William', *Truth*, 30 August 1903, p. 3.

p. 37, 'so long as the indecent exposure remained': 'Indecent exposure', *South Coast Times and Wollongong Argus*, 8 October 1926, p. 10.

p. 37, 'By the mid-1920s, "peeping Tom" ': 'Peeping Tom', *The Mail*, 21 August 1926, p. 31.

p. 38, 'In 1927, an illustrated version of Lady Godiva': 'Exchange and Mart', *World's News*, 24 December 1927, p. 34.

p. 38, 'A copy of this book could be bought': 'Peeping Tom', *World's News*, 26 November 1927, p. 33.

p. 38, 'Geographically, Moore Park is located': Moore Park heritage analysis 2016 prepared for Moore Park 2040 Future Directions report, CAB Consulting Pty Ltd Heritage Urban Design Landscape and Architecture, Church Point.

p. 39, 'The examiner identified six distinct': 'Moore Park tragedy', *Barrier Miner*, 31 October 1922, p. 3.

p. 39, 'From the outset, police found it difficult': 'Moore Park mystery', *The Argus*, 2 November 1922, p. 8.

p. 40, 'Police wondered why the men hadn't': 'Moore Park tragedy', *Maitland Weekly Mercury*, 4 November 1922, p. 6.

p. 41, 'Every possible lead culminated in a dead end': 'Moore Park murder', *Muswellbrook Chronicle*, 17 October 1922, p. 3.

p. 41, 'Then a local van driver': 'Moore Park mystery', *Daily Advertiser*, 31 October 1922, p. 3.

p. 41, 'They'd been seen drinking ale': 'Moore Park mystery', *The Argus*, 2 November 1922, p. 8.

p. 41, 'Ellicombe said it was Jensen': 'Park murder', *Daily Mail*, 4 November 1922, p. 7; 'Jensen's denial', *The Sun*, 8 December 1922, p. 7.

p. 42, 'John Carl Jensen was put on trial': 'Conclusion of trial', *Kalgoorlie Miner*, 9 December 1922, p. 4.

p. 42, 'The body was found lying facedown': 'Todays wires', *Wellington Times*, 15 May 1924, p. 4.

p. 43, 'The device normally had a toothpick': 'A fateful knife', *Evening News*, 17 May 1924, p. 1.

p. 44, 'A brown woollen golf coat': 'Long Bay crime', *Sydney Morning Herald*, 17 June 1924, p. 6.

p. 44, 'In other words, a police informant': 'Long Bay murder', 15 May 1924, p. 1; 'Long Bay murder', *Newcastle Morning Herald and Miners' Advocate*, 16 May 1924, p. 5.

p. 44, 'The attacker had also wounded her internally': 'Long Bay murder', *Daily Standard*, 15 May 1924, p. 1.

p. 46, 'Rebecca's death was a crime': 'Long Bay murder', *Newcastle Morning Herald and Miners' Advocate*, 15 May 1924, p. 5.; 'Long Bay tragedy', *Daily Advertiser*, 17 June 1924, p. 2; 'Long Bay tragedy', *Sydney Morning Herald*, 16 May 1924, p. 9.

p. 46, 'According to him, her murder': 'Long Bay murder', *Daily Standard*, 15 May 1924, p. 1.

p. 46, 'She was dirty, usually drunk': 'Long Bay murder', *Daily Telegraph*, 17 June 1924, p. 11.

p. 46, 'Less than a month before her death': 'Long Bay affair', *Goulburn Evening Penny Post*, 17 June 1924, p. 6.

p. 47, 'Police tried to retrace her steps': 'Long Bay murder', *The Mercury*, 17 June 1924, p. 8.

p. 47, 'Mrs Ethel Wagner': *Newcastle Morning Herald and Miners' Advocate*, 25 June 1924, p. 6.

p. 47, 'A detective named Jake Miller': 'Long Bay murder', *Sydney Morning Herald*, 16 January 1925, p. 7.

p. 47, 'Throughout the investigation': 'Long Bay murder', *The Telegraph*, 21 May 1924, p. 2; 'A fateful knife', *Evening News*, 17 May 1924, p. 1.

p. 47, 'The brief presented to the coroner': 'Long Bay mystery', *Singleton Argus*, 26 June 1924, p. 2; *Newcastle Morning Herald and Miners' Advocate*, 25 June 1924, p. 6.

p. 48, 'Five years passed': 'Perhaps derelict was not murdered', *Evening News*, 3 April 1929, p. 1.

p. 48, 'Police identified her': 'Strangled by woman?', *Tweed Daily*, 25 March 1929, p. 3.

p. 48, 'They eventually connected many aliases': 'Ghastly murder in Hyde Park', *Northern Star*, 23 March 1929, p. 9; 'Found dead', *Maitland Daily Mercury*, 22 March 1929, p. 5.

p. 49, 'the wife of a New Zealand sea captain': 'Mystery', *Sunday Times*, 24 March 1929, p. 2.

p. 49, 'She would disappear for about six months': 'Lonely woman was victim of silk stocking murderer', *Daily Telegraph*, 23 March 1929, p. 3.

p. 49, 'She had no enemies': 'New clues in Hyde Park Mystery', *The Sun*, 24 March 1929, p. 2.

p. 50, 'Vera's murder was quickly regarded': 'Mystery Hyde Park murder. Police search in underworld', *Sunday Times*, 24 March 1929, p. 2.

CHAPTER 4: PENNY IN THE SLOT

p. 53, 'More refinery than refined': Redfern Railway Station Group NSW State Heritage Register Office of Environment and Heritage.

pp. 54–55, 'Arthur and Patience had raised four children': '10' [shillings] per 100', *The Sun*, 8 April 1928, p. 2.

p. 57, 'Swimming and diving had defined': 'A whale in the bay for Arthur O'Connor', *The Referee*, 27 January 1938, p. 3; 'Sunday's swimming carnival', *Narrandera Argus and Riverina Advertiser*, 14 January 1949, p. 2; 'Arthur O'Connor', *Daily Telegraph*, 3 March 1925, p. 5; 'Arthur O'Connor', *Forbes Advocate*, 14 January 1930, p. 6; 'Sunday's swimming carnival', *Narrandera Argus and Riverina Advertiser*, 14 January 1949, p. 2.

p. 59, 'The amount wouldn't be enough': 'National park horror', *Truth*, 18 December 1932, p. 16.

pp. 64–65, 'Not far off the road': 'Mad killer's victim', *Truth*, 18 December 1932, p. 1.

p. 66, 'He had served in World War I': 'Death of Detective Sergeant Geldart', *Sydney Morning Herald*, 11 October 1929, p. 8.

p. 68, 'First they had to identify her': 'Mad killer's victim'.

p. 69, 'The police tracked him down': 'Park inquest', *Goulburn Evening Penny Post*, 30 January 1933, p. 3.

p. 71, 'Bessie wasn't like the other women': 'Mad killer's victim'.

p. 72, 'the police didn't have just one new vehicle': 'Their new car', *The Sun*,
28 September 1932, p. 15.

p. 73, 'She borrowed the train fare': 'Mad killer's victim'.

p. 73, 'The *Daily Telegraph* proposed': 'Startling theory in the park murder
case', *Daily Telegraph*, 17 December 1932, p. 1.

p. 73, 'And then the paper answered itself': 'Mad killer's victim'.

p. 74, 'The charlatan undertaker': 'Attempt to kidnap girls', *Truth*,
25 December 1932, p. 9.

p. 76, 'The guard of honour was composed': 'Funeral of victim 1932', *Daily
Telegraph*, 19 December 1932, p. 7.

p. 76, 'Redfern is not a locality in which': 'Bessie O'Connor's murderer may be
unmasked!', *Truth*, 15 January 1933, p. 13.

p. 76, 'In the late afternoon of 14 December': 'National park horror', *Truth*,
18 December 1932, p. 16.

CHAPTER 5: TRAFFICKING

p. 78, 'He had summoned the most experienced detectives': 'Bessie O'Connor's
murderer', *Truth*, 15 January 1933, p. 13; 'Woman murdered in
Centennial Park', *The Sun*, 27 July 1932, p. 13.

p. 80, 'As one journalist pointed out': 'Police make dramatic moves', *The Sun*,
17 December 1932, p. 5.

p. 80, 'Data from 1927 ranks': 'Ranks fifth', *Casino and Kyogle Courier*,
1 October 1927, p. 2; ABS Commonwealth of Australia Yearbook no 16
for 1923. ABS Yearbook of Australia 2011 ABS Canberra.

p. 81, 'In 1929 they publicly released crime statistics': 'Stolen motor cars',
Western Argus, 7 January 1930, p. 18.

p. 81, 'By the mid-1920s': 'Numbers changed on stolen cars', *Daily Advertiser*,
20 October 1926, p. 1.

p. 83, 'In that year, the winner was an Oldsmobile': 'Brisbane Sydney road
record', *Northern Star*, 16 February 1929, p. 3; 'Brisbane to Sydney',
Armidale Chronicle, 24 February 1923, p. 10.

p. 83, 'Up to 1928 only about 10 per cent': 'Huge turnover', *Narromine News
and Trangie Advocate*, 13 June 1928, p. 1; 'Hudson-Essex show peak
sales in April', *Sunday Times*, 27 May 1928, p. 23.

p. 84, 'While the Ford still remained popular': 'The motor in Sydney', *The
Advertiser*, 29 June 1923, p. 11.

p. 84, 'One editorial claimed': 'Petting parties', *The News*, 24 November 1930,
p. 5.

p. 84, 'Marketed as a family car': E. Swift, *The Big Roads: The Untold Story of the Engineers, Visionaries and Trailblazers Who Created the American Superhighways*, Mariner Books, NY, 2012, p. 88.

p. 84, 'It was perhaps a particularly appropriate': 'Joy riders in Sydney', *West Australian*, 4 January 1930, p. 15.

p. 85, 'Hilda had been moonlighting as a prostitute': 'Gruesome bundle in Centennial Park', *The Arrow*, 29 July 1932, p. 23.

p. 85, 'Police believed that grudge attacks': 'Mystery of naked woman's body found in Queen's Park lantana', *The Arrow*, 16 December 1932, p. 6.

p. 86, 'Red-light districts had flourished': 'A girl who just can't go straight: here's another worst woman in Sydney', *The Arrow*, 11 March 1932, p. 25.

p. 86, 'Networks of brothels': 'Free furniture for underworld', *The Arrow*, 18 March 1932, p. 4.

p. 87, 'They had even begun accepting food coupons': 'Food coupons buy love', *The Arrow*, 27 November 1931, p. 5.

p. 87, 'Prostitutes had to look for new ways': 'It's a good wind that blows no ill', *The Arrow*, 11 March 1932, p. 7; 'Consorting charge', *Sydney Morning Herald*, 15 January 1932, p. 6; 'Consorting: police squad active', *Wagga Wagga Express*, 12 March 1932, p. 17.

p. 88, 'With consorting laws': 'Shocking tale of life of semi slavery', *The Arrow*, 11 March 1932, p. 24.

p. 88, 'The conditions were documented': 'Cheap city residentials need disinfectant: unlicensed hotels are hot beds of iniquity', *The Arrow*, 19 February 1932, p. 6.

p. 89, 'Only the previous year': 'Sensational sequel to "morality squad" clean up', *Truth*, 23 August 1931, p. 11.

p. 90, 'There was also active local trading': 'White girls sold', *Northern Miner*, 13 February 1930, p. 2.

p. 91, 'It was rumoured that her earnings': 'Social outcast battered to death', *Truth*, 11 December 1932, p. 18.

p. 91, 'Detective Sergeants Keogh, Barratt': 'Park murder', *National Advocate*, 8 August 1932, p. 4.

p. 91, 'To the officers assembled': 'Bessie O'Connor's murderer may be unmasked!', *Truth*, 15 January 1933, p. 13.

CHAPTER 6: THE DARK TRIANGLE

p. 93, 'the Slayer's demeanour': 'Bus driver who talked at midnight with park killer said car was out of juice', *Truth*, 1 January 1933, p. 10.

p. 93, 'When lab testing was completed': 'Mystery of naked woman's body found in Queen's Park lantana', *The Arrow*, 16 December 1932, p. 6.

p. 94, 'After Hilda's murder, police had gathered': 'Blood on coat', *Truth*, 7 August 1932, p. 4.

p. 95, 'Despite the bleak economic conditions': 'Christmas Gift Grocery Parcel', *Catholic Press*, 8 December 1932, p. 23.

p. 96, 'On returning home he called Gallard': 'Craig now charged with Bessie O'Connor's murder', *Truth*, 22 January 1933, p. 13.

p. 97, 'Downey's car was spotted the next morning': 'Where killer lived: Police say national park killer lived in this region', *The Sun*, 5 January 1933, p. 11.

p. 98, 'Downey also claimed to have found': 'Craig faced three days of unnerving recital', *Truth*, 5 February 1933, p. 15.

p. 98, 'He said a Texaco oil tin': 'Murder of Bessie O'Connor: Motorist's evidence, *Armidale Express and New England General Advertiser*, 1 February 1933, p. 1.

p. 99, 'The discovery of the vehicles became central': 'Where killer lived', *The Sun*, 5 January 1933, p. 11.

p. 100, 'They were recent photos of a happy girl': 'Desperate attempt to kidnap girls', *Truth*, 25 December 1932, p. 9.

p. 100, 'In reporting the brutal killings of women': 'Mystery of naked woman's body found in Queen's Park lantana', *The Arrow*, 16 December 1932, p. 6.

p. 101, 'They said they anticipated interviewing': 'Man held at CIB', *Daily Telegraph*, 7 January 1933, p. 1.

p. 102, 'Locals were warned': 'The Park murders: police activities', *Northern Miner*, 27 December 1932, p. 2.

CHAPTER 7: MOVING PICTURES

p. 108, 'the moon hadn't been full': 'Bessie O'Connor's murder', *Truth*, 15 January 1933, p. 13.

p. 108, 'But Cook couldn't offer police': 'Craig's trial', *Goulburn Evening Penny Post*, 30 March 1933, p. 3.

p. 110, 'On the first day of 1933': 'Talkie helps in manhunt search for national park slayer', *The Sun*, 1 January 1933; 'Grisly trail of a killer: Clues that may seal park demon's doom', *Truth*, 1 January 1933, p. 1.

p. 110, 'Editors posed a confronting question': 'Bus driver who talked at midnight with park killer said car was out of juice', *Truth*, 1 January 1933, p. 10; 'On the trail of the slayer', *The Labor Daily*, 30 December

1932, p. 5; 'Who is the satyr of the parks?' *The Arrow*, 23 December 1932, p. 5; 'A midnight interview', *The Sun*, 2 January 1933, p. 7.

p. 111, 'Police also made use of state-of-the-art': 'Park horror', *National Advocate*, 2 January 1933, p. 2.

p. 114, 'Police were also still looking for the items':'Park murders', *Northern Miner*, 27 December 1932, p. 2.

p. 115, 'The gold buyer was interviewed': 'National park suspect released', *Labor Daily*, 3 January 1933, p. 5; 'Police make dramatic moves', *The Sun*, 17 December 1932, p. 5.

p. 116, 'And the CIB cinema newsreel': 'Park murder', *Daily Telegraph*, 31 December 1932, p. 5.

CHAPTER 8: THE CONFESSION

p. 124, 'I was at home': Central Criminal Court transcripts, 1933, Rex V Eric Roland Craig.

p. 135, 'The statement contains': 'Mother's sobs in corner', *Daily Telegraph*, 21 January 1933, p. 7.

CHAPTER 9: STAIN REMOVAL

p. 139, 'The scale of the challenge': 'National park murder case: detectives worried', *Newcastle Sun*, 23 December 1932, p. 1.

p. 140, 'Much to the chagrin of police': 'Murder of Bessie O'Connor', *Sydney Morning Herald*, 10 January 1933, p. 11; 'Line up fails to help in murder hunt', *Daily Telegraph*, 11 January 1933, p. 9.

p. 142, 'During intense interrogation': 'Man detained', *The Telegraph*, 16 January 1925, p. 5.

p. 145, 'As the Royal Women's Hospital today': Patient records, Women's hospital, Royal Women's Hospital Melbourne. https://www.thewomens. org.au/about/our-history/patient-records

p. 147, 'Wounded in action': Australian Imperial Force unit war diaries 1914–18, Australian War Memorial holdings.

p. 152, 'A week after Craig's arrest': 'Bessie O'Connor's murderer may be unmasked!', *Truth*, 15 January 1933, p. 13.

p. 154, 'First, one noticed the way Leah': 'Craig now charged with Bessie O'Connor's murder', *Truth*, 22 January 1933, p. 13.

p. 154, 'In contrast, Mary-Caroline': 'Mother's sobs in corner', *Daily Telegraph*, 21 January 1933, p. 7.

p. 157, 'When asked if he wished to apply for bail': 'Second murder', *Tweed Daily*, 23 January 1933, p. 3.

p. 158, 'Craig wasn't talking to her': 'Once gaoled for biting a man's ear', *New Call*, 9 February 1933, p. 19.

CHAPTER 10: WORST CRIME ON THE CALENDAR

p. 160, 'Like the inquest': 'Sequel to Park horror', *Truth*, 19 March 1933, p. 1.

p. 167, 'The cardigan that police claimed': 'Advertising', *The Sun*, 20 March 1932, p. 33.

p. 179, 'March had won an Oscar': 'Movie star competition', *Newcastle Sun*, 7 December 1932, p. 5.

CHAPTER 11: DEAD IN THE WATER

p. 186, 'The process of jury selection': 'Craig's agony of suspense', *Truth*, 2 April 1933, p. 1.

p. 186, 'He was there at every court appearance': 'Sydney Park horrors', *Daily News*, 21 January 1933, p. 1.

p. 187, 'locked in for the night': 'Jury locked up', *Tweed Daily*, 1 April 1933, p. 5.

p. 190, 'One such incident had occurred': 'Tragedy of Sydney Harbour unlocked', *The Sydney Living Museums Magazine*, August 2018.

p. 192, 'police noticed the date': 'Sydney Harbour hoax', *Bowen Independent*, 10 April 1933, p. 3.

p. 193, 'As one newspaper noted': 'Craig's agony of suspense', *Truth*, 2 April 1933, p. 1.

CHAPTER 12: MOTHER-IN-LAW

p. 196, 'Perhaps they identified with Patience': 'Bessie O'Connor's murderer may be unmasked!', *Truth*, 15 January 1933, p. 13.

p. 197, 'Justice Colin Davidson': M. Rutledge, 'Davidson, Sir Colin George Watt (1878–1954)', *Australian Dictionary of Biography* volume 8, MUP, 1981.

p. 198, 'As a legal commentator for the *Sun*': 'Another trial for Craig', *The Sun*, 30 April 1933, p. 3.

p. 200, 'Davidson issued a stern warning': 'Warning!', *Maitland Daily Mercury*, 27 April 1933, p. 7.

p. 216, 'It was Thomas Brown': *Truth*, 30 April 1933; 'National park murder', *Kalgoorlie Miner*, 29 April 1933, p. 5.

p. 217, 'Perhaps that is the best place': 'Sydney park murder', *The Age*, 1 May 1933, p. 11.

CHAPTER 13: RED GALALITH BEADS

p. 224, 'A vast and still developing body of science': T. Albright, 'Why eyewitnesses fail', *Proceedings of the National Academy of Sciences of the United States of America*, vol. 114, no. 30, 2017, pp. 7758–7764.

p. 228, 'At the third trial': 'Craig faced three days of unnerving recital', *Truth*, 5 February 1933, p. 15; 'Perjury third degree', *Truth*, 30 April 1933, p. 15; 'National park', *Sydney Morning Herald*, 31 January 1933, p. 10.

p. 230, 'Watson senior': 'Craig's trial', *Goulburn Evening Penny Post*, 30 March 1933, p. 3.

p. 230, 'Contemporary researchers in the field of neuroscience': T. Albright, 'Why eyewitnesses fail', *Proceedings of the National Academy of Sciences of the United States of America*, vol. 114, no. 30, 2017, pp. 7758–7764.

p. 232, 'Along the chain of witnesses': 'Craig's agony of suspense', *Truth*, 2 April 1933, p. 1.

p. 235, 'Her abject fear became evident': 'Mother's sobs in corner', *Daily Telegraph*, 21 January 1933, p. 7.

p. 237, 'She also noted that, much like her husband's': 'Perjury third degree', *Truth*, 30 April 1933, p. 15.

p. 238, 'Leah whispered through the bars of the dock': 'Craig's defence an alibi', *Daily Telegraph*, 30 March 1933, p. 8.

p. 239, 'His fingers were still curled': 'Averted eyes of jury warned Craig of his doom', *The Sun*, 11 June 1933, p. 2.

CHAPTER 14: CLEANSKINS AND DIRTY MINDS

p. 240, 'In August 1933, Craig's life hung in the balance': M. Donnelly, 'Long Bay jail reformed women before men swung from gallows', *Daily Telegraph*, 24 April 2017.

p. 244, 'At trial, police stated': 'Moxley guilty', *Armidale Express and New England General Advertiser*, 17 June 1932, p. 6.

p. 245, 'Newspapers provide some insight': 'The devil roamed one night', *Truth*, 2 October 1949, p. 22; 'Moxley prays: reads bible', *The Sun*, 14 August 1932, p. 2.

p. 245, 'While standing on the gallows': 'Death is sweet', *Daily Telegraph*, 18 August 1932, p. 6.

p. 246, 'The execution provided the state': 'Amazing defence moves being made for Moxley insanity plea', *Truth*, 29 May 1932, p. 13.

p. 247, 'The Crown was furious over the verdict': 'Moxley's fate in balance', *The Herald*, 17 June 1932, p. 6.

p. 248, 'The suggestion that a sex crime': 'To what extent is automatism responsible for murder?', *Smith's Weekly*, 18 June 1932, p. 2.

p. 249, 'Craig's conviction occurred at a time': R. T. White, 'Sir John Macpherson: the first but sometimes overlooked Professor of Psychiatry at the University of Sydney', *Australasian Psychiatry*, vol. 22, no. 4, 2014, pp. 378–82; 'Mental diseases', *Armidale Chronicle*, 5 August 1922, p. 4.

p. 249, 'The Department of Health expanded': 'Crime in Sydney', *Queensland Times*, 1 August 1928, p. 7.

p. 250, 'an article published in the *Labor Daily*': 'The scientist – not the detective only', *Labor Daily*, 15 May 1924, p. 4.

p. 250, 'In 1928, a special council': 'Crime in Sydney', *Queensland Times*, 1 August 1928, p. 7.

p. 251, 'The definitive medical text on sexual psychopathy': R. Krafft-Ebing, *Psychopathia Sexualis: With especial reference to the antipathic sexual instinct. a medico-forensic study*, Rebman Co., New York, 1900, p. 527.

p. 252, 'The 1930s saw further experimentation': 'Sex offender sentenced operation suggested', *Singleton Argus*, 3 September 1937, p. 1.

p. 252, 'Lionel Davis, a labourer convicted': '"Pitiful case" says judge', *Northern Star*, 14 April 1938, p. 7.

p. 252, 'By the end of the 1930s': 'Sex offender sentenced', *Singleton Argus*, 3 September 1937, p. 1.

p. 253, 'A range of what were perceived': *Psychopathia Sexualis*, pp. 86, 127, 487.

CHAPTER 15: THE INTERVIEWS

p. 256, 'So ended another chapter': 'Nerve gone', *Truth*, 3 September 1933, p. 14.

p. 256, 'It was custom, though not a legal requirement': 'Moxley's fate in balance', *The Herald*, 17 June 1932, p. 6.

p. 259, 'The journalist sat in the chair opposite': 'Two women on Craig's reprieve', *Daily Telegraph*, 19 September 1933, p. 1.

CHAPTER 16: OVERTURE TO DEATH

p. 271, 'On the morning of 9 March 1940': 'Baffling mystery', *Truth*, 17 March 1940, p. 24.

p. 272, 'And as with the other victims': 'Fiendish murder', *The Argus*, 13 June 1946, p. 3.

p. 272, 'There was a stocking around her neck': 'Dead girl's fondness for thrillers', *Tweed Daily*, 12 March 1940, p. 5; 'Still baffled', *Truth*,

26 May 1940, p. 22; 'Stocking death case: suicide, police say', *The Argus*, 4 April 1940, p. 3.

p. 275, '*Truth*, a newspaper known for its unvarnished': 'Murder is indicated', *Truth*, 7 April 1940, p. 20.

p. 275, 'The paper's criticism was scathing': 'Overhaul of police demanded', *Truth*, 28 July 1940, p. 17.

p. 277, 'There could only be one conclusion': 'Police now confess failure', *Truth*, 21 July 1940, p. 17.

p. 278, 'Then, in June 1946': 'Clue on sex murder', *Sydney Morning Herald*, 18 June 1946, p. 4.

p. 278, 'At the scene, police were shocked': 'Fiendish murder of young girl in Sydney cemetery', *The Argus*, 13 June 1946, p. 3.

p. 279, 'Joan was still wearing': 'Murder in a cemetery', *The Mirror*, 16 August 1952, p. 8.

p. 279, 'Interviews with friends': 'Child murder unsolved', *Sydney Morning Herald*, 5 November 1946, p. 4; '8 year man hunt is still on', *The Mirror*, 3 July 1954, p. 11.

p. 280, 'Police followed hundreds of potential': 'Murderer of girl', *Sydney Morning Herald*, 14 June 1946, p. 4.

p. 280, 'There were too many suspects': 'Two park murders', *Smith's Weekly*, 16 November 1946, p. 21.

p. 280, 'Then Joan's mother began receiving': 'Old clothes', *The Mercury*, 22 June 1946, p. 23.

p. 281, 'The hoaxes even crossed the state': 'Impersonated police', *Sydney Morning Herald*, 21 June 1946, p. 3.

p. 281, 'Police pursued every archetype': 'To aid in man hunt', *The Telegraph*, 25 June 1946, p. 7.

p. 281, 'By mid-June, over four hundred': 'Girls murder suspects', *Canberra Times*, 15 June 1946, p. 2; 'New police check on', *Sydney Morning Herald*, 13 September 1950, p. 6.

p. 281, 'Police transcribed three full': 'Police disbelieve three men's confessions', *The Advertiser*, 5 November 1946, p. 7.

p. 282, 'The woman had received heavy blows': 'No clue to stranger', *Courier Mail*, 5 November 1946, p. 3; 'Murder suspect alleged to have snatched bag', *Daily Advertiser*, 6 December 1946, p. 2; 'No trace of murderer', *The Advertiser*, 5 November 1946, p. 7.

p. 284, 'Ada's husband wasn't deemed': 'Body in scrub inquest', *The Herald*, 5 December 1946, p. 3.

p. 284, 'Ada's handbag was found': 'Cooper Park murder', *Daily Telegraph*, 6 November 1946, p. 4.

p. 284, 'Her piano teacher': 'Strangled woman may have known murderer', *Daily Telegraph*, 5 November 1946, p. 4; 'Police seek young bagsnatcher as park murderer', *The Sun*, 5 November 1946, p. 2; 'Cooper park tragedy', *Singleton Argus*, 8 November 1946, p. 4.

p. 284, 'Detectives saw similarities': 'Murdered woman identified', *Scone Advocate*, 5 November 1946, p. 1.

p. 285, 'A sharp stick': 'Evidence opens in Sydney Park murder case', *The Telegraph*, 5 December 1946, p. 7.

p. 285, 'Police followed Clifford Kennedy': 'Man charged with Cooper Park murder', *Daily Telegraph*, 24 November 1946, p. 7.

p. 285, 'During the interrogation': 'Woman's death', *Kalgoorlie Miner*, 25 March 1947, p. 4; 'Cooper park murder', *National Advocate*, 7 December 1946, p. 1.

p. 285, 'Kennedy claimed he had gone': '12 years for Cooper Park killing "merciful" says judge', *Truth*, 30 March 1947, p. 42.

p. 286, 'According to her murderer': 'Kennedy sent for trial on Sydney Park murder charge', *The Telegraph*, 6 December 1946, p. 7; 'Kennedy for trial', *Sydney Morning Herald*, 7 December 1946, p. 5.

p. 286, 'He added that he hadn't': 'Today real life: strangled woman was found in park', *Daily Telegraph*, 8 December 1946, p. 32.

p. 287, 'While acknowledging the "sadism" ': 'Manslaughter verdict', *West Australian*, 26 March 1947.

p. 288, 'At the end of 1946': 'Two park murders', *Smith's Weekly*, 16 November 1946, p. 21.

CHAPTER 18: RELEASED

p. 298, 'At about 2 p.m. on Sunday': 'Murderer escapes at Bathurst', *Newcastle Morning Herald and Miners' Advocate*, 27 October 1941, p. 1; 'Recaptured', *Forbes Advocate*, 28 October 1941, p. 2; 'Break from gaol', *Barrier Miner*, 27 October 1941, p. 1.

p. 299, 'The Eucharistic procession': 'Eucharistic procession', *National Advocate*, 16 October 1948, p. 7.

p. 300, 'An official description of Craig': 'Murderer escapes', *Sydney Morning Herald*, 27 October 1941, p. 7.

p. 301, 'News reports provided more': 'These were tragedies that jolted a nation', *Truth*, 23 October 1949, p. 26.

p. 301, 'Just near the Macquarie River': 'Escaped strangler caught', *Daily News*, 27 October 1941, p. 21; 'Gaol organist escapes', *The Mercury*, 27 October 1941, p. 5; 'Back to prison', *West Australian*, 28 October 1941, p. 6.

p. 302, 'When captured, Craig': 'Short lived liberty', *Barrier Miner*,
    27 October 1941, p. 3; 'Murderer had 15 hours liberty', *Weekly Times*,
    1 November 1941, p. 4.

p. 302, 'On the Thursday morning': 'Lifer at large', *National Advocate*,
    27 October 1941, p. 2.

p. 303, 'Craig had planned his escape': 'Lifer's jail escape', *Daily Telegraph*,
    27 October 1941, p. 2; 'Boasted of jail break', *Daily Telegraph*,
    28 October 1941, p. 5.

p. 305, 'The Act expanded the powers': Section 5.1.c *Commonwealth National
    Security Act 1939*.

p. 306, 'At around the same time': 'Life sentence prisoners', *Sydney Morning
    Herald*, 9 October 1941, p. 4.

p. 307, 'Solicitor-General Cecil Edward Weigall': K. Mason, 'Cecil Edward
    Weigall', *Australian Dictionary of Biography* volume 12, MUP, 1990.

p. 308, 'The prisoner rehabilitation experiment': 'Education in gaol',
    Goulburn Evening Post, 30 September 1949, p. 5; J. F. Nagle (Royal
    Commissioner), Report of the Royal Commission into NSW Prisons,
    vols I, II & III, Parliament of NSW, 1978.

p. 310, 'In 1952, the Prisons Department': 'Psychiatrist for gaols', *Newcastle
    Morning Herald and Miners' Advocate*, 13 February 1952, p. 6.

p. 310, 'One judge sums up the attitude': 'Judge's view of male sex', *Truth*,
    24 February 1952, p. 8.

p. 313, 'McGeorge argued that violence was': 'Grafton gaol in ABC', *Daily
    Examiner*, 9 November 1954, p. 6.

CHAPTER 19: KEEPING WATCH

p. 315, 'Craig was supported on the outside': 'Freeing a murderer', *Sunday
    Telegraph*, 1 September 1957, p. 16.

p. 320, 'It was in the early morning': 'Life sentence in girl murder case',
    Canberra Times, 10 June 1964, p. 18; 'Man questioned on girl's death',
    Canberra Times, 1 February 1964, p. 3.

p. 320, 'The media quickly picked up': 'River body case today', *Canberra
    Times*, 3 February 1964, p. 4.

p. 320, 'Police quickly drew conclusions': Parliament of NSW 1965, Report of
    the Police Department 1964.

p. 321, 'Though it wasn't found': 'River body case today', *Canberra Times*,
    3 February 1964, p. 4.

p. 322, 'He gave a statement to police': 'Life sentence in girl murder case',
    Canberra Times, 10 June 1964, p. 18.

Also by critically acclaimed and awards shortlisted author
Tanya Bretherton

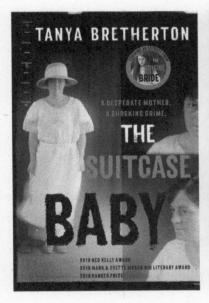 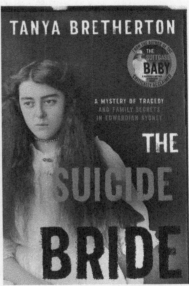

'A chilling story . . . recounted in simple,
often moving writing'
The Saturday Age

'Bretherton's unflinching fact-finding is what makes
this book throb'
The Australian Women's Weekly

'A fascinating story of crime, desperation, abandonment
and poverty . . . expansive and gripping'
The Dictionary of Sydney

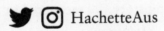